Creativity for Learning

Tools, Strategies, and Environments for Nurturing Creative Thinking in the Classroom

Kristy Doss and Lisa Bloom

Routledge
Taylor & Francis Group

NEW YORK AND LONDON

Designed cover image: Getty Images

First published 2026

by Routledge

605 Third Avenue, New York, NY 10158

and by Routledge

4 Park Square, Milton Park, Abingdon, Oxon, OX14 4RN

Routledge is an imprint of the Taylor & Francis Group, an informa business

ISBN: 9781032561752 (hbk)
ISBN: 9781032557403 (pbk)
ISBN: 9781003434221 (ebk)

DOI: 10.4324/9781003434221

Typeset in Perpetua
by Deanta Global Publishing Services, Chennai, India

Creativity for Learning

Creativity for Learning provides a comprehensive understanding of creativity's role in learning, as well as practical approaches to teaching creative thinking strategies to diverse learners.

This book provides a roadmap for creating instructional practices that allow learners to go beyond knowledge acquisition. Chapters provide research on creativity along with insights from professionals who apply creativity in their work, offering valuable guidance on how to nurture these essential skills in the classroom. Packed with research-based activities to help learners acquire and exercise creative thinking, novel approaches to assessment, as well as suggestions for learning space design, this book has everything you need to orchestrate a classroom that fosters equitable talent development for all students across the content areas.

This must-read guide will be the trusted companion for all educators seeking to transform their students into creative thinkers ready to meet the challenges of an uncertain future.

Kristy K. Doss is an assistant professor at Western Carolina University. She instructs courses in gifted and special education and conducts research in the area of creativity.

Lisa A. Bloom is professor emeritus and the former Jay M. Robinson distinguished professor of instructional technology at Western Carolina University. She teaches in the areas of gifted and special education and engages in research in the field of creativity.

Creativity for Learning

Contents

About the Authors

Kristy Doss

Kristy Doss is an assistant professor at Western Carolina University. She instructs courses in gifted and special education including differentiation methods for gifted and creative learners, education in a diverse society, teacher leadership, social/emotional issues of exceptional and gifted learners, and instructional technology in personalized learning environments to promote collaboration, creativity, and critical thinking. Her research interests include creativity, instructional methods in higher education, problem-based learning, mindfulness, twice-exceptional learners, and curriculum in gifted education.

Lisa Bloom

Lisa Bloom is a professor at Western Carolina University where she has been a member of the faculty since 1989. Her current research interests include using technology to personalize learning environments and to promote creative and critical thinking, problem-based learning, culturally responsive teaching, and the social and emotional well-being of children. She is the author of Classroom Management: Creating Positive Outcomes for All Students published by Pearson, as well as numerous journal articles related to her research interests. She teaches both online and face-to-face courses in instructional technology, classroom management, and creative and critical thinking.

Chapter 1

Introduction to Creative Thinking

INTRODUCTION

During his youth, Tom described himself as a problem child who struggled with attention deficit disorder. Traditional school learning was difficult for him, as he preferred drawing pictures and delving into the world of his imagination. These early struggles shaped his creativity and unique problem-solving approach. As an adult, Tom worked as a hydrologist and land manager for the state of Montana, where he encountered a pressing and complex challenge. Farmers and ranchers often used bulldozers to shove gravel into rivers or constructed concrete dams to channel water into irrigation canals. While these methods met immediate irrigation needs, they destroyed riverbanks, harmed ecosystems, and caused dangerous flooding. Concrete dams also created reverse hydraulics that posed fatal risks to unsuspecting boaters.

Determined to find a solution, Tom embarked on a quest to balance the needs of farmers, the environment, and public safety. He spent countless hours researching how other countries managed similar issues and carefully observing the movement of rivers and streams in Montana. Despite his efforts, Tom felt stuck, unable to find a sustainable solution. Searching for inspiration, he returned to a childhood passion – visual art. Immersing himself in 3-dimensional art, Tom began carving and painting wooden fish, focusing on creating realistic movement with chisel and paint. The process not only reignited his creativity but also led to an unexpected breakthrough.

While working on his wooden fish sculptures, Tom was struck by an idea for a more flexible irrigation solution. He envisioned a system similar to a Swiss army knife – multifunctional, adaptable, and efficient. Drawing from his observations of water movement and his artistic work, Tom designed a channeling system with movable three-dimensional irrigation diversion blocks. These blocks could be easily adjusted as needed, preserving riverbanks, protecting ecosystems, and minimizing risks to boaters. His innovation turned an insurmountable problem into a manageable solution.

Tom's irrigation system has since gained national recognition, becoming a sustainable tool for farmers and ranchers across the country. His story highlights the power of creativity, persistence, and unconventional thinking. By returning to his artistic roots and combining them with his professional expertise, Tom not only solved a significant environmental challenge but also demonstrated how embracing diverse talents and perspectives can lead to groundbreaking solutions.

Tom's "Big-C" creativity demonstrates the kind of groundbreaking innovation that solves large-scale, complex problems. By developing an adaptable irrigation system that balances the needs of farmers, environmental conservation, and public safety, he tackled an issue with nationwide implications. In contrast, Pam, a third-grade teacher in North Carolina, exemplifies "little-c" creativity – the everyday creativity that enriches daily life and learning. Pam finds inventive ways to engage her students in literature by connecting it to their interests and experiences. For instance, she mimics social media platforms in her classroom by having students create "Twitter feed" conversations between main characters in classic novels and develop YouTube-style video advertisements to inspire their peers to read. These creative strategies help bring literature to life for young learners.

Whether it's "Big-C" creativity that changes the world or "little-c" creativity that enhances classroom experiences, both play essential roles in society. Creativity fuels problem solving, innovation, and engagement, yet research suggests it is on the decline. Factors such as rigid educational structures, an emphasis on standardized testing, and limited opportunities for exploration and play contribute to the diminishing cultivation of creativity in schools. This trend underscores the urgent need for educators to prioritize nurturing creativity and critical thinking in their students.

The purpose of this text is to empower educators and others who want to foster creativity to better understand its nature and connection to learning. By exploring theories and strategies for developing creative thinking, the text provides practical tools to inspire and motivate young innovators. It emphasizes the importance of creativity not only as a pathway to personal and professional success but also as a means of addressing societal challenges and enhancing individual fulfillment.

Creating environments that support creativity is critical for developing talent and encouraging innovative thinking. Whether in the classroom, workplace, or community, fostering a culture of creativity helps individuals unlock their potential and approach problems with fresh perspectives. Educators like Pam show how simple, everyday innovations can transform learning experiences, while stories like Tom's remind us of the power of creative thinking to tackle big challenges. Together, these examples illustrate the vital role creativity plays in shaping the world.

WHY CREATIVITY?

As the world encounters increasingly complex and multi-dimensional problems such as political divide, economic disparity, a rise in mental health issues, and climate change, we hope that our children and youth who inherit these problems will be well-equipped with the kind of brain power that will generate innovative solutions. In addition to world problems, technology and the way we do business continue to evolve at a rapid pace. Consider Artificial Intelligence (AI), disruptive technology that may change business as well as education. For one example, ChatGPT is an AI application that can generate human-like responses to user in-puts in real-time. One can ask it to generate poetry, fiction, research papers, essays, etc. This technology may strike fear in teachers who assign research papers and essays. Teachers and their students will need to be creative to ensure that students can demonstrate learning.

In the 21st century, interest in creativity can be seen globally. With such technology in the workforce, the jobs once occupied by middle-class workers are easily replaced by automation. To be competitive in the job market, our future workers will be required to engage in work where answers and procedures are fluid and ambiguous and where innovation and creativity will be highly sought.

Bronson and Merryman (2010) declared in Newsweek that the US was experiencing a "crisis in creativity", although leaders in business and economics had already determined that the crisis was "looming" (Florida, 2004). The European Commission designated 2009 as the European Year of Creativity and Innovation with the slogan "Imagine. Create. Innovate". through their mission of "Raising awareness of the importance of creativity and innovation for personal, social and economic development" (European Commission, 2008). Similarly, in China, creativity is a national priority (Xi Jinping, 2017). In response, schools in China are adopting a problem-based learning approach to education (West-Knights, 2017). At the 2018 World Cup, the fence surrounding the soccer field flashed a digital message that read, "Creativity is the Answer".

In 2011, Kyung Hee Kim described a creativity crisis based on a review of decades of scores on the E. Paul Torrance Test of Creativity that indicate a decrease in scores in the US since 1990. Prior to 1990, scores had been on the rise. Unfortunately, Kyung Hee Kim's recent research indicates that creativity is still declining (Kim, 2016, 2021). And currently, there is a new wave of focus on the urgent need to revive creativity. For example, in the *Washington Post*, Wooldridge (2022) reports a "famine of the mind". In his book, *Another World Is Possible: How to Reignite Social and Political Imagination*, Mulgan (2022) describes

3

an "imaginary crisis", a real crisis involving a dearth of creativity and imagination among our youth, social and political activists, and in the sciences and the arts.

Educational reformers worldwide call for transformations in teaching and learning that put creative and critical thinking at the forefront (Couros, 2015; Robinson, 2015; Zhao, 2012). Critical thinking, problem solving, and creativity have become important goals of international education standards and reform efforts (European Higher Education Area, 2011; Ritchhart, 2015; Zhao, 2009). Reformers argue that "schools kill creativity". Perhaps the emphasis on creativity is a response to a backlash from decades of high-stakes assessment in schools which has created a focus on knowledge acquisition to the detriment of creative thinking. Science, business, and educational leaders have sounded the alarm.

WHAT IS CREATIVITY?

Tom's creativity in stream restoration is the kind of innovation that solves big problems. Pam's everyday creativity is more common and helps solve everyday problems, allows for self-expression, and can be personally satisfying and fulfilling. But what is creativity, what types of thinking do creative individuals use?

Experts agree that creativity involves not only having novel ideas but also using critical thinking processes to develop ideas that are effective, useful, or in some way have value (Runco & Jaegar, 2012). Sir Ken Robinson (2015) defines creativity as the "process of having original ideas that have value" (P.18). Robinson further characterizes creativity as the use of the imagination as well as critical thinking. Creativity is a complex process that involves allowing for imagination, putting new ideas in place, and being reflective about, evaluating, and refining those ideas. According to Pink (2005), creativity involves symphony, the act of putting seemingly unrelated ideas together, assessing ideas, recognizing patterns and relationships, and connecting the dots in new ways to create something original, something no one else has envisioned.

Beghetto and Kauffman (2017) distinguish between "little-c" and "Big-C" creativity. "Big-C" creativity represents the big, breakthrough ideas that most people think of when they think of creativity, such as the invention of the lightbulb. "Big-C" ideas are rare and not the only kind of creative thinking. "Little-c" creativity is equally as important, if not more so, than "Big-C", especially in the classroom. "Little-c" is everyday creativity, the small ideas, moments of inspiration, and creations that may be small contributions but are indeed highly creative.

Helfand et al. (2017) posit that the "little-c" and "Big-C" dichotomy does not adequately describe the full range of creativity. These authors suggest a four-c model of creativity that adds "mini-c" and "Pro-c" creativity to the continuum. "Mini-c" creativity is internal, personally meaningful, and related to process rather than product. Examples include "aha" moments when we create meaning out of previously misunderstood or unknown concepts by connecting unrelated ideas. It also involves applying a skill or idea learned in one setting to a new context. "Pro-c" creativity includes people who engage in creative work for a living but don't reach a significant level of prominence. A creative engineer might regularly find innovative solutions but may not earn notoriety for their work. Similarly, amateurs in the sciences or the arts might be very clever but don't aspire to publish or make a living from their creative endeavors. Still, their creativity might rival that of professionals and would fall under "pro-c" creativity.

Kim (2016) introduces the concept of creativity through the framework of inbox, outbox, and newbox (ION) thinking. Inbox thinking refers to the process of developing expertise within a particular field by researching, learning, and adhering to established rules and practices. It is foundational for building the necessary knowledge and skills to master a discipline. However, creativity also requires thinking beyond traditional boundaries, which is where outbox thinking comes into play. Outbox thinking encourages individuals to break the rules and explore new approaches, styles, and strategies, leading to innovative solutions and ideas.

The third component of Kim's model, newbox thinking, focuses on the critical evaluation of new ideas and their outcomes. It involves assessing the effectiveness and potential impact of novel approaches, ensuring that they are viable and aligned with goals. Newbox thinking combines creativity with critical thinking, allowing individuals to refine and improve their ideas.

Guilford's model of creativity (1950) emphasizes that creative thinking involves both divergent and convergent thinking. Divergent thinking refers to the ability to generate a wide variety of ideas and solutions, while convergent thinking involves focusing those ideas into a coherent and effective solution. According to Guilford, the interplay between these two types of thinking is essential for creativity, as it allows individuals to explore many possibilities and then narrow them down to find the most valuable or practical ideas.

Guilford identified four key components of divergent thinking that are crucial for creativity. Flexibility is the capacity to think in diverse ways and adapt to different perspectives. Fluency, is the ability to generate multiple ideas in a short period of time. Originality highlights the importance of novel and unique ideas that stand apart from conventional thinking, while elaboration involves refining and adding depth to these ideas to make them practical and well-developed. Together, flexibility, fluency, originality, and elaboration form the foundation for creative thought, driving innovation and problem solving.

Wallas (1926) proposed that the creative process unfolds in four distinct stages. The first stage, preparation which involves brainstorming and research, sets the tone for the following stages of incubation, illumination, and verification.

When a creative individual faces a problem or is searching for an innovative idea, they engage in divergent thinking and move through a series of stages to come up with an idea and bring it to fruition. Evaluation is essential in creative problem solving as individuals assess and select the most appropriate or promising idea or solution. These components work together to bring about innovative thinking along the continuum of creativity.

CREATIVITY AS LEARNING

Arguing that "schools kill creativity", Sir Ken Robinson (2006) posits that an emphasis on test scores is at the crux of the problem. Test preparation can kill creativity by moving curiosity, imagination, and play to the back burner. Learners living in poverty, low achievers, and those from minority populations are often subject to scripted curricula and rote learning, further alienating already disenfranchised, vulnerable populations. Children and youth living in poverty have less access to quality education, art supplies, extracurricular activities, and cultural events. These resources and experiences can support a child's development and promote creativity. The good news is that experts agree that creativity can and should be taught and nurtured and that doing so brings many benefits.

Promoting creative thinking contributes to learning and emotional well-being. Teachers who provide opportunities for learners to use their creativity observe higher-order thinking skills in their students, including problem solving, critical thinking, deeper learning, and a transference of learning across subject matters (Saad, 2019). Creativity can help students make connections and encourages exploration, curiosity, and critical thinking.

Recent research suggests that engaging in creative tasks has a positive effect on the brain, elevating feelings of happiness and reducing anxiety (Ceci & Kumar, 2016; Tan et al., 2019). Bloom and Doss (2021) asked children to rate their level of happiness and engagement when doing both school activities that included the opportunity for creativity and activities that did not. Children's ratings overwhelmingly favored activities that allowed for creativity. With increasing concern regarding mental health issues, educators need practices that promote our youth's sense of well-being and engagement in school.

Finally, incorporating creative activity allows access to talent development. It provides enrichment for diverse learners. "Little-c" moments capture the hearts and minds of learners and enhance the learning experience.

Nurturing creativity is essential for many reasons, but can be difficult to achieve as it requires fostering a culture that values and encourages creative thinking as a key component of learning. In this book, we break the necessary components of creative nurturement into four focus areas depicted in Figure 1.1: Cultivating creative thinking and mindsets through metacognition and strategy, providing the opportunity for creativity, creating a nurturing environment, and motivating and inspiring creativity. In this book, we will explore each theme in depth. We use current research and theory as well as what we've learned from creative individuals like Tom and Pam to develop a comprehensive plan for reigniting, refueling, and reawakening the creative potential in our children and youth.

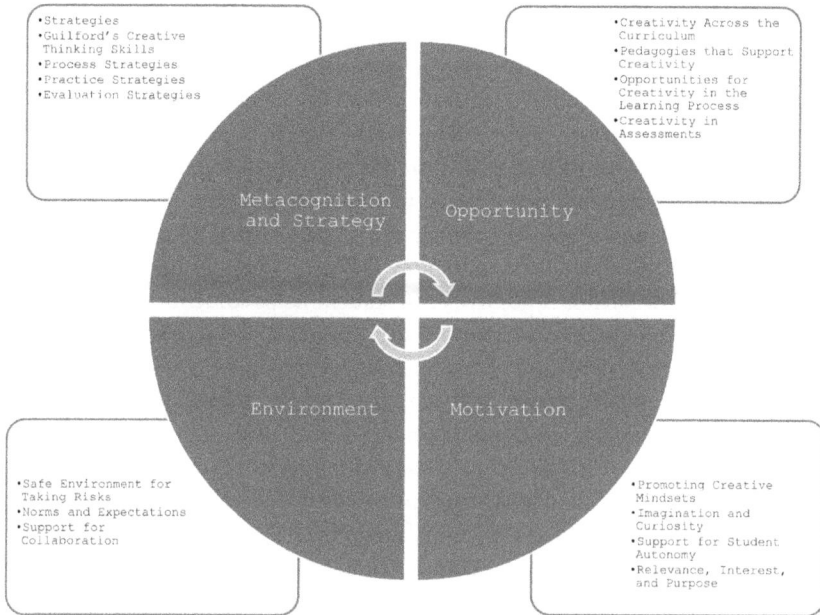

Figure 1.1 Interactive Cycle of Processes Influencing How Educators Can Nurture Creative Thinking.

METACOGNITION AND STRATEGY

Interviews with creative individuals reveal a heightened awareness of metacognition or thinking about thinking. In our interviews with creative people like Tom and Pam, we found they believe that their innovative ideas don't just come out of thin air. Rather, they result from curiosity, imagination, play, observation, effort, research, risk-taking, strategy, and keeping an open mind. For example, Tom describes the ability to induce "hyperfocus". Others describe specific brainstorming and problem-solving processes and ways to generate their own motivation and inspiration. All agree that creativity is something that needs nurturement.

Dweck's (2008) research on mindset indicates that traits such as creativity can be improved through a combination of belief, effort, and strategy. Helping learners to develop the mindset that they can become creative can fuel motivation. But a positive mindset is not enough. Beyond belief and practice, Dweck (2015) explains that individuals with a growth mindset seek, learn, and apply strategy. Helping learners develop strategies for creative thinking will enhance their success by making creativity seem more accessible.

7

ENVIRONMENTS THAT NURTURE CREATIVITY

Providing opportunities and creating an optimal environment for creative and critical thinking are essential for fostering creativity in the classroom. In a caring environment, students are more willing to take risks in their thinking and persist when facing challenges (Niemiec & Ryan, 2009). When students feel supported and encouraged, they are more likely to step out of their comfort zones and experiment with new ideas. This willingness to take risks is a key component of creativity, as it allows students to explore different solutions and think beyond conventional approaches. A positive environment helps students build the confidence they need to be open to innovative thinking and problem solving.

One of the first steps in creating such an environment is ensuring that the classroom is free from sarcasm, bullying, and negative behaviors that could hinder creative expression. Students must feel emotionally safe to express their ideas, ask questions, and take creative risks without fear of ridicule or judgment. When students are afraid of being laughed at or belittled, they may suppress their creative thoughts or avoid sharing ideas altogether. Therefore, it is essential for teachers to establish a classroom culture where respect and kindness are prioritized, and all students feel valued and supported.

Equally important is establishing clear norms and expectations for collaborative work. In a creative classroom, students often work together to brainstorm and develop ideas, and it is crucial to ensure that everyone feels respected as a contributor. Establishing norms for communication and teamwork helps students understand how to interact with one another in a way that fosters trust and mutual support. This foundation of respect and inclusion sets the stage for meaningful interactions, where students can freely exchange ideas, challenge each other's thinking, and work collaboratively toward creative solutions.

In addition to emotional safety, nurturing creativity requires a climate that encourages curiosity, interests, and passions. Allowing students to explore topics they are curious about helps them connect with their own interests, which can drive their creativity and motivation. Providing students with the freedom to pursue projects that align with their passions allows them to invest more deeply in their work, leading to greater innovation and personal satisfaction. By giving students opportunities to explore new ideas and learn in ways that resonate with them, educators can cultivate a sense of excitement and ownership over their creative endeavors.

Fostering creativity requires a classroom environment where failure is seen as a natural part of the learning process. Encouraging students to embrace mistakes as opportunities for growth helps build resilience and the willingness to take risks. By providing appropriately challenging tasks and offering chances to reflect on their learning, educators can inspire students to view setbacks as learning experiences rather than obstacles. These conditions not only enable creativity to thrive but also prepare students to tackle complex challenges with confidence and originality, ready to apply their creative thinking to a wide range of real-world problems.

MOTIVATION

Engaging in creative activity is often inherently motivating for many students, as it offers opportunities for self-expression and exploration. However, this may not be the case for all learners, especially those who are performance-driven or perfectionistic. These students may struggle with the uncertainty and iterative nature of the creative process, finding it difficult to embrace the ambiguity and experimentation that creativity requires. They often prefer clear guidelines, measurable outcomes, and certainty, which may not align with the open-ended nature of creative tasks. As a result, they may become frustrated, disengaged, or hesitant to take risks in their work.

While offering choices in how students demonstrate their learning and allowing for self-expression can help boost motivation, some students need additional support to feel comfortable stepping outside their comfort zones. These students may need extra encouragement to engage with creative tasks that lack clear structure or where outcomes are less predictable. Providing a safe and supportive environment that encourages experimentation, failure, and iteration can help these students overcome their resistance to creative challenges. It's essential for educators to recognize that some learners may need more time and guidance to appreciate the creative process fully.

Performance-driven students benefit from encouragement to take risks, accept mistakes as part of learning, and engage in constructive feedback. Teachers can foster a classroom culture that values growth over perfection by emphasizing the importance of the learning journey, rather than focusing solely on the final product. By creating opportunities for students to reflect on their learning and progress, educators can help students recognize the value of process-based work. Encouraging students to take risks and accept mistakes as part of their learning helps them understand that creativity often involves trial and error, and that innovation cannot happen without occasional setbacks.

Providing specific, useful, and kind feedback is another important aspect of supporting performance-driven students. This type of feedback helps students see mistakes as opportunities for improvement, rather than as failures. When feedback is framed in a way that is both constructive and supportive, students are more likely to feel confident in their ability to explore new and innovative ideas. Teachers can guide students through the process of revision, showing them that creativity involves refining and reworking ideas. By fostering a growth mindset, students are encouraged to embrace challenges and view them as part of the creative process.

For students with perfectionistic tendencies, direct instruction on navigating the creative process can help them better understand and appreciate the setbacks and challenges that often accompany originality. These students may find it hard to start a project or may procrastinate due to fear of not achieving perfection. Explicitly teaching the iterative nature of creativity – where ideas evolve and improve over time – can help perfectionistic learners see that mistakes are not only inevitable but also valuable. Teaching students that creative endeavors are seldom linear and that each step, including failures, is part of the journey to success, allows them to embrace the messy nature of creativity.

By addressing these motivational factors, educators can create an environment where all students feel empowered to think creatively and embrace innovative problem solving. Students who may initially struggle with creative tasks due to their perfectionistic tendencies or performance-driven attitudes can be supported through thoughtful teaching strategies that prioritize process over product. Through these efforts, students can learn to overcome self-doubt and embrace the creative process as a valuable skill set for both personal growth and future problem solving. This approach not only nurtures creativity but also fosters resilience, persistence, and confidence in all learners.

OPPORTUNITY

As with developing any new skill or talent, ample opportunity to engage in creative and critical thinking will help learners sharpen that skill. In addition to the arts, where creativity is typically emphasized, creativity is at play in all areas of life and is valued by virtually every discipline, as well as business and industry (Pfieffer & Thompson, 2013; Wagner, 2008), and subsequently, should be nurtured in all areas of schooling (Robinson, 2015). Learners benefit from opportunities to work across disciplines, allowing them to identify connections between seemingly unrelated ideas. By engaging in interdisciplinary thinking, students can use information or inspiration from one field to fuel creativity in another, fostering the development of novel ideas and solutions. This approach encourages learners to integrate knowledge from various subjects, leading to deeper understanding and more innovative thinking.

Creativity can be nurtured throughout the curriculum by incorporating various teaching strategies that encourage exploration, critical thinking, and innovation. Inquiry-based learning pedagogies, for example, provide students with the opportunity to ask questions, explore topics deeply, and discover answers through active participation and collaboration. This approach allows students to take ownership of their learning and engage in problem solving, both of which are key components of creative thinking. Similarly, Genius Hour, which gives students dedicated time to explore their passions and pursue personal projects, fosters creativity by promoting curiosity and independent thinking.

Flipped learning is another effective strategy for fostering creativity in the classroom. By reversing the traditional learning model — where students learn content at home and apply it in the classroom — teachers can create space for more interactive, hands-on activities that encourage students to use their creativity. This method empowers students to become active problem solvers and critical thinkers as they apply what they've learned in practical, real-world scenarios. Such engagement not only enhances their creative abilities but also reinforces their understanding of the content.

Makerspaces, which provide students with the tools and materials to create, invent, and explore, are also essential for cultivating creativity across subjects. In these environments, students can work on projects that combine various disciplines, from science and technology to art and design. Makerspaces encourage experimentation and iteration, which are vital aspects of the creative process. When students are given the freedom to design and build, they develop problem-solving skills and learn how to express their ideas in concrete, tangible forms. These experiences help students understand that creativity is not limited to one area but can be applied across multiple subjects.

Providing creative outlets within all content areas further enriches students' ability to think outside the box and apply their creativity in meaningful ways. By integrating creative activities such as storytelling, visual arts, and performance into subjects like math, science, and language arts, students can make connections between seemingly unrelated concepts. This holistic approach ensures that creativity is not confined to specific classes but is instead woven into the fabric of their overall learning experience. When students have the freedom to explore their ideas in diverse formats, they build confidence in their creative abilities and develop a deeper understanding of how creativity can be applied to solve real-world problems.

ASSESSMENT AND EVALUATION

In the current educational climate, high-stakes assessments often dominate as the primary focus of evaluation. However, in a personalized classroom where creativity thrives, assessment takes on multiple forms, serving different purposes beyond simply evaluating what students have learned. While assessment "of" learning remains essential, it is complemented by assessment "for" learning and assessment "as" learning. Assessment "for" learning engages both teachers and students in a collaborative process, using assessments to adjust teaching strategies and learning activities. This dynamic approach helps ensure that students are supported in real time as they progress through their learning journey.

Assessment "as" learning encourages students to take ownership of their learning by teaching them to set goals, self-assess, and use their insights to guide their educational growth. This process enables students to become more reflective and metacognitive about their learning, which can enhance their motivation and engagement. By actively involving students in their evaluation, they can develop a deeper understanding of their strengths and areas for improvement, fostering a growth mindset that supports long-term success.

The integration of a rich array of apps and technology tools can further support creativity in assessment. These tools give learners more autonomy and allow for greater choice in how they document their learning. For example, self-evaluation can be enhanced through apps that facilitate goal-setting, rubrics, and progress monitoring, allowing students to track their growth in creative and personalized ways. These digital tools also promote efficiency in the process of self-assessment, enabling students to reflect on their progress in real time.

Moreover, students can use their creativity to document and present their learning in unique ways, such as podcasts, news reports, 3-dimensional models, blogs, or websites. These diverse presentation formats provide students with opportunities to express their understanding in innovative ways, showcasing their creative abilities while demonstrating their mastery of the content. By encouraging students to take an active role in designing their evaluation methods, assessment becomes another avenue for fostering creativity, empowering learners to engage in self-directed learning and expression.

PATHWAYS FOR IMPLEMENTING CREATIVE THINKING PRACTICES INTO THE CLASSROOM

To foster creativity in the classroom, teachers can begin by integrating techniques that improve core components of creative thinking: Fluency, flexibility, originality, elaboration, incubation, and evaluation. By building activities that target each of these skills, educators can nurture a holistic approach to creativity. For example, fluency exercises might involve brainstorming as many solutions as possible to a single problem, while flexibility activities could encourage students to approach a problem from multiple perspectives. Originality can be developed through metaphorical thinking or exploring unusual connections, and elaboration can focus on adding depth and detail to ideas. Structured time for incubation allows students to process ideas unconsciously, while evaluation ensures their creative outcomes are refined and aligned with goals.

Another pathway to foster creativity is through pedagogical approaches such as Project-Based Learning (PjBL), Problem-Based Learning (PBL), and Creative Problem Solving (CPS). These methods are rooted in authentic, real-world applications of learning, which engage students in meaningful problem solving. For instance, PjBL might involve students designing a sustainable community, while PBL could challenge them to address a local environmental issue. CPS, on the other hand, introduces structured steps for tackling complex problems, from identifying the challenge to generating and refining solutions. Teachers who design units based on these methods encourage students to use their creativity in collaborative, purposeful ways.

Developing students' creative mindsets is another essential component of promoting creativity in the classroom. Teachers can model and reinforce a growth mindset by emphasizing that creativity is a skill that can be improved through effort and practice, as proposed by Dweck (2008). Encouraging students to take risks, embrace challenges, and view setbacks as learning opportunities helps foster resilience and confidence in their creative abilities. Teachers can also introduce reflective practices, such as journaling or group discussions, to help students recognize their creative progress over time.

Fostering strong collaboration skills is equally important for creativity. Group projects can help students practice brainstorming, active listening, and constructive feedback. Teachers can assign roles within groups, such as idea generator, evaluator, or elaborator, to ensure all aspects of creativity are addressed and every student participates meaningfully. Activities that simulate real-world team dynamics, such as design sprints or collaborative problem-solving challenges, prepare students to work creatively in diverse settings.

The physical learning environment also plays a crucial role in promoting creativity. Flexible learning spaces equipped with movable furniture, whiteboards, and accessible materials encourage dynamic collaboration and free-flowing idea generation. Teachers can create "creativity corners" or makerspaces with resources like art supplies, technology, and design tools. These areas provide opportunities for students to experiment and explore, helping them feel empowered to think outside the box.

Healthy learning environments, where students feel safe and supported, are essential for creativity to thrive. Teachers can build these environments by fostering mutual respect, encouraging open communication, and celebrating diverse perspectives. Incorporating mindfulness activities, such as meditation or journaling, can reduce stress and enhance students' ability to focus on creative tasks. Additionally, providing unstructured time for exploration and play can stimulate curiosity and innovation.

To embed these practices into daily instruction, teachers can start small by incorporating short, creative exercises into their lessons. For example, warm-up activities like "What if?" scenarios or quick brainstorming sessions can prime students for innovative thinking. Gradually, teachers can expand these efforts by designing units of study centered on creative challenges or interdisciplinary projects that connect various subject areas. Consistent opportunities for creativity will help students build confidence and competence in their creative abilities.

By implementing strategies to develop fluency, flexibility, originality, elaboration, incubation, and evaluation, as well as embracing pedagogical approaches like PBL and CPS, teachers can transform their classrooms into hubs of creativity. Combined with an emphasis on growth mindsets, collaboration, and supportive learning environments, these pathways empower students to think innovatively, solve problems effectively, and approach learning with curiosity and imagination. Through intentional planning and practice, teachers can ensure that creativity becomes an integral part of their students' educational experiences.

CONCLUSION

As the global need for creativity continues to grow, nurturing creative and critical thinking in our youth has become a crucial responsibility for educators. The ability to think creatively is not only essential for problem solving and innovation but also significantly enhances overall learning and well-being. By fostering creativity, educators can provide equitable opportunities for talent development, ensuring that all students have access to the tools they need to thrive in an ever-changing world. In a future where creativity will be highly valued across industries, it is imperative that educators prioritize the development of creative skills in their students.

Research on creativity, along with insights from professionals who apply creativity in their work, offers valuable guidance on how to nurture these essential skills in the classroom. Understanding creative thinking strategies and the environments in which creativity flourishes is key to preparing students for success. Teachers can draw inspiration from these resources to enhance their teaching methods and create spaces that encourage curiosity, exploration, and innovation. By integrating these strategies, educators can help students develop the mindset and skills needed to tackle complex problems and generate novel solutions.

The goal of this text is to provide educators with a comprehensive understanding of creativity's role in learning, as well as practical approaches to teaching creative thinking strategies. In addition to offering guidance on how to motivate and inspire young innovators, this text will emphasize the importance of creating nurturing environments where students can develop their creative potential. By orchestrating classrooms that foster equitable talent development, educators can ensure that all students have the opportunity to grow and succeed as creative thinkers, ready to meet the challenges of an uncertain future.

REFERENCES

Beghetto, R.A., & Kaufman, J.C. (2017). *Nurturing creativity in the classroom*. Cambridge: Cambridge University Press.

Bloom, L.A., & Doss, K. (2021). Can creativity improve engagement and emotional wellbeing? *NCAGT (North Carolina Association for Gifted & Talented) Newsletter*.

Bronson, P., & Merryman, A. (2010). The creativity crisis. *Newsweek*. Retrieved from https://www.newsweek.com/creativity-crisis-74665

Ceci, M., & Kumar, V. (2016). A correlational study of creativity, happiness, motivation, and stress from creative pursuits. *Journal of Happiness Studies, 17*(2), 609–626. https://doi.org/10.1007/s10902-015-9615-y

Couros, G. (2015). *The innovator's mindset: Empower learning, unleash talent, and lead a culture of creativity*. San Diego, CA: Dave Burgess Consulting.

Dweck, Carol S. (2008). *Mindset: The new psychology of success*. New York, NY: Ballantine

Dweck, C.S. (2015). Carol Dweck revisits 'growth mindset'. *Education Week, 35*(5), 20–24.

European Commission (2008, December 16). Decision no 1350/2008/EC of the European Parliament and of the council concerning the European Year of Creativity and Innovation (2009). *Official Journal of the European Union*.

European Higher Education Area. (2011). The official Bologna Process website. Retrieved from the European Higher Education Area website: http://www.ehea.info/

Florida, R. (2004). America's looming creativity crisis. *Harvard Business Review*. October, 2004. Retrieved from https://hbr.org/2004/10/americas- looming-creativity-crisis

Guilford, J.P. (1950). Creativity. *American Psychologist, 5*(9), 444–454.

Helfand, M., Kaufman, J.C., & Beghetto, R.A. (2017). The four C model of creativity: Culture and context. In V. P. Glăveanu (Ed.), *Palgrave handbook of creativity and culture research* (pp. 15–360). New York, NY: Palgrave

Kim, K.H. (2016). The creativity challenge: How we can recapture American innovation. Amherst, NY: Prometheus Books.

Kim, K.H. (2021). Creativity crisis update: America follows Asia in pursuing high test scores over learning. *Roeper Review, 43*(1), 21–41. https://doi.org/10.1080/02783193.2020.1840464

Mulgan, G. (2022). Another world is possible: How to reignite social and political imagination. London: Hurst.

Niemiec, C.P., & Ryan, R.M. (2009). Autonomy, competence and relatedness in the classroom. Applying self-determination theory to education practice. *Theory and Research in Education, 7*(2), 133–144.

Pfeiffer S.I., & Thompson T.L. (2013). Creativity from a talent development perspective. In K.H. Kim, J.C. Kaufman, J. Baer, & B. Sriraman (Eds.), *Creatively gifted students are not like other gifted students. Advances in creativity and giftedness*, vol 5, 231–255. Rotterdam: Sense Publishers.

Pink, D. (2005). *A whole new mind: Moving from the informational age to the conceptual age*. New York, NY: Penguin.

Ritchhart, R. (2015). *Creating cultures of thinking*. San Francisco: Jossey -Bass.

Robinson, K. (2015). *Creative Schools*. New York, NY: Penguin Random.

Robinson, K. (2006, February). Do schools kill creativity? [Video]. TED Conferences. https://www.ted.com/talks/sir_ken_robinson_do_schools_kill_creativity

Runco, M.A., & Jaeger, G. J. (2012). The standard definition of creativity. *Creativity Research Journal*, *24*(1), 92–96.

Saad, L. (2019). Teachers who promote creativity see educational results. Retrieved from https://news.gallup.com/opinion/gallup/245600/teachers-promote-creativity-educational-results.aspx.

Tan, C.-S., Tan, S.-A., Mohd Hashim, I. H., Lee, M.-N., Ong, A. W.-H., & Yaacob, S. nor B. (2019). Problem-solving ability and stress mediate the relationship between creativity and happiness. *Creativity Research Journal*, *31*(1), 15–25. https://doi.org/10.1080/10400419.2019.1568155

Wagner, T. (2008). Rigor redefined. *Educational Leadership*, *66*(2), 20–25.

Wallas, G. (1926). *The art of thought*. New York, NY: Harcourt Brace and World.

West-Knights, I. (2017). Why are schools in China looking west for lessons in creativity? *Financial Times*. Retrieved from https://www.ft.com/content/b215c486-e231-11e6-8405-9e5580d6e5f

Wooldridge, A. (2022). How to reverse the West's creativity crisis. *Washington Post*. Retrieved from https://www.washingtonpost.com/business/how-to-reverse-the-wests-creativity-crisis/2022/07/04/f9267a98-fb56-11ec-b39d-71309168014b_story.html

Xi Jinping (2017). China daily. Full text of Xi Jinping's report at 19th CPC National Congress. Retrieved from https://www.chinadaily.com.cn/china/19thcpcnationalcongress/2017-11/04/content_34115212.htm

Zhao, Y. (2009). Catching up or leading the way: American education in the age of globalization. Alexandria, VA: ASCD.

Zhao, Y. (2012). *World class learners: Educating creative and entrepreneurial students*. Thousand Oaks, CA: Corwin Press.

Chapter 2

Creativity as Learning

INTRODUCTION

Enrique, a highly successful astronomer and physicist, delves into physics theories and takes an innovative approach to helping his students, including those with visual impairments, access physics and astronomy through activities such as sonification. Sonification, the process of representing data in sounds rather than data points on paper, allows students to "hear" stars. Star patterns are used to create musical scores. Through the use of AI to assign harmonies to star patterns, he helps students to anthropomorphize stars and identify when a star sounds happy (major chords) and when it sounds sad (minor chords).

Enrique grew up in Mexico City. He recalls how opportunity for creative expression as a child fueled his thinking and learning. He spent hours upon hours with a hand-me-down set of Legos, constructing contraptions and structures from his imagination. He attributes his math ability to his Lego play. He explains that the Legos helped him visualize in 3D. Enrique also recalls hearing about things in the US such as choose-your-own-adventure books, Dungeons and Dragons, and video games that he had no access to in Mexico City. As a result, he was driven to fill the void of what he thought he was missing out on. His desperation led him to create a project that included a large map of possible storylines and his own version of a choose-your-own-adventure book.

Like Enrique's experience with Legos and book making, creativity aids in learning because it is active, dynamic, and engaging. As learners create, they explore, question, and connect concepts in novel ways. The influence of creativity on learning has long been recognized by educational theorists.

In his theoretical model, Dewey (1899) posited that children possess four natural impulses: To inquire, to communicate, to construct, and to express. These impulses drive how children engage with the world and learn. Dewey's emphasis on building curricula around these impulses rather than separating learning into traditional disciplines aligns with the contemporary understanding

DOI: 10.4324/9781003434221-2

of the importance of creativity in education. It suggests that embedding creativity across various aspects of learning not only aligns with children's natural impulses but also enhances their educational experience. Allowing children to explore, experiment, and express themselves creatively leads to a more motivating and effective learning process.

Like Dewey, Piaget (1952) also viewed creativity as a natural extension of the cognitive development process. Piaget emphasized that creativity stems from the individual's capacity to reorganize and reconstruct knowledge in novel ways. In Piaget's theory of cognitive development, children actively construct their understanding of the world by interacting with their environment and experimenting with different ideas. Creativity, for Piaget, is a form of "assimilation" where individuals incorporate new experiences into existing cognitive structures, but it also involves "accommodation", which means modifying those structures to adapt to new ideas and perspectives. This interplay between assimilation and accommodation is key to creative thinking, as it enables learners to develop original solutions by reconfiguring their understanding of familiar concepts. Piaget also highlighted that true creativity emerges when children are given opportunities for autonomous exploration and problem solving, allowing them to engage in imaginative play and experiment with new ways of thinking.

Like Dewey and Piaget, Vygotsky (2004) also viewed creativity as an essential part of human development and learning. According to Vygotsky, creativity plays a critical role in cognitive development, as it allows learners to transcend existing knowledge, explore new possibilities, and apply their understanding in novel ways. He argued that creativity is not limited to extraordinary individuals but is a universal process that everyone engages in, especially during learning. Vygotsky believed that creativity emerges from a combination of imagination and experience, with both drawing from the individual's cultural and social context. He emphasized the role of social interaction in developing creativity, suggesting that learners expand their creative capacities through collaborative and guided experiences with others.

Harel and Papert (1991) present a foundational theory in education that builds on the ideas of constructivism, particularly those developed by Dewey, Piaget, and Vygotsky. *Constructionism* posits that learners construct knowledge most effectively when they are actively involved in creating meaningful, tangible artifacts. This approach emphasizes learning by making – where students learn through hands-on, project-based activities that allow them to explore concepts, solve problems, and apply their knowledge in practical ways.

How do you view creativity? Is it something that can be nurtured or something individuals are born with? Henriksen and Mishra (2014) describe historical views of creativity as a magical or mystical quality that someone is either born with or has bestowed on them. Teachers with this type of philosophy may describe individual students as creative due to their unique insights about the world or specific skills in writing, art, or music. Contemporary views contend that creative thinking is something that can be taught and nurtured and is within reach of all people. Teachers with this type of mindset see creative potential in all students and orchestrate the opportunity for creative expression in many aspects of life in the classroom.

Creative thinking, like academic achievement, benefits when learners and their teachers believe individuals can improve. They recognize that, as with developing any new skill or talent, time engaged with the skill, as well as explicit instructions about the tricks of the trade, will help learners sharpen that skill. Teaching specific strategies can contribute to the development of creative and critical thinkers. Creative individuals use particular tactics, techniques, and processes to develop their ideas, such as brainstorming ideas, creating mind maps, and journaling about intriguing ideas. Although there are general strategies that help students understand the creative process, teaching creative thinking in generic terms is less beneficial than teaching skills and strategies in the context of the discipline (Mishra, 2012).

USING A CREATIVE APPROACH IN THE CLASSROOM

In Mrs. Gable's fourth-grade class, the unit on the Industrial Revolution served as a springboard for a creative project: Designing and building "dream machines". Students explored concepts like innovation, technological advancement, and the impact of new inventions on society. They researched historical inventions, analyzed their mechanisms, and then applied these principles to design their own fantastical contraptions.

Across the hall, Mr. Davis's class also studied the Industrial Revolution. However, his approach emphasized rote memorization of key dates, inventors, and the chronological order of major events. Students were expected to learn definitions, identify key figures, and complete worksheets on the impact of industrialization.

While both classes covered the same curriculum, their learning experiences differed significantly. Mrs. Gable's students engaged in hands-on activities, collaborative discussions, and presentations, fostering critical thinking, problem solving, and creative expression. They learned to apply historical concepts to novel situations and developed a deeper understanding of the creative process behind technological innovation.

Mr. Davis's students, on the other hand, primarily engaged in passive learning activities, such as listening to lectures and completing worksheets. While they may have been able to recall factual information on the test, such as the year the steam engine was invented or the names of prominent industrialists, their understanding of the underlying concepts and their ability to apply them in new contexts may have been limited.

Six months later, Mrs. Gable's students were likely to remember their "dream machine" projects with fondness. They might recall the excitement of the design process, the challenges they overcame, and the unique solutions they developed. These memories would likely be linked to a deeper understanding of historical concepts, such as how technological advancements can revolutionize industries, the role of innovation in societal progress, and the ethical considerations surrounding new technologies. For example, a student who designed a "pollution-free energy generator" might recall researching the environmental impact of the Industrial Revolution and connect it to contemporary concerns about climate change.

In contrast, Mr. Davis's students were more likely to recall the unit on the Industrial Revolution as a series of tedious facts and figures. Their memories might be fragmented and disconnected, such as remembering that the Industrial Revolution began in England but struggling to explain why or how it impacted the world. They might recall specific dates or the names of inventors, but without a deeper understanding of the historical context, these facts may be quickly forgotten or misremembered.

MYTHS ABOUT CREATIVITY

Creativity is often misunderstood, and these misconceptions can deter people from recognizing its value or investing time and resources into nurturing it. One common myth is that creativity is an innate talent, reserved for a select few individuals with exceptional abilities. This belief overlooks the reality that creativity is a skill that can be developed and strengthened with practice and intention. Just as students can improve their math or writing skills through education, they can also learn to think creatively with proper guidance and support. Tackling this misconception is crucial for educators and parents, as it highlights the accessibility of creativity and ensures that all students have the opportunity to explore and develop their creative potential. Creativity is often left off the list of initiatives, but it must be added to teacher training programs and professional development in order for educators to understand the potential impact and be prepared to implement and experiment with techniques in the classroom (Makel, 2009; Ramlackhan et al., 2024).

Another widespread misconception is that creativity only applies to the arts, such as painting, music, or literature. While the arts certainly thrive on creative thinking, as we see from creative individuals such as Enrique who are referenced in this text, creativity is equally vital in fields like science, engineering, mathematics, and even social studies. For instance, a scientist devising a groundbreaking experiment or an entrepreneur innovating a new business model relies just as much on creativity as a novelist crafting a story. Creativity is not limited to specific disciplines but is a universal skill essential for solving problems, thinking critically, and adapting to challenges in any domain.

A third misconception is that creativity is purely spontaneous and cannot be structured or taught. Many people assume that creative ideas emerge in moments of inspiration, completely separate from deliberate effort. While moments of "aha!" insight do occur, they are often the result of sustained effort, practice, and strategic thinking. Frameworks such as the Guilford Model and Torrance Incubation Model demonstrate that creativity follows processes that can be learned and cultivated. Teaching students to approach creativity systematically — by practicing fluency, flexibility, and elaboration, for example — demystifies the process and empowers them to be more consistently innovative.

Creativity is also frequently dismissed as less important than other skills like critical thinking, literacy, or STEM knowledge. This misconception undermines the fact that creativity is deeply intertwined with these areas. Creative thinking is essential for solving complex problems, generating innovative solutions, and making connections across disciplines. For example, a student designing an app to address a community need must draw on technical STEM skills, but their ability to think creatively enables them to design features that are user-friendly, unique, and impactful. By addressing this misconception, educators and readers can appreciate creativity as a foundational skill that enhances all aspects of learning and professional success.

Finally, there is a tendency to view creativity as an abstract, "nice-to-have" quality rather than a necessity in education and life. However, in a rapidly changing world, creativity is a critical skill for thriving in the face of uncertainty. Employers consistently rank creativity among the top skills they seek, as it drives innovation and adaptability. Moreover, creativity fosters personal growth, resilience, and emotional well-being, enabling individuals to navigate challenges with confidence and optimism. By challenging this misconception, readers can better understand why investing time and resources into cultivating creativity is not only worthwhile but essential for preparing students to succeed in a dynamic, ever-evolving world.

TEACHING CREATIVITY TO PROMOTE EQUITY, DIVERSITY, AND INCLUSION

Creativity has the power to break down barriers and create opportunities, making it a crucial tool for addressing equity, diversity, and inclusion in education. When students are taught to think creatively, they are encouraged to see problems from multiple perspectives and value diverse viewpoints. This mindset fosters empathy and respect for others' experiences, backgrounds, and ideas. For example, when students collaborate on creative projects that explore cultural heritage or address social challenges, they gain an appreciation for diversity while contributing their unique perspectives. Creative education helps level the playing field by allowing every student, regardless of background, to contribute ideas and solutions in ways that highlight their individuality and strengths.

Creative teaching also empowers underrepresented and marginalized students by encouraging self-expression and recognizing the value of their voices. In many traditional classroom settings, certain forms of knowledge or expression may be prioritized over others, unintentionally excluding students who don't conform to these norms. Creativity, however, celebrates nontraditional approaches and values unconventional ideas, giving students from all backgrounds a platform to shine. For instance, a project where students design community improvement initiatives can allow students from different socioeconomic or cultural backgrounds to draw on their lived experiences as assets, creating equitable opportunities for meaningful participation.

Incorporating creativity into the classroom can also address systemic inequities by reducing the emphasis on standardized assessments that often marginalize nontraditional learners. Creativity-focused tasks, such as open-ended projects or collaborative problem-solving activities, allow students to demonstrate their knowledge and skills in diverse ways that transcend rigid testing structures. This inclusive approach ensures that students with different abilities and experiences can thrive. By emphasizing creative problem solving and innovation, schools can create a more equitable environment where all students feel valued and capable of success (Ramlackhan, 2024).

FOSTERING WELLNESS AND RESILIENCE THROUGH CREATIVITY

Teaching creativity not only addresses issues of equity and inclusion, but also plays a vital role in fostering wellness and resilience among students. Creative activities provide an outlet for self-expression, allowing students to process emotions and experiences in constructive ways. For example, students may write reflective journal entries, create artwork that explores their identities, or design solutions to challenges they face in their communities. These activities help students build emotional intelligence and self-awareness, both of which are essential for mental health and well-being. Creative thinking also encourages a growth mindset, teaching students that mistakes and setbacks are opportunities for learning rather than failures.

Creativity inherently nurtures resilience by teaching students how to approach challenges with flexibility and resourcefulness. When students learn to generate multiple solutions to a problem or reframe obstacles as opportunities, they develop the skills needed to navigate uncertainty and adapt to change. For instance, in a STEM project where students design prototypes, they learn to iterate and improve their designs, embracing trial and error as part of the process. These lessons extend beyond the classroom, equipping students with the mental tools to persevere through life's difficulties with confidence and optimism.

Creative activities build a sense of community and connection, which are vital for both individual and collective well-being. Collaborative creative projects encourage students to work together, listen to each other's ideas, and build on one another's strengths. This not only reinforces inclusivity but also fosters a sense of belonging and support among students. In a world where mental health challenges and social isolation are growing concerns, creativity serves as a powerful means of building resilience, enhancing well-being, and creating a classroom culture where every student feels seen, valued, and empowered to thrive.

WHAT IS A CREATIVE TEACHER?

A creative teacher is someone who embraces innovation, flexibility, and adaptability in their teaching approach, inspiring students to think beyond conventional boundaries. Creative teachers go beyond traditional methods, incorporating novel strategies, tools, and activities that make learning engaging and meaningful. They view challenges in the classroom as opportunities to innovate, whether it's finding new ways to differentiate instruction or creating projects that connect academic content to real-world problems. For instance, a creative teacher might design an interdisciplinary project where students use math skills to calculate the cost of building a sustainable home, integrate art by having students sketch designs, and explore science concepts related to energy efficiency.

One of the hallmarks of a creative teacher is their ability to foster an environment where curiosity thrives. These educators encourage students to ask questions, take risks, and explore multiple solutions to a problem, rather than seeking a single "correct" answer. They celebrate originality and support students in experimenting with ideas, even if the outcome is imperfect. For example, a creative teacher might ask students to brainstorm unusual uses for everyday objects, such as a paperclip or rubber band, to develop divergent thinking skills. By modeling curiosity and openness, creative teachers inspire their students to approach learning with enthusiasm and confidence.

Creative teachers also prioritize connection – both in building relationships with their students and in designing lessons that connect to students' lives and interests. They recognize that creativity flourishes in a supportive environment where students feel valued and understood. For example, a creative teacher might adapt a history lesson to include stories of local heroes or cultural narratives relevant to the students' communities, making the content more relatable and engaging. Additionally, they use creative teaching methods, such as storytelling, games, or hands-on experiments, to ensure that lessons resonate with different learning styles and keep students actively engaged.

Creative teachers are lifelong learners themselves, constantly seeking out new ideas and practices to improve their craft. They read, attend workshops, collaborate with colleagues, and embrace feedback to refine their teaching methods.

They are also willing to step out of their comfort zones, experimenting with technology or unconventional approaches to spark interest and curiosity in their students. By embodying creativity, they show students that learning is a dynamic, ongoing process. In this way, creative teachers not only nurture their students' creativity but also equip them with the tools and mindset to be innovative thinkers in their own lives.

Seven habits of highly creative teachers (Costa & Kallick, 2008; Sawyer, 2019; Schrek, 2009) include the ability to actively listen to their students and foster meaningful connections. They embrace flexible thinking, adapting their teaching strategies to meet diverse needs. Creative teachers are also problem solvers, finding innovative ways to address challenges in the classroom. They demonstrate empathy, understanding their students' perspectives and emotional experiences. Humor is welcomed as a way to create a positive and engaging learning environment. Additionally, these teachers practice metacognition, remaining aware of their own thoughts and actions. Finally, they view failures as valuable learning opportunities, modeling resilience and growth for their students.

WHAT DOES A CREATIVE STUDENT LOOK LIKE?

A creative student demonstrates curiosity and a willingness to explore new ideas and concepts, often going beyond the surface level of learning. These students ask thoughtful and unexpected questions that challenge traditional perspectives and show a deep engagement with the subject matter. For example, in a science lesson about ecosystems, a creative student might wonder how urban architecture could mimic natural processes to create more sustainable cities. Their curiosity drives them to connect ideas from different disciplines and explore possibilities that others may overlook. This intellectual curiosity is a hallmark of creativity, laying the foundation for innovative thinking.

Creative students are also characterized by their ability to think divergently, generating multiple ideas or solutions to a given problem. They are not satisfied with conventional answers and instead seek out original approaches or alternative perspectives. For instance, in a classroom discussion about resolving conflicts, a creative student might suggest a community art project to foster understanding among different groups, blending creativity with problem solving. Their flexibility allows them to adapt and see opportunities where others might only perceive obstacles, making them valuable contributors to group work and collaborative projects.

Another key trait of a creative student is their resilience and willingness to take risks. These students understand that failure is a natural part of the creative process and view mistakes as opportunities for growth. For example, a creative student working on a coding project might experiment with different algorithms, even if some of them fail, in pursuit of an innovative solution. They are persistent in refining their ideas and value the process of learning as much as the outcome. This resilience not only enhances their creative abilities but also equips them with the confidence to tackle challenges in all areas of life.

Creative students are often passionate about self-expression and originality. Whether through writing, art, music, or other forms of creative output, they find ways to communicate their unique perspectives and ideas. For example, a student might compose a song to explain a historical event or create a storyboard to present a solution to a community issue. This passion for self-expression fosters a sense of identity and purpose, helping students develop confidence in their abilities. By nurturing their creativity, these students learn to think critically, innovate, and approach the world with curiosity and adaptability – skills that are essential for success in school and beyond.

WHAT DOES CREATIVE LEARNING LOOK AND SOUND LIKE?

Creative learning is a dynamic process where students are actively engaged in exploring ideas, solving problems, and expressing themselves in meaningful ways. In a classroom, creative learning looks like students collaborating in small groups, discussing different perspectives, and using hands-on materials or digital tools to bring their ideas to life. For example, students in a STEM class might construct prototypes for eco-friendly inventions using recycled materials, testing their designs and refining them based on results. The energy in the room is palpable as students engage in trial and error, learning through discovery and experimentation. Creative learning environments are vibrant, often filled with visual cues such as brainstorming maps, project drafts, or student-created artwork, reflecting the diversity of thought and exploration.

The sounds of creative learning are equally distinctive. Instead of a teacher delivering a lecture, you'll hear lively discussions, students asking thought-provoking questions, and peers sharing their ideas and offering feedback. In a history class, this might involve students participating in a debate about the causes of a significant event, exploring perspectives they might not have considered before. You'll also hear moments of quiet reflection as students think deeply about their next steps or work individually on tasks like writing, drawing, or coding. Teachers act as facilitators, guiding discussions with open-ended questions like, "What if we approached this differently?" or "How could you build on that idea?". This creates a space where students feel encouraged to take intellectual risks and express themselves freely.

Creative learning often blurs the lines between subjects, making it interdisciplinary and holistic. In one example, students might combine art, science, and writing to create an illustrated children's book explaining complex environmental issues in simple terms. This type of learning fosters connections between disciplines, encouraging students to see how knowledge can be integrated to solve real-world problems. It also provides opportunities for students to bring their interests and cultural backgrounds into the classroom, making learning more personal and meaningful. When students see themselves reflected in their work, they become more invested and empowered to explore creative possibilities.

Creative learning fosters an atmosphere of curiosity, wonder, and excitement. It prioritizes the process over the product, emphasizing exploration, reflection, and growth. Students take pride in their efforts, even when their ideas don't work out as planned, because they recognize the value of what they've learned along the way. Teachers encourage students to ask, "What did I discover?" or "How can I make this even better?". This focus on metacognition helps students develop critical thinking skills, resilience, and a lifelong love of learning. Creative learning is not confined to a single subject or project; it is a mindset that transforms how students approach challenges, express ideas, and engage with the world around them.

METACOGNITION

Metacognition, often referred to as "thinking about thinking", is an essential skill for students in K–12 classrooms to develop, particularly for enhancing creative thinking and problem-solving abilities. Metacognition enables students to reflect on their own thought processes, assess their strategies, and adjust their approaches to achieve better outcomes (Beyer, 1998; Schunk, 2000). In creative tasks, metacognition helps students evaluate the originality, practicality, and effectiveness of their ideas, fostering a mindset of growth and adaptability. Neuroscience provides valuable insights into the mechanisms behind metacognition, revealing its significant role in learning and cognitive development.

In the classroom, metacognition is already emphasized in several disciplines, serving as a bridge between creative thinking and other essential cognitive skills. For instance, in math and language arts, metacognition is encouraged through critical thinking exercises, such as analyzing problem-solving methods, revising written work, or completing research projects (VanTassel-Baska & Little, 2017). In STEM education, students are often required to reflect on experimental designs, troubleshoot errors, and iterate on solutions, all of which involve metacognitive processes. These practices cultivate an awareness of one's thought patterns and foster a habit of self-improvement, which directly benefits creative endeavors. Similarly, social and emotional learning (SEL) programs emphasize metacognition in the context of self-awareness and emotional regulation, helping students recognize how their thoughts and feelings influence their behavior and decision-making. This awareness is crucial for creativity, as it allows students to manage frustration, persist through challenges, and take intellectual risks.

Metacognition also plays a pivotal role in developing executive function and self-regulation skills, which are foundational for success across all areas of learning. Executive functions, such as working memory, cognitive flexibility, and inhibitory control, are closely tied to metacognitive abilities. When students plan a project, monitor their progress, or adjust their approach after encountering a setback, they are engaging in metacognitive practices that strengthen these executive functions. These skills are not only critical for academic performance but also for fostering creativity, as they enable students to organize their ideas, shift perspectives, and stay focused on their goals.

The intersection of metacognition and creativity is particularly evident when comparing it to its role in other areas of education. For example, critical thinking in math and language arts often involves structured problem solving and analysis, requiring students to evaluate their reasoning and seek evidence for their conclusions. Similarly, STEM education emphasizes iterative thinking and hypothesis testing, processes that parallel the reflective and exploratory aspects of creativity. In social and emotional learning, students develop metacognitive awareness to navigate interpersonal challenges, a skill that enhances their ability to collaborate and innovate in group settings. Even executive function and self-regulation, which are vital for organizing tasks and managing time, contribute to creativity by providing the cognitive resources needed to sustain focus and generate novel ideas.

Metacognition is a cornerstone of creative thinking and problem solving in K–12 education. By fostering self-awareness and reflective thinking, students can better understand their cognitive processes and adapt their strategies to achieve greater success. The neuroscience of metacognition underscores its importance, linking it to brain regions that support the monitoring and regulation of thought. When integrated across disciplines – from math and language arts to STEM and SEL – metacognition empowers students to excel not only in creativity but also in critical thinking, executive function, and emotional well-being. As educators continue to prioritize metacognitive practices, they equip students with the tools to navigate the complexities of learning and innovation in a rapidly changing world.

CREATIVE THINKING MODELS: GUILDFORD MODEL OF CREATIVITY, TORRANCE INCUBATION MODEL, AND WALLAS 4-STAGE MODEL OF THE CREATIVE PROCESS

The Guilford Model of Creativity, developed by psychologist J.P. Guilford, is a framework that emphasizes the cognitive components of creative thinking. At its core, the model identifies four key elements: Fluency, flexibility, originality, and elaboration. Fluency refers to the ability to generate a large number of ideas, which helps individuals explore multiple solutions to a problem. Flexibility is the capacity to think in diverse ways and adapt to different perspectives, allowing people to approach challenges from various angles. Originality highlights the importance of novel and unique ideas that stand apart from conventional thinking, while elaboration involves refining and adding depth to these ideas to make them practical and well-developed. Together, these components form the foundation for creative thought, driving innovation and problem solving. In K–12 classrooms, Guilford's model provides a structured approach to nurturing creativity.

E. Paul Torrance, often referred to as the "Father of Creativity", dedicated his career to understanding and fostering creative thinking. His work focused on identifying and nurturing creative potential in individuals, especially within educational settings. Torrance is best known for developing the Torrance Tests of Creative Thinking (TTCT), a set of assessments designed to measure creative abilities such as fluency, flexibility, originality, and elaboration. These tests remain widely used and have influenced how creativity is understood and evaluated globally. Unlike traditional intelligence tests, the TTCT emphasizes divergent thinking, encouraging students to generate multiple ideas and consider a variety of perspectives, highlighting creativity as a multifaceted and essential skill.

Torrance's research revealed that creativity could be taught and developed through deliberate practice and encouragement. He emphasized the importance of nurturing creativity in schools by creating environments that allow for curiosity, experimentation, and risk-taking. Torrance's Incubation Model of Teaching is one example of his efforts to integrate creativity into the classroom. The model emphasizes three stages – heightening anticipation, deepening exploration, and going beyond – that encourage students to engage with content in meaningful and imaginative ways. For instance, a history teacher might spark curiosity about ancient civilizations by presenting a mystery about their decline, prompting students to investigate evidence and propose unique theories.

Torrance's work also demonstrated that creativity is vital across disciplines, not just in the arts but in STEM, humanities, and everyday problem solving. He argued that fostering creativity builds resilience, as students learn to embrace challenges and persist in the face of failure. Torrance's legacy has significantly impacted education, highlighting the role of creative thinking in preparing students for a rapidly changing world. By valuing creativity alongside traditional measures of intelligence, Torrance shifted the educational focus toward developing well-rounded thinkers capable of innovation and adaptability.

The Wallas Model of Creativity, introduced by Graham Wallas in his 1926 book *The Art of Thought*, provides a foundational framework for understanding the stages of the creative process. The model is divided into four key stages: Preparation, incubation, illumination, and verification. Wallas's approach emphasizes the progression of thinking and problem solving that leads to innovative ideas, making it a widely referenced model in education, psychology, and creative industries.

The first stage, preparation, involves gathering information and exploring the problem at hand. This is a critical step in which individuals immerse themselves in the subject, collect data, and build a foundation of knowledge. For example, in a science classroom, students investigating renewable energy might research various energy sources, analyze case studies, and review existing technologies. This stage not only equips individuals with the tools needed to address the problem, but also trains skills like critical thinking, research, and information synthesis, which are essential for both academic and professional success.

The second stage, incubation, is perhaps the most unique aspect of Wallas's model. During this period, individuals step away from active problem solving, allowing their subconscious mind to process the information gathered during preparation. Neuroscience research suggests that during incubation, the brain's default mode network (DMN) becomes active, facilitating connections between seemingly unrelated ideas. In practical terms, a student struggling with a complex math problem might take a break to work on an art project or go for a walk, giving their mind the space to subconsciously explore solutions. This stage encourages patience, reflection, and trust in the creative process.

The third stage, illumination, is often referred to as the "aha!" moment when a solution or innovative idea becomes clear. This moment of insight often feels sudden but is the result of the mental work done during preparation and incubation. For instance, in a social studies class, a student working on a project about urban planning might suddenly realize that incorporating green rooftops into their city design can address both environmental and economic concerns. Illumination highlights the importance of persistence and open-mindedness, as breakthroughs often arise when individuals least expect them.

Finally, the verification stage involves testing, refining, and validating the idea or solution. This step ensures that creative insights are not only innovative but also practical and effective. For example, a group of students designing a water filtration system in a STEM project might test their prototype, analyze its efficiency, and make adjustments to improve its performance. Verification emphasizes critical thinking and attention to detail, teaching students the importance of iteration and improvement.

GROWTH IN CREATIVE SKILLS AND ABILITIES

This book pulls strategies from different models to provide a structured yet flexible approach to creativity. Each stage fosters distinct skills, from research and analysis in preparation to reflection during incubation and persistence in verification. By guiding students through these stages, educators can help them develop not only creative thinking but also problem solving and resilience, preparing them for real-world challenges.

Fluency

Fluency refers to the ability to generate a large number of ideas or solutions in response to a given problem or question. It is foundational to creativity as it allows individuals to explore a wide range of possibilities without being constrained by initial limitations. For example, in a K–12 classroom, students might be tasked with brainstorming various uses for a common object, like a paperclip, encouraging them to think divergently. This skill is invaluable in careers such as marketing, where generating multiple campaign ideas can lead to the most impactful strategies, or engineering, where numerous prototypes may be explored before identifying the most efficient design. Developing fluency builds confidence and encourages students to take intellectual risks, fostering a mindset open to experimentation.

Flexibility

Flexibility is the ability to approach problems from different perspectives or categories, allowing individuals to adapt and innovate in dynamic situations. In the classroom, flexibility might be demonstrated in a social studies assignment where students analyze a historical event, such as the Civil Rights Movement, from diverse perspectives including activists, government officials, and journalists. This practice not only enhances empathy but also strengthens critical thinking by encouraging students to consider multiple angles. Flexibility is equally crucial in professions like urban planning, where balancing environmental, economic, and social factors requires innovative solutions. By developing flexibility, students learn to navigate complex problems and adapt their thinking to varying contexts.

Originality

Originality is characterized by the ability to produce ideas that are novel and unique. This skill is central to innovation and is highly valued in fields such as scientific research, product design, and the arts. In a science classroom, students might be asked to design an original method for conserving water in their community, pushing them to think beyond existing solutions. Encouraging originality in students involves creating a safe environment for intellectual risk-taking, where unconventional ideas are celebrated. This not only cultivates resilience but also prepares students for careers where groundbreaking contributions are rewarded.

Elaboration

Elaboration involves adding depth and detail to an idea, transforming it from a simple concept into a well-developed solution. In an art class, for instance, students might begin with a rough sketch and gradually refine it into a detailed painting, incorporating symbolism and context. Similarly, in a STEM project, a prototype for a solar-powered car could be elaborated with features that improve its efficiency and usability. Elaboration helps students develop precision and critical thinking, equipping them with the skills needed to implement their ideas effectively in real-world scenarios.

Incubation

Incubation is the stage in which individuals take a step back from actively working on a problem, allowing their subconscious mind to process information and form new connections. This period of reflection is crucial for overcoming creative blocks and achieving breakthroughs. For example, a teacher might encourage students to take a break after being introduced to a challenging math problem, allowing their brains to work on the solution unconsciously. In careers like writing or engineering, incubation often leads to "aha!" moments that result in innovative ideas. Teaching students the value of incubation fosters patience and emphasizes that creativity often requires time and persistence.

Evaluation

Evaluation is the process of assessing ideas for feasibility, practicality, and effectiveness. In classrooms, this might involve students testing and refining their hypotheses in a science experiment or peer-reviewing each other's essays in a language arts class. Evaluation is a critical skill in careers such as medicine, where treatments must be rigorously tested, or technology, where products undergo multiple iterations before being released. By learning to evaluate their work critically, students develop analytical skills and the ability to seek constructive feedback, both of which are essential for continuous improvement.

INDEPENDENT SKILLS OR PART OF A PROCESS

Teachers can use the concepts of fluency, flexibility, originality, elaboration, incubation and struggle, and evaluation as individual skills to be taught separately or as interconnected components of a larger creative process. Each skill serves a distinct purpose in fostering creativity and critical thinking, offering students tools to approach problem solving and innovative thinking in versatile ways. Whether incorporated into specific lessons or as part of a comprehensive creative-thinking framework, these skills can be adapted to suit different age groups, subject areas, and learning objectives.

When teaching each skill independently, educators can focus on developing students' capacity in specific areas of creative and critical thinking. For example, fluency – generating a large number of ideas – can be practiced through brainstorming activities. In an English class, students could list as many possible endings to a story as they can, emphasizing quantity over quality to encourage idea generation. Similarly, flexibility can be taught by asking students to consider problems from multiple perspectives. For instance, in social studies, students could examine a historical event from the viewpoints of different stakeholders, helping them to see beyond a single narrative.

Originality, the ability to come up with unique and innovative ideas, can be fostered through open-ended challenges. Teachers might encourage students in art classes to create an unconventional piece using everyday objects, stretching their imaginative boundaries. Meanwhile, elaboration, the skill of adding depth and detail, can be emphasized in writing assignments where students expand on a simple idea by creating vivid descriptions or layering complex arguments.

Incubation and struggle, which involve stepping back and allowing ideas to develop over time, can be reinforced through reflective practices such as journaling or taking structured breaks during problem-solving activities. Lastly, evaluation can be taught as a self-assessment tool, where students analyze their work to identify strengths and areas for improvement. For example, in a STEM class, students might test a prototype, collect data on its performance, and refine their designs accordingly.

Teachers can also combine these skills into a cohesive process that mirrors real-world problem solving. For instance, a class project on environmental sustainability could begin with fluency, where students brainstorm a wide range of solutions to reduce plastic waste. Next, they could practice flexibility by considering different angles, such as economic feasibility, environmental impact, and societal acceptance. Students would then move to originality, generating unique approaches, such as biodegradable alternatives or innovative recycling methods. Elaboration comes next, where students flesh out their ideas with details like implementation plans and potential challenges.

During incubation, teachers can encourage students to take a step back, reflect, and revisit their ideas after a break, fostering deeper thinking and connections. Struggles during this phase are reframed as opportunities for growth and perseverance. Finally, in the evaluation phase, students can present their ideas to peers, receive feedback, and refine their solutions based on constructive criticism.

Using this approach, students develop a range of essential skills that are valuable not only in the classroom but also in everyday life and future careers. Fluency and flexibility enhance adaptability and resourcefulness, originality cultivates innovation, elaboration sharpens attention to detail, and evaluation builds critical thinking and self-assessment. The incubation and struggle phases teach patience and resilience, encouraging students to embrace challenges as part of the creative process.

By teaching these skills independently or as part of a process, teachers empower students to think creatively, solve problems effectively, and approach tasks with confidence. Integrating these skills across different subjects and grade levels ensures that all students develop the habits of mind necessary for success in a rapidly changing world.

CONCLUSION

Fluency, flexibility, originality, elaboration, incubation, and evaluation are all integral components of creative thinking and problem solving. These skills, when incorporated into K–12 education, not only enhance students' academic performance but also prepare them for success in various professional fields. By engaging with these stages, students become confident, adaptable, and innovative thinkers.

Incorporating these components into the curriculum helps students develop a robust set of cognitive skills. Fluency and flexibility allow them to generate and adapt ideas, while originality and elaboration encourage unique and detailed thinking. Incubation provides time for ideas to mature, and evaluation ensures that solutions are effective and practical. This comprehensive approach to learning fosters a deeper understanding and application of knowledge.

Ultimately, these skills equip students to tackle the challenges of an ever-changing world. They become adept at navigating complex problems and are better prepared for the demands of the modern workforce. By fostering creativity and critical thinking, K–12 education can produce graduates who are not only academically proficient but also innovative and resilient.

REFERENCES

Beyer, B.K. (1998). Improving student thinking. *The Clearing House, 71*, 262–267.

Costa, A.L., & Kallick, B. (2008). *Learning and leading with habits of mind: 16 essential characteristics of success*. Alexandria, VA: Association for Supervision and Curriculum Development.

Dewey, J. (1899). The school and society. Chicago, IL: University of Chicago Press.

Harel, I., & Papert, S. (Eds.) (1991). Constructionism: Research reports and essays, 1985–1990. Norwood, NJ: Ablex Publishing Corporation.

Henriksen, D., & Mishra, P. (2014). Twisting knobs and connecting things: Rethinking technology & creativity in the 21st century. *TechTrends: Linking Research & Practice to Improve Learning, 58*(1), 15–19. https://doi.org/10.1007/s11528-013-0713-6

Makel, M.C. (2009). Help us creativity researchers, you're our only hope. *Psychology of Aesthetics, Creativity, and the Arts, 3*(1), 38–42. https://doi.org/10.1037/a0014919

Mishra, P. (2012). Rethinking technology & creativity in the 21st century: Crayons are the future. *TechTrends: Linking Research & Practice to Improve Learning*, *56*(5), 13–16. https://doi.org/10.1007/s11528-012-0594-0

Piaget, J. (1952). The origins of intelligence in children (M.T. Cook, Trans.). New York, NY: International Universities Press.

Ramlackhan, K., Ince, A., & Brown, N. (2024). Conclusion: Future directions for creativity in education. https://doi.org/jj.5699289.16

Sawyer, K. (2019). *The creative classroom*. New York, NY: Teachers College Press.

Schrek, M.K. (2009). *Transformers: Creative teachers for the 21st century*. Thousand Oaks, CA: Corwin.

Schunk, D.H. (2000). Motivation for achievement: Past, present, and future. *Issues in Education: Contributions from Educational Psychology*, *6*, 161–165.

VanTassel-Baska, J., & Little, C.A. (2017). *Content-based curriculum for advanced learners* (3rd ed.). Austin: Prufrock Press.

Vygotsky, L.S. (2004). Imagination and creativity in childhood. Journal of Russian and East European Psychology, 42(1), 7–97. https://doi.org/10.2753/RPO1061 -0405280184

Chapter 3

Fluency

The Generation of Many Responses, Solutions, Possibilities, or Consequences

INTRODUCTION

Heather, a nature artist, works to inspire connection to nature, awe, and curiosity. She generates ideas for her art while hiking through forests, observing the shapes, textures, and natural forms around her. Rather than approaching her work with a fixed plan, she allows her discoveries to spark new ideas, adapting and expanding them into creative expressions.

Todd, a sculptor and master woodworker, follows a similar process. He finds creative fuel not only in nature but also in junkyards and hardware stores, where he uncovers unexpected materials that he can integrate into functional and aesthetic designs.

Richard, an expert in special education technology, approaches problem solving through a method he calls "nearest neighbor". He looks to disciplines adjacent to his own to see how they address similar challenges. For example, the principles of Universal Design for Learning emerged from architectural efforts to make buildings accessible – an idea borrowed and adapted to improve educational inclusivity.

Blake, a physical therapist and amateur cartoonist, faces the challenge of working with clients who share similar goals but have vastly different physical abilities. His creativity lies in adapting exercises to provide equivalent benefits for each individual. By closely observing his clients, he modifies movements to suit a wide range of needs, ensuring that every person can progress effectively.

In the *Harry Potter* series, costume designers played a crucial role in shaping the visual storytelling through their work on the characters' costumes, contributing to the development of the magical world. Fluency was essential in the design process, as each costume had to reflect the personality, background, and growth of the characters while aligning with the broader aesthetic of the wizarding world.

For example, when designing the costumes for the Hogwarts students, different designers had to generate multiple ideas to differentiate the four houses: Gryffindor, Slytherin, Hufflepuff, and Ravenclaw. Each house had distinct color

DOI: 10.4324/9781003434221-3

schemes and symbolic elements that aligned with its values and attributes. Gryffindor's robes, for example, featured rich red and gold hues, reflecting bravery and courage, while Slytherin's robes were designed with sleek green and silver fabrics, symbolizing ambition and cunning. The designers had to continually adapt their designs to ensure that the clothing reflected the characters' identities and the magical world they inhabited, requiring fluency in generating ideas that could evolve as the characters grew.

Ultimately, the work of the costume designers in *Harry Potter* highlights the importance of fluency in creative problem solving. Scientists, artists, educators, and innovators across disciplines employ a variety of strategies to generate ideas. Whether recombining found materials into artistic expressions, borrowing and adapting solutions from other fields, or modifying movements to meet diverse needs, their approaches exemplify strategies that individuals use across disciplines to generate ideas.

Fluency, a key aspect of creativity identified in Guilford's (1967) model, refers to the ability to produce a large number of ideas, solutions, or responses within a given context. It reflects an individual's capacity for rapid idea generation, adaptability, and flexible problem solving – essential traits seen in each of these creative professionals. Fluency is essential to creativity and the creative problem solving process because it emphasizes the ability to generate a high volume of ideas, which is the foundation of innovation. Creativity often thrives in environments where multiple perspectives are explored, and fluency allows individuals to move beyond the obvious and surface-level solutions. The more ideas one generates, the greater the chance of discovering truly innovative or unconventional solutions. Fluency doesn't just create options – it fosters mental flexibility, enabling individuals to approach problems from various angles and adapt their thinking to unique challenges. Creative individuals use a range of cognitive strategies to reimagine existing concepts, forge new connections, and develop innovative solutions across disciplines.

Fluency is not just a skill for the present but a critical tool for the future, especially in careers that require adaptability and innovation. In today's dynamic work environment, the ability to generate a wide range of solutions is highly valued, as it equips professionals to address challenges efficiently and creatively. Careers in technology, design, marketing, and leadership often demand a creative edge, and fluency in idea generation ensures that individuals are better prepared to meet those expectations. Moreover, fluency fosters collaboration in team settings, where the ability to share and build on ideas leads to stronger group outcomes.

In adjusting to adverse situations, fluency becomes an invaluable tool. Life is filled with unexpected challenges, and those who can quickly brainstorm and implement multiple solutions are better equipped to adapt. Whether facing a personal setback, a sudden career shift, or global challenges like economic downturns, fluency enables individuals to think constructively and act decisively. This skill transforms obstacles into opportunities, fostering a sense of control and optimism even in the face of uncertainty. Ultimately, fluency in creativity and problem solving builds the foundation for lifelong adaptability, success, and emotional resilience.

ENCOURAGING CREATIVITY THROUGH CLASSROOM STRATEGIES: CLASSROOM EXAMPLES

Teachers can foster creative thinking by using innovative brainstorming techniques that engage students in meaningful discussions. By integrating technology and reframing traditional problem-solving approaches, educators create dynamic learning environments that promote collaboration, critical thinking, and self-expression. The following examples illustrate how two teachers – Mrs. Martin and Mrs. Wagner – use creative strategies to enhance student engagement and problem-solving skills.

COLLABORATIVE BRAINSTORMING WITH TECHNOLOGY

Mrs. Martin's use of the Padlet app for brainstorming highlights how technology can effectively enhance collaborative and creative thinking in the classroom. By asking students to list aspects of school that annoy them, she taps into an area that is immediately relatable and relevant to their lives, naturally fostering engagement. The open-ended nature of the prompt encourages students to reflect on their own experiences and frustrations, setting the stage for a rich exchange of ideas. The collaborative aspect of Padlet allows for real-time contributions, which amplifies the creativity and diversity of the responses. As one student posts a thought – such as dissatisfaction with the school cafeteria options – it triggers connections in others, who may think of related issues, like the quality of vegetarian meals or the lack of allergy-friendly options.

This exercise also demonstrates the power of social brainstorming, where the ideas of others serve as catalysts for deeper thinking. Working in collaborative teams gives learners access to more ideas and more information as each person shares knowledge and ideas gleaned from their own understanding and personal experiences (Paulus & Nijstad, 2003). When students see their classmates' posts, they may feel validated in their own frustrations or gain new perspectives on issues they had not considered. For example, a student who initially only thought about wanting to chew gum in class might be inspired by a post about the dress code to consider other school rules they find restrictive. This kind of idea-sharing builds momentum, creating a snowball effect where the collective input leads to a much richer pool of ideas than any individual could generate alone. Additionally, it models for students how to build on others' thoughts, a skill that is invaluable not just in writing but in collaborative problem solving as well.

The list generated through this activity provides a springboard for the students' persuasive essays, making the writing process more authentic and meaningful.

Since the topics stem directly from their own experiences, students are more likely to feel passionate about their arguments, which can lead to stronger and more compelling writing. For example, a student who has struggled with vegetarian meal options in the cafeteria might feel a genuine desire to advocate for change, making their essay both personal and persuasive. Furthermore, having access to a shared list ensures that even students who struggle to come up with ideas independently have a rich repository of topics to draw from, ensuring that no one feels left out of the creative process.

Mrs. Martin's approach also demonstrates how incorporating technology can bridge the gap between brainstorming and formal writing. The Padlet app not only facilitates the brainstorming process but also serves as a living document that students can revisit throughout the writing process. This allows for ongoing reflection and revision, as students may return to the Padlet to refine their topic or draw connections between ideas. For instance, a student writing about the dress code might return to the Padlet and realize they could strengthen their argument by referencing posts about individuality or freedom of expression. The integration of technology, therefore, not only enhances creativity but also supports the iterative nature of writing.

Finally, this activity teaches students an important lesson about the creative process: Ideas rarely emerge in isolation. By fostering a collaborative environment where students share, build on, and refine each other's ideas, Mrs. Martin models the real-world creative processes that students will encounter in their future academic and professional lives. The exercise also illustrates how frustration and annoyance — often viewed as negative emotions — can be reframed as sources of inspiration. By channeling their grievances into constructive arguments, students learn to view their struggles as opportunities for growth, a skill that extends far beyond the classroom. This dual focus on collaboration and personal relevance makes Mrs. Martin's lesson not just an exercise in writing, but a powerful example of how to harness creativity in problem solving.

REVERSE BRAINSTORMING TO ADDRESS BULLYING

Mrs. Wagner employs reverse brainstorming as a creative strategy to help her students develop solutions for bullying. Instead of approaching the problem in a traditional way by asking, "How can we stop bullying?", she flips the perspective and poses the question, "How can we ignite bullying?". This unconventional approach encourages students to think critically and identify behaviors, policies, or environments that might unintentionally promote bullying. By reframing the problem in this way, Mrs. Wagner prompts her students to consider the root causes of bullying from a different angle, leading to deeper insights and more innovative solutions.

As the students brainstorm ways to "ignite" bullying, they identify factors such as spreading rumors, excluding classmates, or allowing unkind behavior to go unchecked. This exercise makes it easier for students to recognize actions or attitudes that contribute to a negative school environment. By exploring these harmful behaviors, they gain a better understanding of the dynamics that perpetuate bullying. This awareness forms the foundation for effective prevention strategies, as students can more clearly see which behaviors to avoid and which policies to advocate for to create a more inclusive and supportive atmosphere.

The reverse brainstorming session naturally transitions into a problem-solving phase, where students flip their ideas and develop solutions for bullying prevention. For example, if one suggestion for igniting bullying is tolerating mean jokes, students might propose fostering a culture where humor is kind and inclusive instead. Similarly, if students suggest that ignoring bullying enables it to grow, they might develop strategies for bystander intervention, such as teaching peers to stand up for victims or report bullying incidents to trusted adults. The process encourages students to take ownership of the solutions, as they have identified the issues themselves and are actively involved in resolving them.

This activity also fosters empathy and self-reflection. By identifying ways bullying can be exacerbated, students are prompted to consider their own behaviors and how they might unintentionally contribute to a negative environment. Mrs. Wagner's approach helps them understand that everyone plays a role in shaping the culture of their classroom or school. This realization empowers students to take responsibility for their actions and make conscious choices to promote kindness and respect. It also gives them a sense of agency, as they learn that small actions – such as including someone in a conversation or stepping in when they witness bullying – can have a significant impact.

Overall, Mrs. Wagner's use of reverse brainstorming transforms the process of addressing bullying into a creative and collaborative experience. By challenging her students to think in unconventional ways, she inspires them to approach the issue with fresh perspectives and innovative solutions. The exercise not only equips students with practical strategies for preventing bullying but also fosters a deeper understanding of the social dynamics at play. Ultimately, this method cultivates a sense of responsibility, empathy, and critical thinking, preparing students to be proactive, compassionate members of their school community. See Table 3.1 for more Reverse Brainstorming Ideas.

Table 3.1 Reverse Brainstorming Prompts

Grade Level	Subject Area	Objective	Reverse Brainstorming Prompt
Elementary (3–5)	Science	Understand the water cycle and its importance.	*How can we stop the water cycle from working?* Explore evaporation, condensation, and precipitation failures.

(*Continued*)

Table 3.1 (Continued)

Grade Level	Subject Area	Objective	Reverse Brainstorming Prompt
Elementary (4–5)	Reading	Improve reading comprehension and engagement.	*How can we make a story impossible to understand?* Include ideas like missing details or jumbled sentences.
Elementary (3–5)	Health	Learn the importance of hygiene.	*How can we make people get sick easily?* Discuss skipping handwashing, eating spoiled food, or poor hygiene.
Elementary (4–5)	Music	Understand melody and harmony in music.	*How can we create a song that no one wants to listen to?* Consider mismatched notes or unpleasant sounds.
Elementary (3–5)	Geography	Learn about the importance of maps and navigation.	*How can we make a map completely useless?* Ideas like leaving out labels, landmarks, or directions.
Middle School (6–8)	Science	Study the importance of ecosystems and biodiversity.	*How can we destroy an ecosystem?* Discuss invasive species, pollution, or habitat destruction.
Middle School (6–8)	Civics	Understand the importance of good leadership in government.	*How can a leader lose the trust of their people?* Include dishonesty, broken promises, or poor decisions.
Middle School (7–8)	Technology	Learn the principles of cybersecurity and protecting information.	*How can we make a password as weak as possible?* Brainstorm using common words, birthdays, or short codes.
Middle School (6–8)	Visual Arts	Explore design principles like balance and contrast.	*How can we make a design look chaotic and unorganized?* Consider uneven spacing or clashing colors.
Middle School (6–8)	Physical Education	Understand the basics of fitness and healthy living.	*How can we make exercising less effective?* Ideas like skipping warm-ups, using improper form, or quitting early.

(*Continued*)

Table 3.1 (Continued)

Grade Level	Subject Area	Objective	Reverse Brainstorming Prompt
High School (9–10)	Biology	Study the function and importance of the human immune system.	*How can we make the immune system weaker?* Discuss stress, poor diet, or lack of sleep.
High School (9–12)	Economics	Understand how supply and demand impact the economy.	*How can we make a product nobody wants to buy?* Consider high prices, low quality, or bad marketing.
High School (11–12)	Literature	Analyze what makes a compelling and engaging character.	*How can we create the most uninteresting character ever?* Think of no personality, no goals, or no growth.
High School (9–10)	Chemistry	Understand how chemical reactions occur.	*How can we stop a chemical reaction from happening?* Brainstorm ideas like removing reactants or energy.
High School (9–12)	Media Studies	Learn the importance of effective advertising.	*How can we create an ad that everyone ignores?* Include boring visuals, no message, or unclear purpose.
High School (9–12)	History	Study the causes of revolutions in history.	*How can a government push its people toward revolt?* Discuss oppression, inequality, or censorship.
High School (9–12)	Physics	Understand how machines reduce effort and improve efficiency.	*How can we design a machine that wastes as much energy as possible?* Explore friction, weight, or poor materials.
High School (11–12)	Environmental Science	Learn about sustainable living practices.	*How can we make a community as unsustainable as possible?* Include wasting resources or overbuilding.
High School (11–12)	Psychology	Explore how habits are formed and broken.	*How can we make it harder for someone to build a good habit?* Discuss lack of consistency or motivation.

(*Continued*)

Table 3.1 (Continued)

Grade Level	Subject Area	Objective	Reverse Brainstorming Prompt
High School (9–12)	Sociology	Understand how social groups function effectively.	*How can we make a group project fail completely?* Explore poor communication, unequal work, or no collaboration.

STRATEGIES

In the age of technology, it is tempting for students to use search engines to generate ideas. Certainly, the internet opens a world of possibilities. With the vastness of ideas at our fingertips, it may be overwhelming for learners to believe they can come up with anything on their own. At the same time, students can learn to use technology effectively in order to see what's out there to spark their interest and share their ideas. Incorporating specific techniques into lesson plans or teaching students how to use idea generation strategies on their own can help provide structure in what could be an overwhelming process.

BRAINSTORMING

Brainstorming or generating multiple ideas only to use one or two may seem like a waste of time, but generating multiple ideas before choosing one can be essential to the creative process. Brainstorming can happen individually or in groups. There is a case and a time for both. Research on brainstorming indicates that individual brainstorming may lead to more ideas in terms of quantity (Goldenberg & Wiley, 2011). Brainstorming individually might be more conducive to idea generation because individuals may feel constrained in a group setting due to being fearful of sharing ideas (Isaksen & Gaulen, 2005) and/or becoming fixated on ideas already generated by others (Smith, 2003).

Solo idea generation may have some advantages, such as reduced anxiety. During group brainstorming sessions, individuals may feel pressure from having to think on the spot in front of others. Even so, in the modern workplace, the ability to problem solve in a group and collaborate with others is essential. Group brainstorming offers the advantage of allowing individuals to build upon the ideas of their teammates. Technology can help learners express the best of both worlds. Students can post their ideas on an app such as Padlet where they can publish their ideas anonymously, without the threat of being criticized or the pressure of being rushed.

Osborn (1963) generated helpful rules for a group brainstorming process that Paulus (2000) refined and expanded. Using the guidelines, teachers can facilitate brainstorming sessions or train student team leaders to be facilitators. Applied to a classroom situation, the guidelines for successful brainstorming include:

- Stay focused on the task. When student ideas begin to stray off the target, the facilitator reminds them to focus on the question or problem at hand.
- Encourage all to participate. Facilitators can encourage quiet students to share their ideas.
- Avoid criticism. The facilitator reminds students that during brainstorming, all ideas are encouraged, and students are told to avoid evaluating ideas in order for all team members to feel encouraged to share their ideas.
- Welcome all ideas, including wild ones. Assure students that all ideas are welcome. Of course, the teacher may impose rules that prohibit profanity, obscenities, or otherwise insensitive ideas.
- Initially, go for quantity. Sometimes the best ideas come when the most common ideas have been exhausted. Encourage students to keep thinking beyond the common ideas.
- Return to previously explored ideas and improve on them. When students seem to have exhausted their mental resources, revisit ideas to see how they may be combined or altered to create new ideas.

EXAMPLES OF REVERSE BRAINSTORMING: IDEA MARATHONS

The Idea Marathon, developed by Takeo Higuchi (2016), is a systematic approach to fostering creativity through a continual brainstorming process. Participants are encouraged to generate a new idea every day for 30 days or longer. Each idea must be recorded, illustrated, and shared with others to enhance understanding and feedback. Higuchi's research indicates that this consistent practice boosts creative thinking, as demonstrated by improvements in Torrance Tests of Creative Thinking (TTCT). The act of regularly producing and refining ideas strengthens the creative process, helping individuals develop their ability to think divergently and generate novel solutions to problems.

In classroom settings, the Idea Marathon can be adapted to suit a variety of learning goals. Students might keep personal idea journals where they document their daily ideas, accompanied by sketches or visual aids to illustrate their thoughts. Sharing sessions can be integrated into the daily or weekly schedule, allowing students to present their ideas and receive feedback from peers. This collaborative exchange not only enriches individual creativity but also fosters a classroom culture of innovation and respect for diverse perspectives. By encouraging students to articulate and refine their ideas, educators help them develop critical thinking and communication skills alongside creativity.

For a more collaborative approach, a class-wide Idea Marathon can be conducted using tools such as a shared notebook, blog, or wiki. These platforms allow students to contribute their ideas to a collective repository, creating a dynamic, shared resource for inspiration. As students read and build upon one another's contributions, they experience the value of collective creativity and learn how to work as a team. This approach also highlights the iterative nature of creativity, as ideas evolve through collaboration and discussion. The collective marathon fosters a sense of shared purpose while encouraging students to view creativity as a process rather than a singular act.

The Idea Marathon is a versatile and powerful tool for fostering creativity in education. By making idea generation a daily habit, students develop the discipline and mindset necessary for creative thinking. Whether approached individually or collaboratively, this technique promotes the consistent practice of brainstorming, reflection, and iteration. In addition to enhancing creativity, the Idea Marathon encourages students to explore their own interests, engage in problem solving, and contribute to a community of thinkers. This process not only benefits individual learners but also creates a vibrant, innovative classroom environment where ideas can flourish.

See Table 3.2 for an example of an Idea Marathon notebook.

MIND-MAPPING

A concept map, as described by Novak (1998), is a visual representation of knowledge that shows the relationships between ideas and concepts. Similarly, mind-mapping involves creating a diagram of a central idea with details branching or radiating outward, often resembling a tree-like structure (Buzan & Buzan, 2010). Both tools serve as effective strategies for visually organizing information in a way that fosters understanding and exploration. By providing a structured yet flexible framework, these methods help learners visualize how concepts are interconnected, which is particularly useful in complex topics or creative problem solving.

These tools also facilitate the generation of ideas and the steps needed for execution. According to Malycha and Maier (2017) and Simper et al. (2016), concept maps and mind maps encourage brainstorming by allowing learners to organize their thoughts in a non-linear fashion. This approach often leads to discovering previously unnoticed relationships or connections between ideas, unlocking creative potential. For instance, as students visually link seemingly unrelated concepts, they can uncover innovative solutions or gain deeper insights into the topic at hand. This makes these tools particularly valuable in subjects that require critical thinking and creativity, such as science, social studies, and literature.

In addition to fostering creativity, concept maps and mind maps help learners process and retain information more effectively. By engaging with content in a dynamic and interactive manner, students actively participate in organizing and restructuring their knowledge. This process not only deepens understanding but also improves memory retention, as visual representations are easier to recall than linear text. These tools can be used as a reference point for further study or collaboration, making them versatile in both individual and group settings.

Table 3.2 Idea Marathon Examples

Grade Level	Invention	Possible Uses	Where the Idea Came From	Person You Shared the Idea With
Elementary	Color-Changing Ball	A ball that changes color based on how hard or soft it's thrown, making games more fun.	Watching mood rings change color.	Best friend in class.
Elementary	Interactive Learning Notebook	A notebook with interactive pages that display facts or play sounds when touched, great for studying.	Playing with pop-up books in the library.	My teacher during recess.
Elementary	Magnetic Backpack	Backpack that sticks to metal surfaces to prevent it from falling.	Seeing a magnet on a fridge.	My sibling at home.
Elementary	Soundproof Pillow	A pillow that cancels noise, helping you sleep in noisy environments.	Thinking about quiet places to sleep.	My mom, who always says I make too much noise.
Elementary	Self-Cleaning Shoes	Keeps shoes clean by automatically removing dirt when walking.	Watching a dog clean its paws.	Best friend in class.
Middle School	Foldable Solar Tent	A tent with built-in foldable solar panels to charge devices and power small lights.	Watching a camping show with solar gadgets.	My science teacher.
Middle School	Floating Bike	A bike that hovers off the ground for smoother rides, especially in rough terrain.	Seeing a hoverboard and imagining it with a bike.	My best friend who loves sci-fi.
Middle School	Temperature-Adjusting Lunchbox	A lunchbox that keeps food at the perfect temperature, either warm or cold, using rechargeable batteries.	Complaining about cold pizza at lunch.	My science teacher who teaches about energy.

(Continued)

45

Table 3.2 (Continued)

Grade Level	Invention	Possible Uses	Where the Idea Came From	Person You Shared the Idea With
Middle School	Automatic Homework Assistant	A device that helps with homework by guiding through steps and providing hints.	Using an educational app.	My older brother, who struggles with homework.
Middle School	Emoji Translator	A gadget that turns emojis into text to communicate better online.	Seeing friends use a lot of emojis in messages.	My classmates who love texting.
High School	Personalized Smart Glasses	Glasses that adjust color and brightness based on your environment.	Looking at sunglasses that change tint.	My art teacher who loves light and color.
High School	Robotic Chef	A robot that can cook your meals with preset recipes.	Watching robots do tasks on TV.	My parents, who like cooking.
High School	Self-Repairing Car	A car that can fix minor issues by itself, like flat tires or low oil.	Watching autonomous vehicles on the news.	My friend who's into cars.
High School	Smart Mirror	A mirror that gives you daily weather, news updates, and reminders while you get ready.	Seeing smart home devices in stores.	My younger sister who loves tech gadgets.
High School	Memory-Boosting Headband	A headband that helps enhance memory and concentration using brainwaves.	Watching documentaries about brain function.	My neuroscience classmate.

They serve as a living document that can evolve as new ideas are added or connections are refined.

Concept maps and mind maps are powerful tools for enhancing learning and creativity. By encouraging students to think critically and visually about the relationships between ideas, they promote deeper engagement with the material. These methods also cultivate important skills such as problem solving, organization, and communication, which are essential for success both in and out of the classroom. Whether used for brainstorming, planning, or studying, these tools offer a dynamic way to explore and connect ideas, making them invaluable resources for learners of all ages. See Table 3.3 for more mind-mapping prompts.

Table 3.3 Examples of Mind-Mapping Assignments Across the Curriculum

Assignment	Grade Level	Subject Area	Description
Mind Map on Historical Figures or Events	7–12	Social Studies	Students create a mind map to illustrate relationships and connections between ideas, events, and concepts related to a political leader (e.g., Thomas Jefferson), historical region (e.g., Mesopotamia), or era (e.g., the Great Depression).
Mind Map of Geometric Shapes	6–8	Math	Students create a mind map of geometric shapes that shows the relationship between geometric figures, with pictures of each shape.
Mind Map for Writing Structure	6–12	English, Writing	Students create a mind map to organize the structure of their writing topic, including main arguments, supporting details, and story plot elements.
Historical Event Mind Map	7–12	Social Studies	Students create a mind map of a historical event, showing connections between key figures, dates, and significant outcomes or consequences.
Math Operations Mind Map	6–8	Math	Students create a mind map that links mathematical operations (addition, subtraction, multiplication, division) with real-world applications or examples.

(Continued)

47

Table 3.3 (Continued)

Assignment	Grade Level	Subject Area	Description
Mind Map on Ethical Issues in Technology	9–12	Technology, Ethics	Students create a mind map exploring the ethical dilemmas related to modern technology (e.g., AI, data privacy), with key arguments and potential solutions.
Visual Timeline as a Mind Map	6–12	History, Social Studies	Students create a mind map that acts as a visual timeline, connecting historical events, figures, and movements in chronological order.
Environmental Issues Mind Map	7–12	Science, Social Studies	Students create a mind map on a local environmental issue, showing causes, effects, and potential solutions.
Mind Map of Literary Devices	6–12	English, Literature	Students create a mind map of literary devices used in a novel or poem, linking each device to examples from the text.
Monument Design Mind Map	7–12	Art, Social Studies	Students create a mind map to design a monument, including key elements like symbolism, historical relevance, and artistic features.
Mind Map for Public Service Announcement (PSA)	6–12	Social Studies, Media Studies	Students create a mind map to plan the structure of their PSA on a social or environmental issue, identifying key messages, target audience, and media used.
Mind Map for Interview Project on Historical Events	9–12	Social Studies, History	Students create a mind map to organize their research on a historical event, identifying key figures, significant dates, and the impact of the event.
Math Art Mind Map	6–8	Math, Art	Students create a mind map linking mathematical concepts (like symmetry, patterns, shapes) to examples in art, demonstrating the connection between math and artistic design.

BENDING, BREAKING, AND BLENDING

Composer Anthony Brandt and Neuroscientist David Eagleman (2017) indicate that the cognitive routines underlying creative inspiration in everything, from great works of art to innovative feats of engineering, are similar. The ability of humans to generate novelty and innovation is a result of our neural wiring for cognitive fluency and flexibility. Cognitive fluency and flexibility allow us to tap into our knowledge, memories, and experiences and use them to create new ideas. Brandt and Eagleman identify three "B"s or three basic strategies that are at the root of all creative thinking: Bending, breaking, and blending.

In blending, the brain combines two or more ideas in novel ways. Consider, for example, the post-it note, which is a blend of note paper and glue. Superheroes are often a blend of animal and human characteristics, such as the combination of a spider, bat, or cat with a person (Spider-Man, Batman, Catwoman). While the idea of combining animal and human traits may fuel comic books, it also has fed scientific endeavors. Brandt and Eagleman (2017) describe the example of Freckles the Spidergoat. Scientists spliced the DNA of a silk-producing spider into Freckles, resulting in a goat who secretes silk with her milk. Examples of blending can be found almost anywhere. Smartphones blend the functions of traditional telephones with the capacity of a personal computer. Candy producers create new products by offering new combinations of food, such as pretzels with peanut butter. In Mrs. Martin's class, students blend time periods of the classics with modern times. For example, they make speed dating profiles and create chat and Twitter feeds of conversations that characters from *Pride and Prejudice* might have had.

In bending, an idea or product is modified from its original version. In the movies *Honey, I Shrunk the Kids*, *The Borrowers*, and more recently, *Antman*, humans are shrunk to encounter worlds of giant objects. Manufacturers took our favorite candy bars and made them huge, family-size, and bite-size. The telephone is an example of technology that continues to "bend" from something tethered to the wall to a device that goes with us everywhere. While Facebook was essentially our first "social media", the idea of a platform for posting to friends and/or the public has been bent to include the posting of pictures (Instagram), posting short bursts of words (Twitter), saving and sharing ideas (Pinterest), and so forth.

According to Brandt and Eagleman (2017), breaking is the process of breaking a whole into parts and reassembling the parts to create something new. They describe the Cubism movement in art as an example of breaking. The images of Cubists such as Picasso appear broken and put back together from different angles and perspectives. Brandt and Eagleman cite numerous examples of breaking in medicine, science, and technology, such as the technology behind compressed data files. By breaking acoustical data into its smallest frequencies, the frequencies the human ear does not miss can be discarded, allowing music files to be compressed. See Table 3.4 for more examples of bending, breaking, and blending exercises.

Table 3.4 Examples of Bending, Breaking, and Blending Technique

Bending, Blending, and Breaking Concepts	Teach students the concept of "bending, blending, and breaking" and have them search for examples in art, music, technology, and engineering.
Creating New Characters	Have students combine characteristics from two characters in novels to create a new character.
Blending Time Frames	In literature, have students blend time frames (e.g., historical periods, future scenarios).
Twitter Feeds from Classic Literature	Students create Twitter feeds for characters from classic literature like *Pride and Prejudice, Catcher in the Rye,* or *To Kill a Mockingbird.*
Inventions Inspired by Nature	Students research inventions that were inspired by nature, such as Velcro or the Shinkansen Bullet Train.
Blending Technology and Animals	Students generate and illustrate their own ideas that blend technology with animals.
Creating New Characters from Favorite Stories	Students list traits of a character from a favorite story and change each to create a new character.
Reassembling Technology into Art	Students take apart old technologies like a landline telephone or an analog clock and reassemble the pieces into a work of art.
Creating Settings from Real Scenes	Students take apart a scene from their home, neighborhood, or community, using sensory details (sights, sounds, smells, tastes, textures) to create a new story setting.

FLUENCY FOR SOCIAL AND EMOTIONAL WELLBEING

Collaborative Brainstorming for Conflict Resolution

A guidance counselor can use collaborative brainstorming to help students creatively resolve interpersonal conflicts. During the session, the counselor begins by introducing a hypothetical scenario, such as a disagreement between two friends over a group project or a misunderstanding in class. The counselor emphasizes that the goal is to explore as many solutions as possible without judgment.

Students are invited to suggest ideas, which are written on a whiteboard or large sheet of paper. Suggestions can range from practical steps like discussing feelings openly to imaginative approaches like creating a "peace contract". Once a comprehensive list has been generated, the group works together to evaluate the ideas and identify the most effective or feasible options. This activity encourages students to think beyond typical solutions and fosters empathy by considering multiple perspectives. It also creates a supportive environment where students feel comfortable expressing their thoughts and emotions, ultimately building their problem-solving skills and confidence in managing conflicts.

Strength-Focused Mind-Mapping

Another effective activity is strength-focused mind-mapping, which helps students recognize and celebrate their unique strengths and potential. The counselor provides each student with a blank sheet of paper and asks them to write their name in the center, surrounded by branches labeled with categories such as "Skills", "Interests", "Accomplishments", and "Dreams". Students then fill in each branch with words, phrases, or drawings that represent their personal attributes, past successes, and future aspirations. Once the mind maps are completed, students are encouraged to share their work with the group. The counselor facilitates a discussion that highlights commonalities and unique strengths, fostering mutual respect and understanding. This activity boosts self-esteem by focusing on the students' positive qualities and achievements, encourages self-reflection, and helps build a sense of belonging and appreciation for diversity within the group.

Group Idea Marathon for Kindness Initiatives

To foster collaboration and kindness, a counselor can lead a group idea marathon focused on improving the school environment. In this activity, students are asked to brainstorm acts of kindness that they could implement to positively impact their peers or school community. Each idea is written on a sticky note and added to a shared "Kindness Wall". For example, students might suggest ideas like writing thank-you notes to teachers, organizing a lunchtime buddy program, or creating a welcoming committee for new students. Over the course of the session (or week), the students continue to add ideas to the wall, creating a growing collection of actionable suggestions. At the end of the activity, the group selects a few ideas to implement collaboratively. The counselor guides students in planning and executing these initiatives, fostering a sense of teamwork and accomplishment. This activity reinforces the value of helping others, encourages creativity in addressing social needs, and builds pride in contributing to a positive and inclusive school climate.

These activities combine creativity, collaboration, and emotional intelligence to promote social and emotional well-being. By engaging students in brainstorming, mind-mapping, and kindness-focused initiatives, counselors can help students develop critical skills such as empathy, self-awareness, and resilience. These activities not only strengthen interpersonal relationships but also empower students to become proactive problem solvers and contributors to a supportive school community.

SPOTLIGHT: INVENTORS UNDER 18

Keiana Cavé, a young scientist from New Orleans, gained international attention for her groundbreaking work on combating oil spills. At just 18 years old, she researched chemical compounds capable of detecting and neutralizing cancer-causing compounds found in oil spills. Her inspiration stemmed from the devastating Deepwater Horizon oil spill in 2010, which prompted her to explore ways to mitigate the environmental and health impacts of such disasters. By combining her passion for chemistry with her dedication to environmental preservation, Keiana demonstrated remarkable innovation and problem-solving skills.

Keiana's research began during high school. She explored how oil interacts with sunlight, discovering that PAHs become even more toxic when exposed to ultraviolet radiation. This finding inspired her to create a compound that could detect these toxic byproducts before they could harm marine ecosystems or human health. Her invention not only contributed to the field of environmental science but also highlighted the critical intersection of chemistry and environmental conservation.

In recognition of her efforts, Keiana received numerous awards and honors, including a $1.2 million grant from Chevron to continue her research. She also earned a spot on *Forbes'* "30 Under 30" list in the energy sector in 2017. Her success underscores the power of youth-led innovation and the ability to tackle global challenges with creativity and determination. Keiana has become a role model for young scientists, especially women and minorities in STEM fields, inspiring them to pursue their ideas and make a meaningful difference in the world.

Today, Keiana continues her journey in science and entrepreneurship, expanding her work into other areas of research and business. Her story serves as a testament to the importance of fostering curiosity, resilience, and critical thinking among young innovators. By addressing one of the most pressing environmental issues of our time, Keiana has proven that young minds can have a profound impact on the world.

CONCLUSION

Developing fluency skills is essential for fostering creativity, problem solving, and adaptability in students, equipping them to thrive in an ever-changing world.

Teaching strategies for fluency empower learners to explore multiple perspectives, uncover hidden connections, and refine their ideas, which are critical for innovation and critical thinking. By practicing fluency through activities like brainstorming, Idea Marathons, and mind-mapping, students gain the ability to break down complex problems into manageable parts, develop original solutions, and navigate uncertainty with resilience. Moreover, fluency skills contribute to students' long-term success by fostering self-confidence, collaboration, and emotional intelligence, nurturing a growth mindset, and contributing thoughtfully to their communities.

REFERENCES

Brandt, A., & Eagleman, D. (2017). *The runaway species: How human creativity remakes the world* (p. 204). Catapult. Kindle Edition.

Buzan, T., & Buzan, B. (2010). *The mind-map book: Unlock your creativity, boost your memory, change your life*. London, England: BBC.

Goldenberg, O., & Wiley, J. (2011). Quality, conformity, and conflict: Questioning the assumptions of Osborn's brainstorming technique. *Journal of Problem Solving, 3*(2), 96–118. https://doi-org.proxy195.nclive.org/10.7771/1932-6246.1093

Guilford, J.P. (1967). The nature of human intelligence. New York, NY: McGraw-Hill.

Higuchi, T. (2016). *Generating creative ideas: Enhancement effects of the Idea-Marathon System (IMS) on creativity for university students*. Retrieved from https://www.creativity-journal.net/contact-us/item/337-generating-creative-ideas#.XFswQKeZPys

Isaksen, S.G., & Gaulin, J.P. (2005). A reexamination of brainstorming research: Implications for research and practice. *The Gifted Child Quarterly, 49*(4), 315–329.

Malycha, C.P., & Maier, G.W. (2017). Enhancing creativity on different complexity levels by eliciting mental models. *Psychology of Aesthetics, Creativity &the Arts, 11*(2), 187–201. https://doi-org.proxy195.nclive.org/10.1037/aca0000080

Novak, J.D. (1998). *Learning, creating, and using knowledge: Concept maps as facilitative tools in Schools and corporations*. Mahwah, N.J.: Taylor & Francis. Retrieved from https://login.proxy195.nclive.org/login?url=https://search.ebscohost.com/login.aspx?direct=true&db=nlebk&AN=19391&site=ehost-live&scope=site

Osborn, A.F. (1963). Applied imagination: Principles and procedures of creative problem-solving (3rd ed.). New York, NY: Scribner's Sons.

Paulus, P. (2000). Groups, teams, and creativity: The creative potential of idea-generating groups. *Applied Psychology, 49*(2), 237–262. https://doi.org/10.1111/1464-0597.00013

Paulus, P.B., & Nijstad, B.A. (2003). *Group creativity: Innovation through collaboration*. New York, NY: Oxford University Press. https://doi.org/10.1093/acprof:oso/9780195147308.001.0001

Simper, N., Reeve, R., & Kirby, J.R. (2016). Effects of concept mapping on creativity in photo stories. *Creativity Research Journal*, *28*(1), 46–51. https://doi-org.proxy195 .nclive.org/10.1080/10400419.2016.1125263

Smith, S.M. (2003). The constraining effects of initial ideas. In P. Paulus & B. Nijstad (Eds.), *Group creativity: Innovation through collaboration* (pp. 15–31). Oxford: University Press.

Chapter 4

Flexibility

The Ability to Think of Alternatives to an Idea, a Problem, or a Solution

INTRODUCTION

Emma, a designer of outdoor clothing and gear, sees creativity as the intersection of form and function. For her, true innovation means ensuring that a product not only serves a practical purpose but also empowers the user – offering solutions they would find for themselves.

Rich, who designs clothing for sports broadcasters and also leads an organization supporting individuals through the fostering and adoption process, takes a similar approach to creativity. He thrives on uncovering opportunities where others see obstacles. "I like to find the opportunity in what others may consider a major problem", he explains. To him, creativity isn't about imposing a radical new idea but about reshaping existing challenges into tangible, effective solutions. Rather than selling people on an abstract innovation, he prefers to show them a better way forward – one that directly addresses their needs.

Both Emma and Rich exemplify Guilford's concept of *flexibility* – the ability to shift perspectives, reframe problems, and explore multiple solutions. Emma's designs require her to constantly adjust to changing demands in outdoor performance, weather resistance, and consumer expectations, all while maintaining a balance between comfort and challenge. Rich, on the other hand, applies flexibility in both design and social advocacy, recognizing that the most creative solutions are not always the ones that make the boldest statements but the ones that seamlessly solve pressing issues.

Their experiences highlight the value of stepping back from a challenge to analyze it from multiple angles. Emma understands that a good design isn't created in isolation – it emerges from a deep understanding of the user's needs and a willingness to explore unconventional solutions. Rich has learned that creative solutions are often more convincing when framed as answers to real, existing problems rather than abstract innovations. They have both witnessed how

DOI: 10.4324/9781003434221-4

quick-fix approaches, where immediate answers are demanded in meetings or brainstorming sessions, often result in frustration and ineffective outcomes.

Instead, their success comes from patience, adaptability, and the ability to think beyond the obvious – hallmarks of flexibility in creativity. By embracing alternative viewpoints, challenging assumptions, and allowing space for exploration, they prove that creativity isn't just about generating ideas – it's about refining, adapting, and transforming them into something truly meaningful.

For another example of flexibility, *Connections*, a popular game from the *New York Times*, relies upon using flexibility to group ideas or terms together in unique ways. The problem of the day offers 16 words that must be organized into 4 categories, each containing 4 words. The player is not given categories to consider, so they must use flexibility to create their own groupings and consider which words align. For example, words such as friend, pal, buddy, and mate could potentially be a category that refers to friendship. This game requires flexibility because the terms could potentially belong to more than one category. Here is an example: Fly could be a term that refers to how objects move through the air, or it could refer to an annoying insect. "On the fly" refers to catching on quickly or picking things up without hesitating. At the same time, a fly can also be the zipper on a pair of pants or the place above the stage in a theater for the pulleys and supports that allow the stage crew to fly (hoist) curtains, lights, or scenery. It takes flexibility to evaluate all of the 16 words in the puzzle to consider the possible categories and rearrange words as necessary so that, with the final outcome, each word becomes part of a four-word category.

For yet another example, athletes practice drills to master certain skills, but when they are in the game, they must use flexible thinking as they make decisions. The practice drills help them to complete these tasks so that they can rely on their bodies to complete the activities they intend to put into action. Where fluency might be the drills, flexibility is the ability to look at options and make the right decision. Flexibility can also be seen as individuals master skills in the kitchen, moving from imitation to invention. Starko (2021) describes experiences with learning a foreign language as a process involving flexibility and risk-taking.

Cognitive flexibility occurs at the micro-level throughout the day. Flexibility is a component of popular tests of creative potential (Guilford, 1968; Torrance, 1994) and is recognized in numerous theories of creative problem solving (Isen, 2002; Runco, 1986; Russo, 2004; Silver, 1997; Treffinger, 1995). It allows an individual to adapt to new situations, tolerate and accept changes, see multiple points of view, and have the mental strength to shift between tasks or challenges (Dodge, 2019). It involves seeing a problem from different perspectives, looking for unique alternatives or directives, and the ability to change the approach or thought process. Kim (2016) describes flexible thinking as an even better predictor of innovation than fluent thinking as it allows an individual to consider options, envision items in unique ways, and comprehend opposing views. It provides the opportunity to think independently, disregard presumptions, and break barriers (Kim, 2016).

IQ scores are often viewed as a predictor of success, but that might not be the case. IQ involves measures of working memory and pattern recognition. Lawrence et al. (2008) found entrepreneurs of multiple companies had higher cognitive flexibility than managers of similar age and IQ. Cognitive flexibility involves being able to move through the process, switch between concepts, and adapt behaviors in a novel setting changing the process for ultimate success (Sahakian et al., 2021). The process involves learning how to learn – perhaps in the form of metacognition. Artists and entrepreneurs of multiple companies use their cognitive flexibility to create, design, and invent. Cognitive flexibility is important where individuals must quickly adjust to the situation while making decisions. Cognitive flexibility can be measured using the Wisconsin Sorting Test, and cognitive training programs such as Structural Learning have been introduced to enhance flexibility (Sahakian et al., 2021).

Open-mindedness is one of the most consistent attitudes found in innovative individuals (Kim, 2016). Flexibility can help children work through uncertain events and unexpected changes by incorporating new information into plans and ideas (Jacobson, 2022). It is a key aspect for self-regulation which, in turn, helps children to handle emotions and understand that setbacks are not permanent. Validating children's emotions can be a step in helping to develop flexible thinking. Letting them know that disappointment is frustrating or confusing can be a first step in the process allowing them to move forward from the negative emotions and become able to seek solutions while playing a role in the problem-solving process (Jacobson, 2022).

We see flexible thinking, or the lack of flexible thinking, all around us. When a child is not flexible, it can be challenging to help them understand other perspectives or navigate situations in healthy ways. Rigid or black-and-white thinking can prompt an individual to think in extremes. Educators might recognize students struggling with flexible thinking in the classroom as individuals who resist experimenting with new ideas or strategies. If the lack of flexibility is causing excessive frustration, practicing flexible thinking skills can have the potential to help the students understand themselves better.

FLEXIBILITY IN THE CLASSROOM

Charlie's teacher recommended him for a support group the school counselor was offering. Her major concerns were that Charlie was not meeting his potential in the classroom and struggled to maintain relationships. In addition, Charlie's rigid thinking also seemed to cause trouble in his relationships. He could often be seen scowling, being sarcastic or rude to his peers, or marching down the hallway with his fists clenched in anger.

His teacher wanted to help Charlie understand other perspectives and help him find topics he was passionate about studying in order to increase his motivation to learn. When working through the writing process during language arts, Charlie typically settled on a topic or an idea quickly, wrote a brief passage, and then either refused or could not elaborate on his thoughts. He stopped at the first draft, unwilling to consider new techniques to implement. His teacher hoped that targeting flexible thinking would help him be able to see alternatives and develop skills to persevere.

One of the goals for the small group was to have the students understand themselves on a deeper level by taking personality assessments and tests. One of the tests was the Big Five Personality Test which assesses five dimensions of the personality. These dimensions include conscientiousness, extraversion, agreeableness, openness to experience, and neuroticism. There are no right or wrong answers for the five-factor model. They explain behaviors and traits.

A person scoring high on openness to experiences is described as seeking out a variety of experiences, being more comfortable with the unfamiliar, and having the ability to pay attention to inner feelings. Those scoring low are described as enjoying familiar routines, people, and ideas, and can be perceived as close-minded. Charlie scored a zero on openness to new experiences. This score frustrated him to such an extent that he retook the assessment three times trying to earn a different score in this category. The counselor made it a goal to work on flexibility in thought. She decided to begin each session by having the students in the group play a simple game of questions with choices such as: Would you rather have the ability to fly or be able to turn invisible? Her goal was to have the students learn more about others' perspectives and their reasons for making specific choices that might differ from their own.

TECHNIQUES TO USE ACROSS DISCIPLINES

Flexibility includes brainstorming ideas that are very different and investigating topics even though you feel your initial idea or solution is correct. Taking the time to plan out ideas can be beneficial, especially in the brainstorming phase. Promoted throughout school, it can help build a culture of caring, as well as boost critical thinking skills. Specific strategies can be used in lessons across the curriculum to build cognitive flexibility so that students understand where their ideas are born and prompt them to investigate and understand other perspectives. In addition, cognitive flexibility is a skill that can be used across the curriculum as a strategy for nurturing underserved populations and students in K–12 classrooms.

These strategies begin with building fluency skills where students can generate a multitude of ideas to the next stage where they can seek out very diverse ideas, problems, and solutions. Creative thinking such as lateral thinking, synectics, and metaphorical thinking can also be used to expand initial conceptions.

In addition, using evaluation tools, students can assess specific problems or solutions by using concepts and considering a list of ten common factors that align with the human experience.

SHIFTING PERSPECTIVES

Kim (2016) suggests techniques that can be used to promote flexibility that include turning a design upside down, seeking out friendships beyond one's peer group, role-playing different perspectives such as individuals, animals, objects, and/or shifting time periods to the past, present, or future, or in other places, cities, or countries. Looking at opposite perspectives becomes essential, as does looking for alternative options or possibilities using unique materials, methods, steps, or processes. Kim (2016) also explains the importance of reviewing patents and describes the idea of "checking annoyances" – the process for how burs became Velcro or mold became penicillin. Students can practice this technique in all subject areas.

Language Arts – Select a fictional piece of text students are reading in class. Ask students to reinvision the order of events by exploring a different point of view. These picture books can serve as guides for how perspectives change based on different viewpoints:

Voices in the Park by Anthony Browne: The same walk in the park is told from the perspectives of four different characters – a mother, her son, a man, and his dog. Each character brings a unique point of view and tone to the story.

They All Saw a Cat by Brendan Wenzel: A cat walks through the world, and each creature it encounters sees the cat differently – through their own senses and perspectives.

The True Story of the Three Little Pigs by Jon Scieszka: Told from the wolf's perspective, this retelling of *The Three Little Pigs* claims the wolf has been misunderstood all along.

Mirror by Jeannie Baker: This wordless picture book compares the daily lives of two boys – one in Australia and one in Morocco – through parallel illustrations.

Science – Encourage flexibility by presenting the results of an experiment. Allow students to consider what the process entailed to reach those results. Here's a simple science experiment –The Mysterious Floating Water Experiment – that encourages students to observe, think creatively, and come up with multiple explanations for what they see:

Materials: A clear glass or cup, water, food coloring, a small piece of cardboard, a card from a deck of cards, thick paper, or a plastic lid that can cover the top of the cup.

Procedure: Fill the clear glass or cup with water almost to the top. Place the piece of cardboard (or plastic lid) flat on top of the glass, ensuring it covers the opening completely. Hold the cardboard in place with your hand and carefully flip the glass upside down. Slowly remove your hand from the cardboard while keeping the glass upside down. The water does not fall out, and the cardboard stays in place. Ask the students how the water floats in the upside-down glass without spilling. Encourage them to come up with multiple explanations for the phenomenon. The scientific explanation is that the air pressure pushing up on the cardboard is greater than the pressure of the water pushing down. This keeps the cardboard in place and the water inside the cup. Water molecules stick together (cohesion), and this surface tension helps keep the water from leaking around the edges of the cardboard.

Math – Challenge students to think of all the ways to get to 40 using addition, multiplication, subtraction, and division.

Social Studies – Select an event students are learning. How would this unfurl if it occurred in a different country or during a different time period?

Art – What would happen if you rearranged the characters in the painting? What if one of the characters was staring away from the viewer instead of at the viewer? What if the colors were darker? What if the artists used a different medium?

Theater – Students will use different acting techniques – moods, actions, facial expressions – to say the same lines on stage. Have students consider how the same words can be delivered through different methods to alter their meaning.

Outdoor Education – Keep a log of the insects and animals on campus. Have students write about what the animals observe happening around the school and in the classrooms.

SEMINARS

An individual develops a toolkit for expanding their flexibility by considering multiple perspectives. In the classroom, there are different approaches to help students understand, explore, and respect other perspectives. Using Socratic Seminars or Paideia Seminars can be a starting point. During this process, there are stages the students move through where they read a text or explore a nuanced topic. This can be a poem, short story, mathematical problem, or a scientific hypothesis. Students engage in reading, analyzing, forming discussion questions, and taking part in respectful conversations where they build on ideas and disagree respectfully by asking to find out more information from the person offering the opinion. Asking for textual support or pivoting can be excellent ways to show students how to complete this process.

Example: Jenny, I see that you believe that the author might be describing an actual path in the forest based on the details about the snow on the trees and the roots in the road. However, I think it might also refer to a metaphor for the decisions we make in life. I wonder what your thoughts are about this idea.

The following sentence starters can help students consider a variety of diverse perspectives, identify gaps, and imagine new possibilities:

What are the strengths and weaknesses of this argument?
How does this idea connect to other concepts we've discussed?
What evidence supports or challenges this claim?
Are there alternative perspectives or interpretations?
How does this idea compare to others we've encountered?
What are the key differences between X and Y?
In what ways does this perspective align or conflict with other readings?
How does this approach differ across contexts, fields, or cultures?
Do you agree or disagree with this argument? Why?
What assumptions are being made here? Are they valid?
What might be missing from this discussion?
How reliable is the evidence being used?
What might happen if this idea were implemented or ignored?
How could this concept evolve or change over time?
What would this argument look like in a different context or time period?
What new questions does this raise for you?

FINDING THE GRAY SPACE

This strategy is geared to foster cognitive flexibility in students as they address personal dilemmas, community problems, and global issues. Cognitive flexibility involves understanding personal opinions while investigating others' perspectives, providing the pathway to shift behaviors and beliefs. In a world that often defaults to black-or-white thinking, this strategy explores the gray.

Standardized testing, innovations in AI, and a culture of right-versus-wrong (fueled by social media) have left our society in a vulnerable place. Educators stand at the forefront of helping the next generation learn to work with and understand others while building a global society that nurtures all individuals. Students must receive the tools to be able to problem solve, evaluate, and implement solutions that guide our future.

The first step in the process is to select a problem for students to explore. Problems are everywhere. It can be beneficial to find ones that students have a personal interest in exploring or if they can make personal connections with the topic. Here is a list of problems to investigate.

- Personal or Family: Social Media, Healthy Eating, Mental Well-Being, Happiness, Opportunities to Explore Interests, Exercise, Education, Religion and Spirituality, Sexuality and Gender.
- School: Classroom Issues, Friendships, Bullying, Food, Attendance, Subjects, Sports.
- Community: Traffic, Safety, Economy, Land Development, Sports, Opportunities.
- State: Finances, Poverty, Education, Economic Growth.
- National: Political Atmosphere, Civil Rights, Reproductive Rights, Firearms.
- Global: AI, War, Food Security, Water.

The next step in the process is to examine the topic and brainstorm issues surrounding the problem. Take the following prompt for example: *How can the school help students develop an awareness of the environment?*

Use this list of basic human factors.

1. Safety and Physical Well-Being
2. Social, Emotional, and Mental Well-Being
3. Environment and Water Quality
4. Family
5. Relationships and Friendships
6. Personal Growth, Self-Expression, and Creativity
7. Opportunity (Educational, Spiritual or Religious, Financial, and Entrepreneurial)
8. Community and Meeting the Basic Needs of Others
9. Local, National, and World Impact
10. Innovation

From the list, students might brainstorm that environmental issues are associated with safety, physical well-being, environment, water quality, community, meeting the needs of others, local impact, and perhaps innovation if they consider avenues for what has already occurred to help make improvements or what could be accomplished in the future. By having students look at this list and brainstorm issues surrounding the topic, you are teaching them how to consider critical issues beyond their initial thoughts. See Figure 4.1 for concepts surrounding environmental awareness.

The next step is to begin brainstorming potential solutions. A student might consider the first idea that pops into his or her head, perhaps to increase recycling efforts across the school. This idea has great potential to explore and implement, but it is an ordinary response. By evaluating diverse ideas, students will have the potential to embark on a different initiative. Brainstorming a diverse list of ideas might include the following: Implementing a river restoration or wildlife

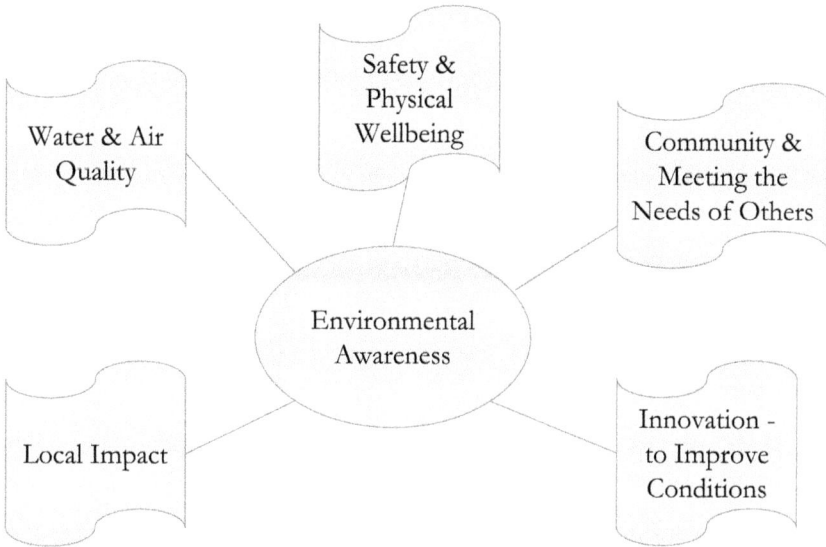

Figure 4.1 Important Concepts Surrounding Environmental Awareness.

rehabilitation project, planting a vegetable garden and designing a composting system, reducing perishable resources throughout the school, designing an upcycling club to repurpose old items into new or useful ones, starting a podcast series with conservation tips and expert interviews, initiating a plastic-free cafeteria, designing an art installation using recycled items that promotes important themes, or creating an advertising campaign to raise awareness about important aspects that families can do at home. See Figure 4.2 for a brainstorming map of potential solutions.

Grouping project ideas can help students understand flexibility. You can teach students to see how topics or ideas are similar in nature. So, in this case, have them consider the long-lasting impacts of the projects. These projects will

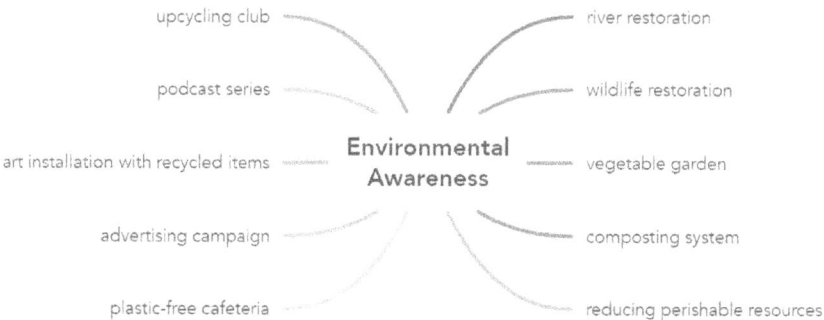

Figure 4.2 Brainstorming Map of Potential Solutions.

involve resources, physical labor, monitoring, and learning about the needs of the environment.

- River Restoration
- Wildlife Restoration
- Vegetable Garden
- Composting System

These projects can be conducted in the classroom:

- Podcast Series
- Art Installation
- Upcycling Club

These projects will need to have support from the administration and may happen without a great deal of student effort:

- Plastic-Free Cafeteria.
- Reducing Perishable Items across the School.

The next step is to consider different stances individuals might take in regard to the solution and return to the same list that students used to think about the initial problem in order to think about implementing the solution. Who would be involved in the solution and what would their perspective entail? For this problem, the following people could potentially be involved depending upon which solution the students choose: Classroom teachers, principal or other administrators, parents, local agencies, county office personnel, media specialist, art teacher, volunteers to help with the garden, river, or wildlife restoration.

DEVELOP STANCES

Describe three different perspectives about the problem and solution using items from the basic human factors list. For example:

1. The students in the classroom might want to make sure that as many people as possible (**community**) are aware of the topics impacting the **environment**, especially the existential thinkers.
2. The teacher might want to focus on certain standards from science, language arts, and math in order to be sure she is covering topics that students need to master (**personal growth**).
3. The principal might be concerned with the **safety** of the students as they implement a solution and may need to seek out permission from those above her at the county office level as there might be a certain protocol to follow.

SOLUTION

Based on these three perspectives, students can then move to the next step in finding a solution that all three can agree upon pursuing. To begin this project, students will write questions and contact experts for a podcast series. Based on what they learn and share with others, they will write a detailed plan to implement a hands-on project at the school. They will include all actions and address any safety issues before presenting their ideas to the principal.

Students can then think about the logistics involved and consider their goals. If the goal is to contribute to environmental improvement and to take an active role in creating positive change within their communities, they can consider combining ideas to create a multifaceted project. For example, students can choose to begin a vegetable garden and composting system and initiate an advertising campaign about products in the cafeteria where they encourage other students to reduce waste by using Bento Boxes or Tupperware instead of plastic bags. Once a potential solution to the problem has been identified, students can begin the next stage of outlining their plan of action and justifying why their idea is worth implementing. See Figure 4.3 for a visual of how the three stances funnel down to a final solution.

Table 4.1 explores how this method can be used to address other school problems students can investigate.

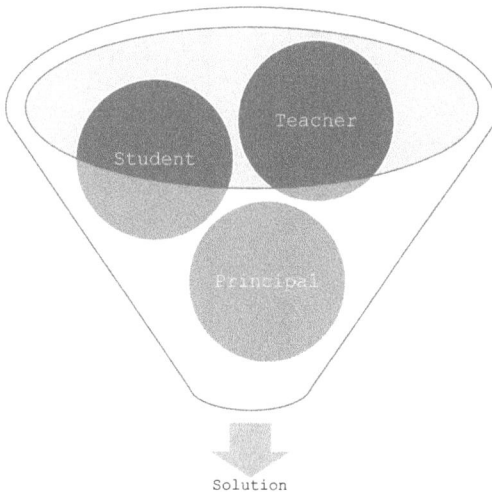

Solution

To begin the project, students will write questions and contact experts for the podcast series. Based on what they learn, they will write a detailed plan to implement a hands-on project at the school. They will include all actions and address any safety issues before presenting their ideas to the principal.

Figure 4.3 Three Stances Funneling Down to a Final Solution.

Table 4.1 Examples of Topics to Explore Using "Into the Gray" Technique

Topic	Who, What, Where, How, Why (Problem Analysis)	Brainstormed Solutions	Different Perspectives	Consensus Solution
Classroom Issues	*Problem*: Students report feeling unsafe to express ideas in class. **Who:** Students, teachers. **What:** Fear of ridicule or judgment. **Where:** Class discussions and group activities. **How:** Harsh criticism, lack of inclusive norms. **Why:** Limited emphasis on emotional safety and creativity.	– Create a "classroom charter" to establish shared norms promoting emotional safety. – Encourage creative self-expression through optional projects and presentations. – Use anonymous Q&A tools or discussion platforms to reduce pressure.	**Students:** Want a safe and supportive learning space. **Teachers:** Need methods to foster open dialogue. **Parents:** Concerned about children's social-emotional growth.	Introduce a classroom charter and train teachers in fostering emotionally safe discussions. Use anonymous tools to empower quieter students, enhancing creativity and expression.
Friendships	*Problem*: New students feel excluded from peer groups. **Who:** New students, peers, teachers, and counselors. **What:** Social isolation. **Where:** Cafeteria, hallways, and extracurricular spaces. **How:** Lack of structured opportunities for interaction. **Why:** Existing friendships dominate, and new students struggle to find their place socially and emotionally.	– Create structured "friendship-building" activities during advisory periods. – Implement peer-buddy programs that focus on emotional support. – Celebrate cultural diversity through events to encourage social-emotional and creative growth.	**New Students:** Seek acceptance and belonging. **Peers:** Worry about changing their social dynamic. **Teachers:** Want to promote kindness and creativity. **Parents:** Concerned about students' emotional health.	Develop peer-buddy programs supported by advisory friendship-building activities. Host monthly cultural celebration events to promote inclusion and social growth, boosting emotional safety for all.

(Continued)

Table 4.1 (Continued)

Topic	Who, What, Where, How, Why (Problem Analysis)	Brainstormed Solutions	Different Perspectives	Consensus Solution
Bullying	*Problem:* Cyberbullying creates emotional and social distress. **Who:** Students, school counselors, parents. **What:** Hurtful messages and exclusion. **Where:** Social media and school. **How:** Anonymity online and lack of emotional empathy. **Why:** Misuse of technology and lack of social-emotional learning opportunities.	– Launch a digital citizenship curriculum to address emotional safety and innovation in online behavior. – Create a reporting system that emphasizes emotional well-being and confidentiality. – Organize restorative circles to promote relationship repair and community building.	**Victims:** Need emotional safety and accountability. **Bullies:** Require empathy education and family support. **Parents:** Want children protected from harm. **Teachers:** Seek tools for preventing and managing bullying.	Introduce a digital citizenship program combined with restorative justice circles. Use anonymous reporting apps to ensure emotional and community safety. Focus on relationship repair and building social skills.

(Continued)

67

Table 4.1 (Continued)

Topic	Who, What, Where, How, Why (Problem Analysis)	Brainstormed Solutions	Different Perspectives	Consensus Solution
Food	*Problem:* Students feel the food offered lacks nutritional and environmental value. **Who:** Students, cafeteria staff, administration. **What:** Limited healthy, sustainable meal options. **Where:** School cafeteria. **How:** Cost restrictions and lack of innovation. **Why:** Budget prioritization and limited student input.	– Conduct surveys to explore students' food preferences. – Partner with local farms to provide fresh, eco-friendly produce. – Use composting to reduce food waste and involve students in innovation projects like "grow your own vegetables" for personal growth and sustainability.	**Students:** Want healthy, sustainable, and tasty food. **Cafeteria Staff:** Face budget constraints. **Parents:** Concerned about nutritional and environmental impact. **Local Farmers:** Interested in school partnerships.	Partner with local farms for sustainable ingredients, launch a composting program, and include students in creating a school garden. This supports physical, environmental, and personal growth while fostering community partnerships.
Attendance	*Problem:* Chronic absenteeism impacts students' educational opportunities. **Who:** Students, families, school counselors. **What:** Inconsistent attendance. **Where:** Home and school. **How:** Mental health issues, lack of transportation, or uninspiring school environment. **Why:** Students may lack emotional support or resources to stay engaged.	– Develop mentoring programs for at-risk students focused on personal growth and opportunity-building. – Provide flexible start times for students facing family or mental health challenges. – Use attendance incentives tied to student-led community projects.	**Students:** Need support for emotional and logistical challenges. **Families:** Struggle with resources and routines. **Teachers:** Need consistent attendance to deliver quality education. **Counselors:** Want to address root causes.	Implement mentoring programs and flexible scheduling for students facing challenges. Incentivize attendance through meaningful student-led community service projects to promote social, emotional, and personal growth.

(Continued)

Table 4.1 (Continued)

Topic	Who, What, Where, How, Why (Problem Analysis)	Brainstormed Solutions	Different Perspectives	Consensus Solution
Subjects	*Problem:* Students find some subjects disengaging and disconnected from real life. **Who:** Students, teachers, and curriculum developers. **What:** Lack of interest or creativity in learning. **Where:** Classrooms. **How:** Rote learning methods and lack of personal relevance. **Why:** Limited focus on creativity and application.	– Use project-based learning centered on real-world innovation (e.g., environmental clean-ups or entrepreneurial ideas). – Incorporate creativity-building tasks such as multimedia projects. – Invite guest speakers from diverse fields to show subjects' relevance to personal growth and global impact.	**Students:** Want lessons to feel meaningful and exciting. **Teachers:** Seek tools for engagement. **Parents:** Want education to prepare children for opportunities. **Communities:** Benefit from student involvement.	Integrate project-based learning with real-world relevance, supported by guest speakers and multimedia projects. Engage students in creating community impact initiatives tied to subject content.
Sports	*Problem:* Limited access to inclusive and diverse sports programs. **Who:** Students, coaches, parents, and school staff. **What:** Competitive programs exclude casual or less-skilled players. **Where:** Sports facilities. **How:** Focus on elite performance. **Why:** Lack of opportunities for social, emotional, and physical well-being for all students.	– Create intramural leagues for different skill levels to foster inclusivity and relationships. – Introduce non-traditional sports (e.g., ultimate frisbee, yoga) to encourage creativity and personal growth. – Promote teamwork and innovation by organizing "sports for good" events tied to community causes.	**Athletic Students:** Want advanced competition. **Casual Players:** Need opportunities for social and physical well-being. **Coaches:** Focus on team performance. **Parents:** Want children to be active and included.	Establish inclusive intramural sports leagues for all levels. Add non-traditional sports options and host community service events through sports to promote teamwork, emotional growth, and physical well-being.

69

PRODUCTIVE THINKING

Productive thinking involves problem solving with an emphasis on flexible thinking. It involves a series of steps that allow individuals or groups to solve business or personal problems (Hurson, 2008). The process focuses on repeatable steps that allow for critical and creative thinking to generate fresh solutions.

The steps include:

Step 1: *What's Going On?* Investigate the problem.

Step 2: *What's Success?* Consider the optimal outcome and define criteria for success.

Step 3: *What's the Question?* Define the actual problem or opportunity.

Step 4: *Generate Answers.* Brainstorm many possible solutions.

Step 5: *Forge the Solution.* Select the best solution and refine it.

Step 6: *Align Resources.* Design a plan of action.

In the following math-focused example, productive thinking is used to help students approach a real-world scenario using mathematical concepts. Throughout this lesson, the instructor should emphasize moments where students are practicing flexibility. By emphasizing flexibility, students can learn about their thinking process while improving their ability to respond to feedback. This approach can enhance mathematical understanding, effective decision-making, and prepare students for similar challenges in their lives.

DESIGNING A BUDGET FOR A SCHOOL FIELD TRIP

A middle school math teacher wants to engage students in a real-world application of math concepts, particularly budgeting, percentages, and financial planning. The goal is to plan a field trip while staying within a specific budget. The first step involves the instructor presenting the problem, such as: How can we design a field trip with a $1,200 budget? Students brainstorm ideas based on different aspects of the field trip including destinations, transportation options, food options, and entry fees for various activities. Each group presents their findings to the class and explains how their aspects will impact the overall budget. As students consider different options, they must use flexibility to consider the best option. The instructor can encourage students to understand this process by emphasizing how the groups are being flexible by changing the destination, seeking out the most educational experiences, and considering unique travel or dining options. Based on these conversations, groups can create a budget proposal with an itemized list of expenses and present their report to the class for feedback. Based on these presentations, groups can collaborate to combine ideas or select one that provides the most educational opportunity at the best price. The final component should involve a reflection where students identify moments when they used flexibility throughout the problem-solving experience.

ATTRIBUTE LISTING

Attribute listing is a technique where individuals assess an item, idea, or problem by analyzing different components or attributes. After listing the attributes, they can consider how aspects can be improved. This process encourages flexibility as the individual can think about how the product can be improved in order to be more successful. It allows the individual to consider individual components that contribute to the overall product such as size, shape, color, material, or function. This provides the opportunity to disrupt fixed thinking patterns and explore multiple perspectives as attributes can be altered or combined in different ways.

For example in a high school science class, students can be asked to create an eco-friendly water filtration system. The attributes might include materials, cost, maintenance, functionality, efficiency, and sustainability. Students can consider diverse aspects of materials such as physical components like sand, gravel, and charcoal. They can also consider environmental aspects such as if the materials are recycled or biodegradable. Another part of the process could involve if the materials are found or produced locally or transported from far away. For cost, students can consider a list that comprises materials and one for construction. Maintenance can be organized by access to certain filters or ease of replacing items. Functionality can include removal of sediment, reduction of pathogens such as bacteria and viruses, and elimination of chemicals or toxins. Efficiency can include time to filter water or energy required to complete a certain process. Finally, sustainability can include environmental impact, longevity of materials purchased, and work required to maintain the operating system.

After deconstructing these components, students can prioritize the attributes in order to complete their designs. This might involve sketching different filtration systems and conducting research about unique solutions. Designs can be shared with classmates in order to evaluate the attributes and make adjustments. By utilizing this process, students are given tools to understand how to think flexibly when creating a product design.

MORPHOLOGICAL SYNTHESIS

Similar to attribute listing, morphological synthesis involves breaking items into categories, but the goal for this technique is the generation of novel ideas. The process is more complex with students considering all of the potential solutions or outcomes. For example, in a middle school social studies class, students could be given the prompt to plan a new community. The key categories involved could include community type, transportation systems, public services, cultural features, and environmental considerations. Based on these concepts, students can create a matrix with the identified categories and list different options for each category.

MORPHOLOGICAL MATRIX: DESIGNING A NEW COMMUNITY

Category	Option 1	Option 2	Option 3	Option 4
Community Type	Urban	Suburban	Rural	Eco-Village
Transportation Systems	Extensive public transit	Biking paths	Walkable areas	Combination of all
Public Services	Large community center	Local schools	Parks and playgrounds	Healthcare facilities
Cultural Features	Multi-ethnic festivals	Local farmers' markets	Art exhibitions	Cultural exchange events
Environmental Considerations	Solar energy	Community gardens	Waste recycling program	Natural habitats

Students can generate combinations by selecting one option from each category. For example: Community Type: Urban; Transportation Systems: Extensive public transit; Public Services: Large community center; Cultural Features: Multi-ethnic festivals; and Environmental Considerations: Solar energy. After generating their combination, students can create a name, community layout, transportation plan, public services, and events that promote cultural awareness and diversity.

MORPHOLOGICAL MATRIX: DESIGNING A CAR

For this example, students are challenged to design a new car. They must consider Power Source, Body Material, Tires/Wheels, Special Features, Design Style, Size, and Environmental Impact.

Components	Option 1	Option 2	Option 3	Option 4
Power Source	Gasoline	Electric	Solar	Hydrogen fuel cell
Body Material	Steel	Aluminum	Carbon fiber	Biodegradable plastic
Tires/Wheels	Traditional tires	Off-road tires	Airless tires	Hover technology
Special Features	Self-driving system	Built-in Wi-Fi hotspot	Smart climate control	Augmented reality (AR) windshield
Design Style	Sporty	Minimalist	Futuristic	Retro
Size/Capacity	Two-seater (compact)	Five-seater (family)	Seven-seater (SUV)	Customizable size
Environment Focus	Low emissions	100% renewable energy	Recyclable parts	Carbon capture tech

Students can choose one option from each row to create their car design. For example: Power Source: Solar; Body Material: Carbon fiber; Tires/Wheels: Airless tires; Special Features: Augmented reality (AR) windshield; Design Style: Futuristic; Size/Capacity: Two-seater (compact); and Environment Focus: 100% renewable energy. After creating a profile, students can consider customers, pricing, and how it addresses current predicaments in the transportation industry.

This process prevents defaulting to familiar or conventional ideas and can allow students to shift thinking from rigid, single-solution patterns to adaptable, multi-faceted perspectives. It provides the opportunity to explore a wide range of solutions and encourages the student to connect unrelated or unlikely ideas, boosting creativity and adaptability. Instead of focusing on a single "right" answer, morphological synthesis opens up multiple possibilities. Morphological synthesis is useful for multi-dimensional problems and helps individuals tackle challenges that require flexible and adaptive problem solving.

LATERAL THINKING

Edward de Bono designed lateral thinking as an approach that involves assessing challenges from different and unconventional perspectives. Instead of focusing on solving a problem in a logical or step-by-step manner, lateral thinking encourages individuals to reframe the problem asking probing questions. For example, instead of asking how to make a bridge stronger, ask if a bridge is needed at all. Individuals are encouraged to generate unusual ideas through brainstorming or random word association. For example, instead of improving a cup to keep coffee warm, think about whether a self-heating coffee container is possible. In addition, individuals are encouraged to consider problems from different stakeholders or alternative scenarios. For example, designing a school from the perspective of students, teachers, and parents to uncover new insights. Finally, individuals are encouraged to break free from traditional constraints or rules. For example, if a store wants to increase customer visits, instead of focusing on ads, consider creating a space for community events. Lateral thinking promotes cognitive flexibility because it requires people to break out of habitual patterns, adapt to new ideas or perspectives, and explore alternative solutions.

There are steps to help students move through the lateral thinking process. For example, students in a high school art class can be challenged to reimagine everyday objects with the goal of exploring new perspectives in art and design. The instructor can start with a statement that challenges assumptions about the object. This step is called po (Provocation). For example, what if chairs did not exist as places to sit, but rather as interactive art pieces? Students could design chairs that changes shape or colors. The next step, exaggeration, asks the student to amplify a feature or characteristic. The teacher could ask what would happen if a chair had eight legs instead of four. Students could experiment with whimsical furniture design and explore concepts with stability. The next stage, distortion, asks the individual to alter the object's form, function, or context in surprising ways. The teacher could ask the students to consider how chairs could be made to float. They could explore materials or textures that evoke this concept. The final aspect, random input, asks the individual to introduce a random word or idea into their design. For instance, the word "ocean" could be introduced. Students could add colors, textures, and sounds, or evoke change in overall design to resemble a coral reef or octopus. Based on these different techniques, students could sketch, draw, paint, or build their designs. An important component to encourage students' understanding of flexible thinking would be the final reflection for how the lateral thinking process encouraged flexible thinking.

SOCIAL AND EMOTIONAL CHALLENGE – SHIFTING PERSPECTIVE THROUGH JOURNALING

Encouraging students to explore new perspectives can foster cognitive flexibility and empathy. For one week, challenge students to shift their point of view and keep a journal capturing how objects or individuals might see or experience events differently. For example, they might consider what the classroom clock thinks about its role in the learning environment or how the playground feels about being overrun by the energy of a Kindergarten class. Through this imaginative exercise, students can better understand how shifting perspectives deepens emotional awareness and broadens creative thinking.

In their journals, students should describe the imagined perspective of their chosen object or individual in both words and visuals. Encourage them to draw pictures that express not only the point of view but also the emotion the item might be experiencing. For example, the clock might "feel" tired as it watches over busy students all day, or the playground might "feel" joyful and alive during recess but lonely after school ends. These illustrations add depth and creativity to the reflective process, allowing students to express themselves in multiple ways.

At the end of the week, ask students to reflect on their journal entries and select one object or perspective that resonated most with them. They can then create a detailed picture representing the chosen perspective, combining their descriptive writing and artistic interpretation. For example, a student might illustrate the clock with drooping hands to convey exhaustion or depict a cheerful playground surrounded by children. This final piece should be designed to communicate the emotions and story of the chosen perspective vividly.

The completed pictures can be displayed in a hallway gallery to share students' creative and emotional insights with others. This public sharing fosters a sense of pride in their work and encourages discussions about empathy and different perspectives. By engaging in this activity, students develop emotional awareness, creative thinking, and the ability to see the world through multiple lenses, essential skills for navigating social and emotional challenges.

SPOTLIGHT: INVENTORS UNDER 18

At just 11 years old, Gitanjali Rao invented "Tethys", a groundbreaking lead detection device inspired by the devastating Flint water crisis. Tethys offers a quicker, cost-effective, and user-friendly solution for detecting lead contamination in water, a problem that affects millions of people worldwide. Named after the Greek goddess of freshwater, the device utilizes carbon nanotube sensors to identify lead particles with precision, transmitting the results to a smartphone application via Bluetooth. Rao's innovative approach has made it easier for individuals and communities to test their water for contamination and take appropriate action to ensure their safety.

Gitanjali was motivated to create Tethys after learning about the Flint crisis, where thousands of residents were exposed to unsafe drinking water due to lead contamination. She conducted extensive research on the problem and found that existing lead detection methods were often expensive, time-consuming, or difficult for everyday users to access. Driven by a desire to find a solution, she applied her interest in science and engineering to create a device that could empower individuals to take control of their water quality. Her invention highlights the potential of young minds to address real-world issues with creativity and determination.

In 2017, Rao's invention earned her the title of "America's Top Young Scientist" at the Discovery Education 3M Young Scientist Challenge. Her innovative work caught the attention of media outlets and industry professionals, showcasing the impact of youth-driven solutions in addressing global challenges. In addition to receiving recognition for her work, Gitanjali has become an advocate for STEM education, particularly for young girls. She frequently speaks at events and collaborates with organizations to inspire others to pursue scientific inquiry and innovative thinking.

Beyond Tethys, Gitanjali has continued to innovate and contribute to the world of science. She has developed additional tools and solutions to address pressing problems, solidifying her role as a leading voice among young innovators. Her story is a powerful reminder of the importance of encouraging curiosity, resilience, and creativity in the next generation.

CONCLUSION

Flexibility plays a vital role in the creative process, as it allows individuals to explore various alternatives, generate diverse ideas, and approach problems from multiple angles. By fostering this skill, learners can engage in divergent thinking, moving beyond conventional solutions to uncover new possibilities. Grouping ideas into categories and utilizing strategies such as shifting perspectives, exploring gray areas, and applying productive thinking enable individuals to identify patterns and broaden their approach to problem solving. Techniques like attribute listing, morphological synthesis, and lateral thinking further encourage unconventional and innovative solutions. Through the integration of these methods, creativity becomes more accessible and actionable. By combining practical strategies with opportunities for reflection, practice, and application, flexibility empowers individuals to think expansively, navigate challenges with confidence, and approach learning with a sense of curiosity and openness.

REFERENCES

Dodge, A. (2019, December 31). *How to improve the cognitive flexibility of your students.* Ozobot. https://ozobot.com/how-to-improve-the-cognitive-flexibility-of-your-students/

Guilford, J.P. (1968). Intelligence, creativity, and emotional implications. San Diego: Knapp.

Hurson, T. (2008). *Think better: An innovator's guide to productive thinking* (your company's future depends on it, and so does yours). New York, NY: McGraw-Hill.

Isen, A.M. (2002). Missing in action in the AIM: Positive affect's facilitation of cognitive flexibility, innovation, and problem solving. *Psychological Inquiry, 13*(1), 57–65.

Jacobson, R. (2022, September 21). *Helping kids with flexible thinking*. Child Mind Institute. https://childmind.org/bio/rae-jacobson/

Kim, K.H. (2016). *The creativity challenge: How we can recapture American innovation* (1st ed.). Guilford: Globe Pequot Press.

Lawrence, A., Clark, L., Labuzetta, J.N., Sahakian, B., & Vyakarnum, S. (2008). The innovative brain. *Nature (London)*, *456*(7219), 168–169. https://doi.org/10.1038/456168a

Runco, M.A. (1986). Divergent thinking and creative performance in gifted and non-gifted children. *Educational and Psychological Measurement*, *46*(2), 375–384. https://doi.org/10.1177/001316448604600211

Russo, C.F. (2004). A comparative study of creativity and cognitive problem-solving strategies of high-IQ and average students. *Gifted Child Quarterly*, *48*(3), 179–190. https://doi.org/10.1177/001698620404800303

Sahakian, B.J., Langley, C., & Leong, V. (2021, June 26). *IQ tests can't measure it, but cognitive flexibility is key to learning and creativity*. The Conversation. https://theconversation.com/iq-tests-cant-measure-it-but-cognitive-flexibility-is-key-to-learning-and-creativity-163284

Silver, E.A. (1997). Fostering creativity through instruction rich in mathematical problem solving and problem posing. *ZDM–Mathematics Education*, *29*(3), 75–80.

Starko, A.J. (2021). *Creativity in the classroom* (7th ed.). Taylor & Francis. https://bookshelf.vitalsource.com/books/9781000479232

Torrance, E.P. (1994). *Creativity: Just wanting to know*. Pretoria: Benedict Books.

Treffinger, D.J. (1995). Creative problem solving: Overview and educational implications. *Educational Psychology Review*, *7*, 301–312.

Chapter 5

Originality

The Ability to Think of New or Unusual Products or Going Beyond the Common or Obvious Answers

INTRODUCTION

The Reebok Pump, released in 1989, was a revolutionary product designed to provide athletes with a customizable and secure fit in their footwear. Reebok recognized a gap in the market for shoes that could offer a more personalized fit, especially for high-impact sports. To address this, Reebok partnered with engineer Paul Litchfield and his team to develop an inflatable air bladder that could be adjusted by the user. This innovation allowed athletes to "pump up" the shoes for a tighter fit and "release" the air for more flexibility, targeting comfort and performance.

The design process involved creating a small, discreet pump in the tongue of the shoe, which inflated the air chamber inside the shoe, tightening it around the foot and ankle. Extensive testing with athletes ensured the product was both durable and effective in real-world conditions. Once refined, the Reebok Pump was marketed as a groundbreaking innovation in sports footwear, with notable athletes like Dee Brown endorsing the product during high-profile events such as the NBA Slam Dunk Contest.

The Reebok Pump's success was driven by its originality and the combination of engineering, design, and creative marketing. It became a cultural icon and a symbol of performance and customization in athletic footwear, influencing future designs and leaving a lasting legacy in sneaker culture. Through the Pump, Reebok introduced a unique concept that went beyond typical shoe designs, offering consumers a novel and interactive experience with their footwear.

Emma, our outdoor gear designer from Chapter 4, believes the best designs exist on the edge of discomfort. A backpack that is too safe, too familiar, fails to challenge expectations or improve performance. The creative sweet spot, she argues, is on the "edge of discomfort" and lies in pushing the limits just enough to introduce something new, something that refines and enhances the user's experience.

DOI: 10.4324/9781003434221-5

Originality is a cornerstone of creativity, reflecting the ability to produce ideas, concepts, or works that are novel and unique. It serves as the essence of creativity, setting apart imaginative endeavors from routine or derivative ones. Originality introduces fresh perspectives and solutions, pushing boundaries and fostering authenticity by showcasing the creator's unique voice and vision. It drives innovation by challenging the status quo and inspiring breakthroughs across fields such as technology, art, and science. Many groundbreaking inventions and transformative changes stem from original thinking, as it disrupts traditional frameworks and redefines industries or societal norms.

Original works have a powerful ability to captivate attention, evoke emotions, and provoke thought. Their novelty and unexpected nature inspire others to think differently while fostering deeper connections with audiences. However, originality does not exist in isolation; it often builds on existing knowledge, ideas, or cultural contexts. Many creative works reinterpret or adapt influences in innovative ways, and originality frequently emerges from collaborative efforts that blend diverse perspectives.

Striving for originality can be both liberating and challenging. It requires courage, experimentation, and resilience to explore uncharted territory, often involving risks of failure or rejection. The instructor can play a powerful role in designing an environment and implementing techniques for risk-taking (Massie et al., 2022; Ramlackhan, 2024). Creators must navigate the fine line between drawing inspiration and imitation, ensuring that their work stands out as truly innovative. In today's rapidly evolving world, originality takes on new dimensions, shaped by digital tools, global connectivity, and cultural exchange. While these developments expand the possibilities for innovation, they also raise questions about the nature of originality in a world saturated with existing ideas. Ultimately, originality remains integral to creativity, driving progress, inspiring change, and shaping the future through its blend of imagination, knowledge, and influence.

METAPHORICAL THINKING

Metaphors and analogies involve applying a word, phrase, or idea to something it is not usually associated with, such as "windows are the eyes of a house". Metaphorical thinking is a sign of creativity (Piirto, 2004; Runco, 2014). While metaphors and analogies are obviously used in literature, they are also important to other areas such as visual arts, science, math, and engineering (Hendrinana & Rohaeti, 2017; Runco, 2014; Sanchez-Ruiz et al., 2013). For example, engineers often refer to medical/health-related terms such as stress and fatigue of metal beams and bleeding of concrete. Finding similarities in unrelated objects and concepts can change the way a person perceives a problem or idea (Veale, 2006) and hence is helpful in generating solutions to problems. Starko (2005)

79

recommends teaching metaphorical thinking to nurture creativity. Teachers can use this strategy by asking students to find and create content-specific metaphors. Examples of questions that prompt metaphorical thinking include:

- Which animal are you most like in the morning? At noon? At night?
- How is time like a thief?
- How might the relationship between the handloom and the power loom be a metaphor for the changes brought about by the Industrial Revolution?
- How are neurons like trees?
- How are brains like forests?

Table 5.1 Examples of Metaphorical Thinking

Challenge	Possible Responses (Metaphorical Thinking)
How can we explain how a cell functions using something familiar?	**The Cell as a Complex Machine**: The cell is like a well-designed machine. The nucleus is the "control panel" where decisions are made, mitochondria are the "energy generators", and the endoplasmic reticulum is the "assembly line" where parts are created and transported.
How can we understand electric current if we've never seen it?	**Electricity as a Stream of Traffic**: Think of electricity as cars on a highway. The battery is the "engine" driving the cars, while resistors act like toll booths that slow down the flow of traffic, and wires are the lanes that guide the cars to their destination.
How could we describe the function of DNA in an organism?	**DNA as a Recipe Book**: DNA is like a recipe book that provides step-by-step instructions for creating an organism. Each gene is like a recipe for a specific dish (protein), and when followed, it ensures the organism develops and functions properly.
How can we visualize the Earth's layers in a creative way?	**Earth as an Onion**: The Earth is like an onion with multiple layers. The outermost layer, the crust, is thin and easy to peel away, while the inner layers (mantle and core) are much denser and harder to reach, just like the deeper layers of an onion.
How could we explain photosynthesis in a more adventurous way?	**Photosynthesis as a Plant's Cooking Recipe**: Imagine photosynthesis as a plant "cooking" its own food. It mixes sunlight, water, and carbon dioxide in the "kitchen" (chloroplasts), and the result is glucose (food) that fuels the plant's growth, with oxygen as a "side dish" released into the air.

(Continued)

Table 5.1 (Continued)

Challenge	Possible Responses (Metaphorical Thinking)
What could represent the relationship between the sun and planets?	**The Solar System as a Dance Performance**: The planets are dancers moving gracefully around the "center stage" (the sun), each following their own path and timing but all contributing to the overall harmony of the performance.
How do we understand energy transfer in a system?	**Energy as a Relay Race**: Energy transfer is like a relay race where one runner (molecule) passes the baton (energy) to the next. Each runner is responsible for keeping the energy moving smoothly to the next stage of the race until it reaches its final destination.
How could we explain the role of the heart in the body?	**The Heart as a Pumping Station**: The heart acts like a pump in a water system, pushing blood (like water) through pipes (blood vessels) to ensure oxygen and nutrients reach all parts of the body, maintaining the body's circulation and health.
What could help us understand atomic structure?	**The Atom as a Mini Solar System**: Picture an atom like a small solar system, with electrons orbiting the nucleus, similar to planets orbiting the sun. The nucleus is the center of the atom, and the electrons are like planets moving in their specific orbits.
How could we visualize the water cycle in an unconventional way?	**The Water Cycle as a Journey**: Think of the water cycle as a journey where water travels in a loop. It starts as water in rivers or lakes (the "starting point"), evaporates into the air (taking a "flight"), condenses into clouds (rests at a "hotel"), and then falls as rain ("arriving" back on Earth).

SYNECTICS

Synectics is a creativity-enhancing technique developed by George Prince and William J.J. Gordon (Gordon, 1961) that encourages innovative problem solving through the use of analogies, metaphors, and creative associations. The name "synectics" comes from the Greek words "syn" (meaning together) and "ektos" (meaning different), emphasizing the concept of bringing together seemingly unrelated ideas to stimulate creative thinking. This approach plays a significant role in fostering creativity by helping individuals move beyond conventional thought patterns and encouraging them to approach problems from new perspectives.

One of the key aspects of synectics is its ability to break mental barriers by urging participants to make connections between unrelated concepts, which often leads to fresh insights and innovative solutions. By promoting out-of-the-box thinking, synectics challenges individuals to explore unusual or unexpected ideas that they might not consider through traditional problem-solving methods. This technique also encourages team collaboration, as participants work together to generate diverse ideas and solutions by looking at a problem from different angles.

Synectics differs from free-form brainstorming by providing a structured approach that guides participants in making new associations and refining raw ideas into workable solutions. It also emphasizes the importance of emotional and intuitive thinking, encouraging individuals to connect with their feelings and experiences to generate more holistic ideas. As a result, synectics is widely applied across various fields, such as business, design, engineering, education, and the arts. In business, it is used to drive innovation and develop new products, while in design and engineering, it helps solve technical challenges creatively. In education, it fosters critical thinking and creativity in students, and in the arts, it supports new ways of artistic expression. Synectics enhances creativity by providing a structured framework for thinking in fresh, unconventional ways. It helps individuals and teams solve problems innovatively and generate novel ideas, making it a valuable tool across a wide range of industries and disciplines.

The process of using synectics involves a series of structured steps that guide individuals or groups through creative problem solving and idea generation. This process combines both divergent (generating many ideas) and convergent (narrowing down ideas) thinking, encouraging participants to make new connections and see problems in a different light. Here are the specific steps typically involved in using synectics.

UNDERSTANDING THE PROBLEM

- **Clarifying the Challenge**: The first step is to ensure that all participants fully understand the problem or challenge at hand. This may involve providing background information or setting up the context in which the problem exists. The group must define the scope of the issue, making sure that everyone is aligned with the objectives of the session.
- **Reframing the Problem**: Instead of approaching the problem in the usual way, synectics encourages participants to reframe or look at the problem from a different angle. For example, asking "What would this problem look like if it were a completely different kind of problem?" helps challenge assumptions and leads to new perspectives.

MAKING ANALOGIES

- **Using Direct Analogies:** One of the core techniques of synectics is the creation of analogies. Participants are asked to think of a situation or object that is similar to the problem but not directly related. These direct analogies could be anything – like comparing a business problem to a sports strategy or a biological system to a city's infrastructure. The goal is to spark new ways of thinking that move beyond the immediate context of the problem.
- **Using Personal Analogies**: Personal analogies involve asking participants to relate the problem to their own life experiences or feelings. This can provide a deeper, more intuitive connection to the problem. For example, a participant might relate a difficult decision in a business setting to navigating a tough choice in their personal life.
- **Using Fantasy Analogies**: Fantasy analogies involve more imaginative thinking. Here, participants might be asked to think about the problem as if they were in a completely different world or as if there were no limitations to what could be achieved. This type of analogy frees the mind from conventional boundaries, encouraging highly creative and out-of-the-box thinking.

IDEA GENERATION AND EXPLORATION

- **Generating Ideas**: Once analogies are established, participants brainstorm solutions and ideas based on these connections. In synectics, the emphasis is on quantity rather than quality at this stage – participants should freely offer as many ideas as possible without worrying about their practicality. The goal is to unlock novel, unexpected possibilities by applying the analogies to the original problem.
- **Exploring the Analogies**: Participants can delve deeper into the analogies, thinking about how the original problem connects to the analogy on multiple levels. This exploration can lead to the discovery of new insights that were not initially obvious and might offer entirely new ways of solving the problem.

EVALUATING AND REFINING IDEAS

- **Converging Ideas**: After generating a wide variety of ideas, the next step is to begin evaluating and refining them. Participants narrow down the ideas by discussing their feasibility, practicality, and relevance to the original problem. This is the point at which the group converges on a few promising ideas to focus on.

83

- **Testing Ideas in Context**: Once a set of potential solutions has been selected, it is useful to test these ideas in the context of the real-world problem. How do these ideas hold up when applied to the actual situation? Are they as innovative as they seemed initially? The group may need to iterate on these solutions, using additional rounds of analogical thinking to tweak and refine their ideas.

IMPLEMENTATION AND REFLECTION

- **Creating an Action Plan**: After narrowing down ideas, participants develop an action plan to implement the most viable solutions. This may involve identifying steps, resources, and timelines to bring the ideas to life.
- **Reflecting on the Process**: Finally, synectics involves reflecting on the overall process to see what worked well and what could be improved. This reflection helps to refine the approach for future creative problem-solving sessions.

SYNECTICS IN ACTION: EXAMPLE

Let's take an example to illustrate the process of synectics in action. Imagine a team working on designing a new product for a tech company. The challenge they face is coming up with a unique design that addresses customers' concerns about durability and portability.

1. **Understanding the Problem**: The team defines the problem clearly – they need to create a durable yet portable device that stands out in the market.
2. **Making Analogies**:
   - Direct analogy: The team compares the device design to a Swiss Army knife, which is known for being compact and multifunctional. They brainstorm ways to make the device flexible without sacrificing strength.
   - Personal analogy: One team member compares the challenge to carrying a heavy backpack for a hike. The solution might involve thinking of ways to reduce weight while maintaining strength, similar to how modern hiking backpacks are designed.
   - Fantasy analogy: The team imagines designing the product as if it were to be used on another planet, where durability and portability are key to survival in extreme environments.
3. **Idea Generation**: Based on these analogies, they generate ideas like modular components, collapsible features, or advanced materials that are lightweight but strong.

4. **Evaluating and Refining**: The team discusses the practicality of each idea, testing them against criteria like cost, user experience, and manufacturability.
5. **Implementation and Reflection**: The best ideas are turned into prototypes, and the team plans further development. Afterward, they reflect on how the analogies helped them think outside the box.

Synectics is a powerful, structured creative process that encourages innovative thinking by making connections between unrelated ideas. By using analogies and metaphors – direct, personal, and fantasy – participants are guided through generating, refining, and implementing creative solutions. This process not only enhances problem solving but also fosters a deeper, more expansive approach to creativity. Table 5.2 illustrates how synectics can be used in a world history classroom to prompt deeper exploration of historical topics through creative analogies. By making connections between history and other areas of knowledge, students are encouraged to think critically and creatively about the forces that shaped the world.

Table 5.2 Analogies in a History Classroom

Historical Topic	Challenge	Analogies
Causes of World War I	What were the underlying causes of World War I, and how can we better understand their complexity?	– **Direct Analogy**: A complex chess game with political alliances as the moves. – **Personal Analogy**: A personal group disagreement that escalates. – **Fantasy Analogy**: A kingdom on another planet with a collapsing government due to sudden alliances.
Impact of the Industrial Revolution	How did the Industrial Revolution change society and shape the modern world?	– **Direct Analogy**: The Industrial Revolution as a high-speed train revolutionizing travel. – **Personal Analogy**: Comparing the smartphone's impact to the Industrial Revolution. – **Fantasy Analogy**: A futuristic society adjusting to automation.
The French Revolution	What caused the French Revolution, and how did it impact France and the world?	– **Direct Analogy**: The French Revolution as a pressure cooker. – **Personal Analogy**: Reflecting on personal oppression and how it leads to rebellion. – **Fantasy Analogy**: A rebellion on another planet against unjust rulers.

(Continued)

Table 5.2 (Continued)

Historical Topic	Challenge	Analogies
Role of the Silk Road in Cultural Exchange	How did the Silk Road facilitate cultural exchange and shape civilizations?	– **Direct Analogy**: The Silk Road as a global marketplace for goods and ideas. – **Personal Analogy**: Modern communication across cultures via social media. – **Fantasy Analogy**: A space station where different planets trade resources and ideas.
Fall of the Roman Empire	What led to the fall of the Roman Empire, and what lessons can we learn from it?	– **Direct Analogy**: The Roman Empire as an overextended bridge collapsing under pressure. – **Personal Analogy**: A person taking on too many responsibilities and failing. – **Fantasy Analogy**: A futuristic mega-city collapsing under its own expansion.
Rise of Nationalism in the 19th Century	How did nationalism in the 19th century influence world events?	– **Direct Analogy**: Nationalism as the rise of a sports team fanbase growing too intense. – **Personal Analogy**: The impact of identifying strongly with a group. – **Fantasy Analogy**: Different planets forming powerful nations that assert their sovereignty.
Cold War and Space Race	How did the Space Race reflect Cold War tensions between the US and Soviet Union?	– **Direct Analogy**: The Space Race as a high-stakes race between two runners. – **Personal Analogy**: Competing to show off skills or abilities against a rival. – **Fantasy Analogy**: Two planets racing to demonstrate their technological superiority in space.

SIX THINKING HATS

The Six Thinking Hats technique, developed by Edward de Bono (Debono, 1985), is a structured framework for problem solving and decision-making that encourages individuals or groups to approach issues from multiple perspectives. Each "hat" represents a specific type of thinking, helping participants focus their mental energy in distinct ways. By metaphorically "wearing" different hats, individuals can explore ideas holistically, fostering balanced discussions and creative solutions. The approach is particularly effective in classrooms, team meetings, and brainstorming sessions, as it ensures diverse viewpoints are considered systematically.

The **White Hat** focuses on facts, data, and information. Participants examine what is known, what needs to be learned, and the evidence available. The **Red Hat** encourages emotional and intuitive thinking, giving space for feelings, gut instincts, and subjective reactions without requiring justification. The **Black Hat** emphasizes critical thinking, identifying risks, weaknesses, and potential challenges. In contrast, the **Yellow Hat** highlights optimism, exploring benefits, opportunities, and positive aspects of ideas or proposals.

For more divergent thinking, the **Green Hat** fosters creativity and innovation, pushing participants to brainstorm new ideas, alternatives, and possibilities. Finally, the **Blue Hat** oversees the process, guiding the group to stay focused, manage transitions between different hats, and ensure all perspectives are addressed. Together, these six hats create a dynamic system that balances analytical, creative, emotional, and practical thinking, reducing bias and fostering comprehensive analysis.

The Six Thinking Hats technique can be a powerful tool for developing originality during the creative process by encouraging individuals to explore ideas from multiple perspectives and push beyond conventional thinking. By systematically adopting different mindsets, the technique breaks the tendency to approach problems from a single viewpoint, fostering deeper insights and more innovative solutions.

One key way the technique aids originality is through the **Green Hat**, which explicitly focuses on creativity, brainstorming, and thinking outside the box. This phase encourages participants to suspend judgment and generate a wide range of ideas, no matter how unconventional or impractical they may seem. This mindset creates a safe space for experimentation, where novel concepts are embraced and nurtured rather than dismissed prematurely.

The other hats also play crucial roles in enhancing originality. The **Red Hat** allows for the incorporation of intuition and emotional responses, which are often the source of unexpected and unique ideas. The **Yellow Hat** emphasizes optimism and potential, encouraging participants to explore the possibilities of even the most unconventional ideas. Conversely, the **Black Hat** provides critical feedback, helping to refine and strengthen creative ideas by addressing weaknesses without stifling innovation.

Finally, the **Blue Hat** ensures that the creative process is organized and balanced, preventing groupthink or an over-reliance on one perspective. By cycling through the hats, individuals and teams are pushed to challenge their usual thinking patterns and consider new angles, resulting in more original, well-rounded, and impactful ideas. This structured approach not only fosters creativity but also helps individuals build confidence in their ability to think differently and innovate.

GROUP PROJECT EXAMPLE

Using the Six Thinking Hats to Create a Real-World Math Application

Scenario: A group of four middle school students is tasked with using math concepts like linear equations, area, surface area, and measurements to design and create a hands-on product. They decide to create a solar-powered mini greenhouse and apply various math concepts to calculate costs, dimensions, and energy consumption. The group will use the Six Thinking Hats technique to guide their process and ensure the project is both original and mathematically sound.

WHITE HAT – GATHERING FACTS AND INFORMATION

The group starts by researching all the components required for building a solar-powered greenhouse. They look up information about the dimensions needed for the greenhouse, materials (e.g., wood, plastic), and costs. They also learn about how much water the plants will need and the energy consumption of the solar panel required to water them.

The students measure the available space in their classroom to determine how large their mini greenhouse should be. They also review how to calculate the **area** of the greenhouse's base, as well as the surface area of the sides and roof, in order to understand how much material they will need.

Example Calculations

- The greenhouse will have a rectangular base of 2 meters by 1 meter.
- Area of the base: Area = Length × Width = 2m × 1m = 2m^2.
- They also research how to calculate the surface area of the four walls and roof to cover them with plastic, noting that the height of the greenhouse will be 1.5 meters.

RED HAT – EXPLORING FEELINGS AND INTUITION

The group shares how they feel about the project. One student feels excited to apply math to something hands-on, while another feels uncertain about whether the solar panel will generate enough power for the watering system. They all agree that they want the greenhouse to not only work effectively but also be something from which everyone can learn.

Example Insight

One student expresses excitement about making the greenhouse eco-friendly, while another feels concerned about the size and cost. They agree that the project must be both functional and cost-effective, with careful attention to measurements and budget.

BLACK HAT – IDENTIFYING CHALLENGES AND RISKS

The group discusses potential challenges. They worry about several things.

- Will the solar panel generate enough energy to power the watering system consistently?
- How can they be sure they are using the right amount of materials without overspending?
- How will they ensure the greenhouse is the correct size to maintain the right temperature for the plants?

They identify that a key math challenge will be determining the area and surface area for covering the greenhouse and ensuring they don't overspend on materials. Additionally, they need to make sure their solar panel can generate enough energy based on the size of the greenhouse.

Example Solution

They decide to calculate the surface area of the entire structure, including the roof and sides, to determine how much plastic is required. They also plan to conduct a small test with a solar panel to confirm it generates enough power for the watering system.

Surface Area Calculation Example

The greenhouse has a rectangular base with four sides and a slanted roof. Using the height and length, they calculate the total surface area of the walls and roof to determine how much plastic to buy.

YELLOW HAT – HIGHLIGHTING POSITIVES AND POTENTIAL

The group reflects on the benefits of their project. They realize that by using a solar-powered system, they will help the environment by reducing energy consumption. Additionally, by incorporating math concepts like area, surface area, and linear equations, they will learn how to apply real-world math to solve practical problems. They also see the project as an opportunity to build something that could be used for future educational purposes.

Example Potential

By using **area** and **surface area**, they can accurately measure how much material they need for the greenhouse. Additionally, by using linear equations, they can adjust the price of materials based on the size of the greenhouse or calculate the energy output of the solar panel based on sunlight hours.

GREEN HAT – GENERATING CREATIVE IDEAS

Now, the group uses their creativity to add new features to the greenhouse. One member suggests including a temperature sensor to trigger the watering system when the temperature reaches a certain threshold. Another proposes making the roof adjustable to let in more sunlight during the day, which could improve the plants' growth.

They also brainstorm ideas for making the structure more efficient.

- They think about using PVC pipes for the frame to reduce cost and weight.
- To make sure they don't waste materials, they want to design the greenhouse to fit precisely within the given space, factoring in the dimensions and surface area to minimize material waste.

Example Creative Ideas: They decide to incorporate a shelving system inside the greenhouse to maximize plant space and also calculate the surface area of the shelves to ensure they don't exceed the greenhouse's volume.

BLUE HAT – ORGANIZING AND MANAGING THE PROCESS

The group organizes the tasks for the project:

- **Week 1**: Finalize the design and calculations (including dimensions and surface area).
- **Week 2**: Purchase materials based on calculated area and surface area, and begin construction of the greenhouse.
- **Week 3**: Set up the solar panel system, test the energy output, and finalize the watering system.
- **Week 4**: Test the greenhouse functionality, complete the presentation, and demonstrate the energy and water-saving benefits.

MATH CONCEPTS USED

1. **Linear Equations**: Used to calculate the total cost of materials and energy consumption of the solar-powered watering system based on time and the number of plants.
   Example Linear Equation:
   If the solar panel costs $20 and generates enough power for 10 plants, the equation for the total energy cost per plant could be:
   Total Cost $= 20 + (x \times 0.5)$ where x is the number of plants.
2. **Area**: Used to calculate the **area** of the greenhouse's base ($2m \times 1m = 2m^2$) to determine how much space is available for plants.
3. **Surface Area**: Calculated to determine how much material (plastic) is needed to cover the walls and roof of the greenhouse.
   Example Surface Area:
   If the height is 1.5 meters and the greenhouse is 2 meters by 1 meter, the total surface area for the four walls can be calculated using the formula for the area of a rectangle: Area $=$ Length $\times$ Width.
4. **Volume**: Used to determine the internal volume of the greenhouse to ensure it can hold enough air for plant growth and regulate temperature.
   Example Volume Calculation:
   For a greenhouse that is 2 meters long, 1 meter wide, and 1.5 meters high, the volume is:
   Volume $= 2 \times 1 \times 1.5 = 3m^3$

Outcome

By the end of the project, the group has successfully built a solar-powered mini greenhouse that integrates several important math concepts: area, surface area, linear equations, and volume. They have used these concepts to calculate the material costs, determine the necessary size of the greenhouse, and ensure the solar panel provides enough energy to power the watering system.

The group presents its finished greenhouse to the class, demonstrating how they used math to design and construct it. They explain the mathematical calculations they performed to ensure the greenhouse functions efficiently, the solar panel works as expected, and the cost remains within budget.

In high school or AP courses, the Six Thinking Hats technique can help students tackle complex topics or debates with depth and structure. For instance, when analyzing a historical event, students might use the White Hat to outline key facts, the Black Hat to assess the event's failures, and the Yellow Hat to evaluate its benefits. This approach teaches students to think critically while respecting diverse perspectives and encourages creativity and collaboration, making it a valuable tool for academic growth.

Table 5.3 provides examples for how the Six Thinking Hats can be implemented in AP Courses.

Social and Emotional Well-Being

Metaphorical thinking can allow students to express complex emotions or challenges through symbolic language, making their feelings more tangible and understandable. For example, a student struggling with anxiety might describe it as "feeling like a balloon about to pop", which gives them a way to communicate their inner experience. This approach encourages students to think creatively about their emotions, fostering self-awareness and emotional articulation. In the classroom, a teacher could introduce an activity where students create visual or written metaphors to represent how they feel about a specific challenge, such as a difficult project or a conflict with a peer. By doing this, students not only gain clarity about their emotions but also feel validated when others recognize their struggles through a new lens.

Using synectics can help students draw connections between unrelated concepts, encouraging them to view their emotions or relationships in novel ways. For instance, a teacher might ask, "How is a storm like an argument with a friend?". This question prompts students to consider the unpredictable and overwhelming nature of both situations while also identifying the potential for resolution, like a storm eventually clearing. Synectics fosters perspective-taking and deep reflection, helping students gain insights into their challenges. In a classroom setting, students could participate in group discussions where they explore connections between personal experiences and abstract ideas, such as likening a growth mindset to the process of planting and nurturing a seed. This activity builds empathy and allows students to approach their problems with a fresh perspective.

The Six Thinking Hats method can encourage students to approach problems from multiple perspectives, breaking down complex social or emotional issues into manageable parts. For example, a teacher could use the hats to guide a student through a conflict with a peer. Wearing the "red hat", the student could explore their emotions, such as frustration or sadness, while the "yellow hat" helps them identify positive outcomes, like improved communication or stronger friendships. This structured approach not only reduces feelings of overwhelm but also promotes balanced decision-making by encouraging students to consider emotions, logic, creativity, and solutions separately. In a classroom setting, the teacher might organize a peer mediation session where students use the hats to analyze a disagreement, brainstorm resolutions, and reflect on the lessons learned. This method teaches valuable social-emotional skills like emotional regulation, empathy, and problem solving.

Table 5.3 Examples of Activities Using the Six Thinking Hats in High School AP Courses

Hat	AP Biology	AP Literature	AP Economics	AP Environmental Science	AP US History
White Hat	Summarize the structure of DNA, providing key facts about its double-helix model and base-pairing rules.	Collect textual evidence about the themes of identity in *The Great Gatsby*.	Present GDP data for a nation and analyze recent trends.	List the carbon emissions from various energy sources, such as coal, natural gas, and solar energy.	Outline key dates and events leading to the Civil War, focusing on the Missouri Compromise and the Dred Scott decision.
Red Hat	Share how you feel about the ethical implications of genetic engineering in humans.	Express an emotional reaction to a poem like "Do Not Go Gentle Into That Good Night".	Discuss personal feelings about income inequality or government taxation policies.	Reflect on the urgency of climate change and how it makes you feel about the future of the planet.	Share an emotional response to a historical event, such as the Trail of Tears, and discuss its personal impact.
Black Hat	Analyze the limitations of CRISPR technology, such as unintended genetic mutations or ethical concerns.	Critique the weaknesses in a character's motivations or actions, like Macbeth's ambition clouding his judgment.	Identify the potential negative effects of inflation on savings or purchasing power.	Highlight challenges in implementing renewable energy solutions, such as high costs or land-use conflicts.	Discuss flaws in policies like the Articles of Confederation, focusing on weaknesses in centralized government authority.
Yellow Hat	Highlight the benefits of genetic modification in improving food security and combating diseases.	Discuss the strengths of a literary work, such as the compelling imagery or the universal themes in *To Kill a Mockingbird*.	Explore the advantages of trade agreements for economic growth and global cooperation.	Discuss the long-term benefits of transitioning to renewable energy, including reduced pollution and biodiversity conservation.	Identify the successes of the New Deal, such as reducing unemployment and stabilizing the banking system.

(Continued)

Table 5.3 (Continued)

Hat	AP Biology	AP Literature	AP Economics	AP Environmental Science	AP US History
Green Hat	Propose a new method to genetically modify plants that increases drought resistance.	Rewrite the ending of *Of Mice and Men* to explore alternative outcomes for George and Lennie.	Brainstorm creative policies to reduce wealth inequality without discouraging economic growth.	Suggest an innovative solution, like vertical farming, to meet food demands while conserving land and resources.	Imagine how American history might have changed if the South had won the Civil War.
Blue Hat	Organize a discussion on biotechnology by assigning roles – some focus on technical details, others explore ethical implications.	Guide a class discussion on multiple interpretations of symbolism in *Lord of the Flies*, ensuring each perspective is addressed.	Facilitate a structured debate on government intervention in markets, ensuring all viewpoints are fairly heard.	Plan a step-by-step approach to assess the sustainability of a local environmental policy.	Develop a timeline of the Revolutionary War and assign small groups to analyze key turning points.

Spotlight: Inventors Under 18

Kenneth Shinozuka, a young inventor and innovator, gained widespread recognition for his groundbreaking work in creating a wearable device designed to assist Alzheimer's patients and their caregivers. Inspired by his personal experiences with his grandfather, who suffered from Alzheimer's and frequently wandered away from home, Kenneth sought a solution to address this common and potentially dangerous issue. At the age of 15, he developed a sensor-based device that could detect movement and alert caregivers via a smartphone app. This invention not only improved safety for patients but also alleviated stress for caregivers, offering peace of mind and better monitoring.

Kenneth's device incorporates a pressure sensor placed on the patient's foot or within their socks. When the patient gets out of bed or begins to walk, the sensor detects the movement and immediately sends a notification to the caregiver's smartphone. This early-warning system is simple yet effective, allowing caregivers to respond quickly and prevent accidents or wandering incidents. Kenneth's innovative approach to a pressing problem earned him the Scientific American Science in Action Award at the Google Science Fair in 2014.

The inspiration for Kenneth's work stemmed from observing his grandfather's struggles and the toll it took on his family. He wanted to apply his passion for science and technology to create a practical solution to improve the quality of life for both patients and caregivers. His dedication and empathy highlight the importance of using innovation to address real-world problems. The success of his project demonstrated not only his technical skills but also his ability to connect science with social impact. Kenneth has since become a prominent advocate for youth innovation, encouraging young people to tackle challenges in their own communities.

Kenneth's work has been featured in numerous media outlets and scientific forums, highlighting the potential for wearable technology in healthcare applications. His story underscores the importance of combining creativity, empathy, and technical expertise to solve complex problems. Kenneth continues to explore new ideas and has expressed interest in developing additional technologies to address healthcare challenges.

CONCLUSION

In conclusion, Chapter 5 highlighted the crucial role of originality in the creative process. Originality empowers individuals to go beyond conventional solutions and generate fresh, unconventional ideas. By exploring strategies like metaphorical thinking, synectics, and the Six Thinking Hats method, this chapter provides practical tools for fostering originality in the classroom. Detailed explanations and step-by-step instructions will help educators integrate these strategies into their teaching, with examples and exercises designed for K–12 content areas. The chapter also emphasizes the connection between originality and social-emotional well-being, offering activities that create a supportive, creative environment for students. By implementing these strategies, teachers can cultivate an atmosphere where students feel inspired to think outside the box, building their creative confidence and problem-solving abilities. Ultimately, encouraging originality equips students with essential skills for innovation and success in the modern world.

RESOURCES

DeBono, E. (1985). *Six thinking hats*. Boston, MA: Little, Brown.

Gordon, W.J.J. (1961). *Synectics: The development of creative capacity*. New York, NY: Harper and Row.

Hendriana, H., & Rohaeti, E.E. (2017). The importance of metaphorical thinking in the teaching of mathematics. *Current Science* (00113891), *113*(11), 2160–2164. https://doi.org/10.18520/cs/v113/i11/2160-2164

Massie, M., Capron Puozzo, I., & Boutet, M. (2022). Teacher creativity: When professional coherence supports beautiful risks. *Journal of Intelligence*, *10*(3), 62. https://doi.org/10.3390/jintelligence10030062

Piirto, J. (2004). *Understanding creativity*. Tucson: Great Potential Press.

Ramlackhan, K., Ince, A., & Brown, N. (2024). Conclusion: Future directions for creativity in education. https://doi.org/jj.5699289.16

Runco, M.A. (2014). *Creativity: Theories and themes: Research, development, and practice* (2nd ed.). Elsevier Science & Technology. https://doi.org/10.1016/C2012-0-06920 7

Sanchez-Ruiz, M., Santos, R., & Jiménez, J. (2013). The role of metaphorical thinking in the creativity of scientific discourse. *Creativity Research Journal*, *25*(4), 361–368. https://doi.org/10.1080/10400419.2013.843316

Starko, A.J. (2005). *Creativity in the classroom: Schools of curious delight* (3rd ed.). Mahwah: L. Erlbaum Associates.

Veale, T. (2006). An analogy-oriented type hierarchy for linguistic creativity. *Knowledge-Based Systems*, *19*, 471–479.

Chapter 6

Elaboration

The Process of Expanding an Idea or Product by Adding Details

INTRODUCTION

Ricardo, a successful poet and Diversity Officer at a university, describes creativity as the ability to act on our ideas and elaborate on them in meaningful ways. "You got it", he says. "You gotta invest in it, if you set aside between 10 and midnight every night to write, even if you don't write between 10 and midnight – just give it something. Even if all you do is put a line down. Just do something. If all you do is rearrange your poems in their folders or reread the last thing you wrote, that's still part of the process". Creativity isn't just about starting fresh – it's about expanding, refining, and building on what's already there.

His perspective highlights the role of elaboration in creativity, emphasizing that progress doesn't always mean generating something entirely new. Sometimes, the most creative work happens in the details – reworking a phrase, deepening an idea, or finding new meaning in an existing draft. Each small action contributes to a larger creative evolution, reinforcing the idea that persistence and iteration fuel artistic growth.

Elaboration is a vital component of the creative process as it enables individuals to expand, refine, and deepen their initial ideas, transforming them into more innovative and impactful outcomes. By adding layers of detail, exploring various perspectives, and integrating diverse elements, elaboration enriches the creative work, making it more compelling and meaningful. This process allows creators to move beyond surface-level thinking, pushing the boundaries of their imagination to generate new possibilities and connections.

In the creative process, elaboration fosters a deeper understanding of concepts by encouraging individuals to explore nuances, consider implications, and address potential challenges. For example, when designing a product, elaboration may involve refining features, anticipating user needs, or incorporating feedback to enhance functionality. It also invites emotional and intellectual investment, increasing engagement and motivation. By connecting ideas to real-world

DOI: 10.4324/9781003434221-6

contexts, analogies, or personal experiences, elaboration allows creative work to resonate with its audience. Elaboration can promote innovation by creating space for breakthroughs, refining ideas into impactful solutions, and fostering a mindset of continual exploration and growth.

When using elaboration techniques, individuals can explore options for adding depth, detail, and complexity to a product, idea, or concept. Elaboration techniques help students integrate specific examples, vivid details, anecdotes, or additional information to provide clarity. In writing, elaboration may include supporting an argument with evidence, developing character backstories, or using descriptive imagery to immerse readers. The goal is to provide a richer, more comprehensive explanation that connects with the audience and deepens their understanding.

Elaboration often involves drawing connections through analogies, real-world applications, historical comparisons, or pop culture references. It encourages imaginative thinking, exploring various perspectives, and examining the potential implications of ideas. This process provides opportunities to enhance comprehension, retention, and application of knowledge. It also helps individuals identify potential weaknesses in an idea through self-reflection or peer feedback.

Collaboration can play a key role in elaboration, as diverse perspectives can lead to more refined and robust outcomes. Constructive discussions and the building of consensus can unify goals and improve the quality of the final product. To foster collaboration, it is essential to create an environment where all ideas are valued and individuals feel comfortable contributing. Different approaches, such as allowing time for individual reflection before group discussions, can help accommodate varying needs and encourage meaningful participation.

ELABORATION IN THE REAL WORLD: LOCAL BAKERY ADVERTISING CAMPAIGN

Elaboration is an important element for small business owners, marketers, and advertisers. Advertising is essential to help others become aware of products or services offered. In the following example, the role of elaboration is described as part of the process for designing an advertising campaign for a local bakery. The first stage involves generating ideas by using fluency techniques with the focus on the quantity of ideas without judgement. Possible slogans might include: *Sweeten your day*, *baked fresh daily*, *warm bread – warm hearts*, *a slice of happiness*, *morning freshness*, or *bite into bliss*. Possible formats might include social media posts or posters.

Next, the team can work on flexibility by exploring different approaches to consider how the message can reach diverse audiences. For example, they might consider families with the slogan of *baking smiles for every age* or gearing toward premium quality with the slogan *artisan breads made with love* or emphasizing convenience for busy professionals with *grab freshness on the go*. Formats might include social media reels or visually-driven advertisements in local publications and magazines.

With the next stage, the team would explore originality by finding unique angles. This might involve evaluating what other bakeries are currently using for their slogan and marketing techniques in order to find an avenue that has not been explored. Originality means focusing on unique aspects of the bakery that can be highlighted to attract attention. For example, perhaps the bakery is known for its special crusty sourdough using a recipe that has been passed down for generations. The team could use the slogan *sourdough – a hundred years in the making*. Visuals could include family members, tradition, and craftsmanship.

Elaboration is the next component necessary where the team would flesh out this idea bringing it to life. This would include writing a script, designing visual images, selecting fonts, creating a storyboard, and selecting social media formats. During this process, the team is adding detail to make the advertising engaging and effective. The team can present different ideas to the bakery such as a social media video advertisement with a close-up of the dough being kneaded, transitioning to the bread baking in the oven, and ending with a family enjoying the fresh loaf at a dining table. The video includes text overlays, the slogan, and a call to action: "Visit us today and taste the tradition". The color palette is warm, earthy tones to evoke a cozy, home-like feel.

After allowing time for reflection, known as incubation, the team might find additional aspects to include. This is a period where no direct work is done on the advertisement, giving the mind time to subconsciously process the project. New insights or improvements might emerge during this phase such as sound effects like the sound of a bustling bakery or having the owner describe the tradition in order to add a personal touch. The final step is to assess the final product and make any final changes. The team can make sure the message is clear, the visuals are appealing, and the advertisement resonates with the intended audience. It could be possible to test the ad with a small focus group of loyal customers in order to collect feedback. Based on suggestions, the team can consider adjusting images, changing the length of the social media reel, and modifying the slogan if necessary.

During this process, elaboration plays a key role in moving from ideas to final product. The final advertisement features a concise, engaging video that showcases the bakery's unique selling point: A sourdough bread made with a recipe passed down through generations. It uses warm, inviting visuals, background sounds from the bakery, and a heartfelt tagline that conveys tradition and quality. The advertisement ends with a clear call to action, inviting viewers to visit the bakery and try the product.

STRATEGY: SCAMPER

SCAMPER is an idea generation technique developed by Alex Osborn and popularized by Bob Eberle that provides learners with a mnemonic for coming up with new or different ideas. Studies across all ages have demonstrated the benefits of using SCAMPER for creative thinking skills. Gündoğan (2019) found increased creative imagination and fluency with Kindergarten students using SCAMPER as an integrated part of the curriculum. Ozyaprak (2016) found an increase in creative thinking skills among students in teacher training programs using the Test for Creative Thinking-Drawing Production (TCT-DP).

In addition to increased creativity in general, researchers have found that SCAMPER is also important in specific content areas. ALKaab (2024) found using SCAMPER improved the creative writing abilities of EFL (English as a Foreign Language) undergraduate students. In addition, participants noted their appreciation for having this tool to use for developing their ideas. Boonpracha (2023) found increased fluency, flexibility, originality, and elaboration in product designs among third-year product design students after moving through the SCAMPER process. Buser (2011) described the outcomes of using SCAMPER with counselors in training through journal analysis with three themes emerging: As a method to "stretch our thinking"; b) value of "structured creativity"; and c) shifting from "right or wrong" application to flexibility and "flow".

This strategy can be used for different approaches based on the objective of the exercise. For instance, it can be used to generate ideas, to think of very different ideas, or to consider ways to elaborate on ideas for a product or design by modifying combining and adapting different concepts. The steps of SCAMPER prompt individuals to consider a product or idea from multiple angles. The acronym stands for:

- **Substitute**: What can be replaced or swapped?
- **Combine**: How can different elements be merged for new possibilities?
- **Adapt**: What can be modified to suit a different purpose?
- **Modify**: How can you change or alter aspects to improve the idea?
- **Put to another use**: Can the idea serve a different function?
- **Eliminate**: What can be removed to simplify or enhance it?
- **Rearrange**: How can elements be reorganized for better outcomes?

Learners use each word to prompt thinking, helping them view a product or problem through different lenses. For example, learners ask themselves questions such as, "What could I substitute in this invention for a part that is not working?", "What rules of this game could I substitute to create a new game?", "What traits of this character could I substitute to make him more interesting?", or "Which parts of this product could be eliminated to make it more appealing?".

Figure 6.1 A Teacher Practices the SCAMPER Technique during Rocket to Creativity, a Field Experience at Western Carolina University.

Table 6.1 Examples of Each Stage of the SCAMPER Technique

SCAMPER Technique	Question	Example
Substitute	What can we replace in the backpack?	Instead of using fabric, what if the backpack was made of waterproof material?
Combine	What can we combine with the backpack?	How about adding a built-in lunchbox compartment that can keep food warm or cold?
Adapt	How can we adapt the backpack for different uses?	What if the backpack could be adjusted to turn into a small chair for sitting during breaks?
Modify	What can we change to improve the backpack?	Let's make the straps wider and padded for more comfort when carrying heavy books.
Put to Another Use	Can the backpack serve a different purpose?	What if the backpack could also be used as a small tent for outdoor adventures?
Eliminate	What can we remove to make it simpler?	What if we eliminated all the extra pockets to make it lighter and easier to carry?
Rearrange	How can we rearrange the features of the backpack?	What if we placed the water bottle holder on the front instead of the side for easier access?

Each letter of SCAMPER can encourage new questions and new ideas. By applying SCAMPER, individuals and teams can stimulate innovative thinking and generate fresh ideas through guided inquiry. The following is an example of how to use SCAMPER to modify a product such as a backpack.

A final product created from the SCAMPER technique could be a multifunctional, ergonomic, waterproof backpack designed for students who enjoy outdoor activities or require versatile storage options for school and after-school needs. Here's how elaboration contributed to the final design.

Substitute: The material of the backpack was replaced with a high-quality waterproof fabric. Elaboration in this case included considering different materials that would provide both durability and resistance to weather conditions. Further investigation into various fabric types (such as ripstop nylon or waterproof canvas) was explored to provide the best balance of strength and weight.

Combine: The addition of a built-in lunchbox compartment that keeps food warm or cold was elaborated by brainstorming potential features like insulation material, size adaptability for different meal containers, and the placement of the compartment within the backpack for easy access. The elaboration focused on maximizing convenience for students who might not want to carry an additional lunchbox.

Adapt: The backpack's ability to adapt into a small chair required creative elaboration. Students envisioned how the structure would work, considering aspects like comfort, durability, and portability. They elaborated on features such as collapsible mechanisms and secure locking systems that would allow the chair to be set up easily without compromising the integrity of the backpack itself.

Modify: Wider and padded straps were added for more comfort when carrying heavy loads. Elaboration in this case involved researching ergonomic design principles for backpacks, including strap placement, padding materials, and adjustable straps, to improve comfort and prevent strain on the shoulders.

Put to Another Use: Transforming the backpack into a small tent for outdoor adventures required an extensive brainstorming process. Students explored different folding techniques, materials that would provide insulation, and how to ensure the backpack remained functional as both a carrier and a shelter. The elaboration focused on practical usage scenarios such as a camping trip or emergency preparedness.

Eliminate: By eliminating extra pockets, the design became simpler and lighter. Elaboration here involved thinking through which features were truly necessary for the user and how reducing bulk could enhance the backpack's portability while ensuring enough storage space for essential items.

Rearrange: The water bottle holder was moved to the front for better access. Elaboration in this case included considering different ergonomic approaches to carrying water bottles, ensuring that students could easily grab their bottles while walking or carrying the bag.

Through elaboration, students added depth to each idea by considering multiple possible variations, analyzing the pros and cons of different designs, and revising them until they produced a functional and innovative final product. By expanding on each SCAMPER prompt, they refined their ideas to create a backpack that not only met basic needs but also provided creative and practical solutions that could serve a wide range of uses, thereby making the product both innovative and more appealing.

SCAMPER can be used in language arts to help students dig deeper into elements of a story and generate ideas for their own writing by taking an element of the story such as a character, an event, or a setting, and walking it through the SCAMPER steps. In math, students can create their own word problems using SCAMPER with a model problem generated by the teacher. For example, they can modify elements of the word problem by substituting (S) operations or variables, or by modifying (M) the problem to make it more challenging or easier to solve. Instructors can provide students with a list of modern inventions and ask them to identify a step of SCAMPER that might have been used to modify an earlier invention to create the modern one. Or, take an object and identify ways it could be modified to make it more useful. Table 6.2 describes how SCAMPER can provide an avenue for teaching students how to elaborate in different content areas.

SCAMPER helps students elaborate on their ideas across various contexts. It encourages deeper thinking and allows students to refine, expand, and connect ideas in meaningful ways. By using the complete process or one aspect of SCAMPER, students can develop deeper comprehension while developing creative thinking skills.

STRATEGY: 6-3-5/COLLABORATIVE SKETCH

Processes that combine individual and group brainstorming can be productive for elaboration. 6-3-5/Collaborative (C) Sketch is a process that allows students to initially generate their own ideas that are then enhanced with team members' suggestions. White, Wood and Jensen (2012) describe the 6-3-5/C Sketch brainstorming process used in various disciplines such as engineering and marketing. In this process, members of a team of 6 each create concept sketches for or describe 3 ideas for solving a problem within 5 minutes. The team members rotate their sketches and notes around the table so that each team member adds to, enhances, or starts a new idea that was sparked by the original sketch.

Table 6.2 SCAMPER Technique Examples Across the Curriculum

SCAMPER Technique	How It Helps Students Elaborate	Example in Writing	Example in Science	Example in Social Studies
Substitute	Encourages students to replace or change elements of their work, helping them explore new ideas and perspectives, adding depth to their understanding.	A student replaces a common setting with an unfamiliar one, such as changing a cityscape to a remote village, to develop more unique and detailed descriptions.	Substitute a common material in an experiment (e.g., a different type of soil or water) to see how different variables affect the outcome, encouraging deeper analysis.	Substitute a well-known historical event with a lesser-known one to uncover new insights, expanding their understanding of historical patterns and impacts.
Combine	Helps students merge different concepts or ideas, encouraging them to connect ideas from various areas, enriching their thinking and output.	Combining two different themes, such as courage and resilience, in a story to create a multi-layered narrative that explores both concepts in depth.	Combine two scientific concepts, such as chemical reactions and energy transfer, to explore how they interact and impact real-world phenomena.	Combine political, social, and economic factors when analyzing historical events to see the complex relationships and deeper causes of change.
Adapt	Encourages students to adjust existing ideas or frameworks to fit new situations, promoting creative thinking and offering alternative perspectives.	Adapting a traditional plot structure to fit a non-linear narrative, which challenges the student to explore different storytelling techniques.	Adapt a standard experiment to test how external factors like temperature or time of day might alter the results, deepening the investigation.	Adapt lessons from the past to apply them to current social issues, helping students draw connections between historical events and present-day challenges.

(Continued)

Table 6.2 (Continued)

SCAMPER Technique	How It Helps Students Elaborate	Example in Writing	Example in Science	Example in Social Studies
Modify	Encourages students to refine or alter their work, focusing on small details or making significant changes that enhance the clarity or quality of their ideas.	Modifying the description of a scene by adding more sensory details, such as the sound of waves or the feel of the wind, to make it more immersive and vivid.	Modify the design of a scientific experiment to address potential flaws, improving the accuracy of the results and making the findings more robust.	Modify historical interpretations by analyzing them from multiple viewpoints, helping students expand their understanding of the causes and effects of historical events.
Put to Another Use	Prompts students to think about how their ideas, tools, or materials can be repurposed, encouraging them to see connections and possibilities beyond the obvious.	A student reimagines an object in their story, such as a letter, not just as a message but as a symbol of hope, expanding its significance.	Put scientific tools or resources to another use, such as using a microscope not just for biology but also for examining materials in physics experiments.	Put historical artifacts or documents to another use by interpreting them to understand contemporary issues, making historical study more relevant to current events.
Eliminate	Helps students identify what is unnecessary or repetitive in their work, allowing them to focus on the core ideas and deepen their exploration of essential concepts.	Eliminate unnecessary descriptions or events from a story to focus on a central theme or character development, making the writing more focused and powerful.	Eliminate variables in an experiment that aren't relevant to the hypothesis, helping to clarify the results and focus on the key scientific question.	Eliminate non-critical details from a historical analysis to focus on the most important causes and consequences of an event, streamlining the study for deeper understanding.

(Continued)

105

Table 6.2 (Continued)

SCAMPER Technique	How It Helps Students Elaborate	Example in Writing	Example in Science	Example in Social Studies
Rearrange	Helps students consider different orders or structures, allowing them to reframe their ideas and explore new ways of presenting or organizing information.	A student rearranges events in a story to create a more engaging build-up, heightening suspense or emotional impact through a strategic sequence.	Rearrange the steps in a scientific experiment to see how the results may change, allowing students to understand the importance of procedure in obtaining valid results.	Rearrange historical events or timelines to explore alternative scenarios, deepening students' understanding of cause and effect in history.

Of course, variations might include the number of members in a group or the number of original ideas on the initial go-round.

Process

- **6 participants** each generating **3 ideas** in **5 minutes**.
- Each participant writes down their ideas on paper, and then passes it to the next person, who builds upon or modifies those ideas.
- This cycle continues until each participant has contributed to every idea.

This method fosters a dynamic exchange of thoughts, allowing for the development of concepts through collaborative elaboration and ensuring that multiple perspectives are considered. Here's how to adapt this activity for middle school students.

Objective: Students work in small groups to quickly generate multiple visual ideas or solutions to a problem.

Materials

- Blank sheets of paper (one per student).
- Pencils, markers, or colored pencils.
- Timers or clocks.

Steps

1. **Form Groups**: Divide the class into groups of 6 students.
2. **Identify a Problem/Theme**: Present a problem, question, or theme for students to address. For example, "Design a new playground feature", or "Create a logo for a school event".
3. **First Round (5 minutes)**:

   - Each student gets a sheet of paper and has 5 minutes to draw 3 different ideas or sketches related to the problem.
   - Encourage quick, rough sketches – they don't have to be perfect, just visual representations of their ideas.
4. **Pass and Repeat**:

   - After 5 minutes, students pass their sheet to the person on their right.
   - The next student looks at the sketches and uses them as inspiration to draw 3 new sketches on the same sheet. This continues until each student has contributed to each sheet.

5. **Repeat for 6 Rounds:**

   - Continue this process for 6 rounds, with each round lasting 5 minutes.

6. **Review and Discuss:**

   - After all rounds are completed, the group reviews the sketches and discusses its favorites.
   - Each group can then present its top ideas to the class.

Let's say the theme for the 6-3-5 Sketch activity is to design a new piece of playground equipment. After completing all the rounds, one of the groups might end up with a final product that looks something like this.

Final Group Presentation: The students can present "Adventure Park", explaining how each element of the design came together through collaborative sketching. They might show how the features are interconnected and explain the purpose of each addition, creating a more well-rounded and imaginative playground concept. This final product is a collaborative and detailed playground design with each student's ideas merged into one creative solution.

In order to meet the needs of different circumstances, the facilitator can adjust the number of group members to meet your needs, as well as adjusting the timeframe, the number of rounds, or the use of words versus pictures. It is important to encourage creativity and emphasize the safe atmosphere free of criticism. Allowing students to describe what they have drawn after the rounds might allow those with perfectionistic tendencies to quickly sketch without focusing on having to have every aspect perfect.

6-3-5/C SKETCH IN THE CLASSROOM

In a classroom where teams are assigned a problem or project, have team members start with this process to generate initial ideas for solving the problem. For example, when Mrs. Watson starts a PBL unit where students are hypothetically granted $1,000,000 dollars to solve a problem faced by their community, teams use the 6-3-5/C Sketch to generate ideas and build upon solutions to the problem they have identified.

Table 6.3 Sample 6-3-5 Activity

Round	Student	Sketch/Modification
Round 1	Student 1	– Sketch 1: A basic climbing wall with handles and ropes.
		– Sketch 2: A spiral slide with a ladder.
		– Sketch 3: A monkey bar structure shaped like a jungle vine.
Round 2	Student 2	– Adds to Sketch 1: A zipline starting at the top of the climbing wall.
		– Modifies Sketch 2: Converts the slide into a tube with transparent sections.
		– Enhances Sketch 3: Adds hanging platforms connected to the monkey bars.
Round 3	Student 3	– Combines Sketch 1 and Sketch 3: Creates a climbing wall leading to monkey bars, transitioning to a zipline.
		– Adds to Sketch 2: Includes a water mist sprayer for cooling off on hot days.
		– Creates a new sketch: A bungee trampoline area.
Round 4	Student 4	– Refines combined Sketch 1: A rock wall with monkey bars leading to a platform connecting to a spiral slide and zipline exit.
		– Modifies Sketch 2: Adds LED lights inside the tube slide for night play.
		– Adds to Sketch 3: Includes climbing nets between the hanging platforms.
Round 5	Student 5	– Adds final touches to Sketch 1: Labels features like "rock wall", "zipline", "slide", and "hanging platforms".
		– Modifies Sketch 2: Adds a safety net beneath the trampoline area.
		– Creates a new sketch: A balancing beam path with obstacles.
Round 6	Student 6	– Combines all ideas into a single cohesive design, called "Adventure Park", featuring:
		– A rock wall leading to an overhead platform.
		– A spiral tube slide with LED lights.
		– Hanging platforms and monkey bars.
		– A connected zipline leading to a bungee trampoline area.

STRATEGY: LAUNCH

LAUNCH is a framework for design-based learning that guides students through the problem-solving process, and can be an excellent tool for teaching students about the elaboration process. Designed by Spencer and Juliani (2016), the LAUNCH framework encourages a structured yet flexible approach to elaboration, promoting critical thinking and creativity throughout the project lifecycle. Students are required to think critically about the ideas, to consider multiple possibilities, and build on initial concepts to make adjustments to clarify and strengthen their ideas with the goal of making the final product as thorough and complete as possible. The acronym stands for the following steps:

- **Look**: Observe the problem or idea closely.
- **Understand**: Gather insights and data to deepen comprehension.
- **Ask**: Pose questions that challenge assumptions and explore possibilities.
- **Navigate**: Plan the path forward, identifying resources and steps needed.
- **Create**: Develop the product or solution based on elaborated ideas.
- **Highlight**: Share and reflect on the process and outcomes.

Table 6.4 provides three examples of how LAUNCH might be used in a middle school or high school setting.

STRATEGY: LITERARY DEVICE BRAINSTORMING SESSION

When students are either beginning the writing process or are revising a draft of a piece of writing, it can be beneficial to take a class period to brainstorm different examples of literary devices they could use in their memoir, story, essay, poem, or article. Elaboration is critical in the writing process because it helps students add depth, detail, and dimension to their work, making their writing more engaging and impactful. By exploring literary devices such as metaphors, similes, imagery, allusions, and symbolism, students can enrich their narratives, evoke emotions, and create vivid mental pictures for their readers. This process encourages them to think critically about their ideas and explore new ways to communicate their message effectively.

Brainstorming literary devices can help students focus on specific elements that enhance their writing while encouraging creativity. For example, a student writing a memoir might brainstorm ways to incorporate sensory details to bring a childhood memory to life or use symbolism to evoke a deeper theme in their story. Encouraging students to experiment with these techniques also improves their ability to express abstract ideas and develop a personal voice. The following is a list of literary devices with examples that could be used in a memoir.

Table 6.4 Sample LAUNCH Activities

Step	Art: Designing a Collaborative Mural	Music: Composing a School Anthem	Physical Education: Developing a New Team Sport
L: Look, Listen, and Learn	Study famous murals and discuss their symbolism. Analyze how artists use colors, shapes, and symbols to convey meaning.	Explore school anthems and their role in fostering pride. Discuss how music conveys emotions and unifies groups.	Watch videos or analyze examples of unconventional team sports (e.g., Quidditch, ultimate frisbee) to identify what makes them fun and engaging.
A: Ask Questions	Ask, "What themes represent our school community?" "How can art reflect diversity and inclusion?"	Ask, "What themes best represent our school?" "What emotions do we want the anthem to evoke?"	Ask, "What physical skills can the sport develop?" "How can we design rules that encourage teamwork and inclusivity?"
U: Understand the Process or Problem	Brainstorm values and symbols that represent the school. Discuss how different elements can come together to tell a story.	Research anthem structure, lyrics, and melody. Examine examples to learn how to write meaningful lyrics and engaging melodies.	Brainstorm what elements make a sport enjoyable (e.g., fast pace, strategy, low barriers to entry). Discuss potential challenges and how to address them.
N: Navigate Ideas	Sketch individual mural ideas, combining them into one cohesive design. Refine sketches based on group discussions.	Write rough drafts of lyrics and brainstorm melodies in small groups. Share and discuss drafts for improvement.	Develop and test ideas for equipment, rules, and scoring. Brainstorm creative ways to ensure fairness and inclusivity in the game structure.
C: Create	Create a scaled-down prototype of the mural, testing colors and layout. Plan and assign painting roles.	Compose a demo version of the anthem, combining lyrics and melody into a cohesive piece.	Playtest the sport in small groups. Adjust rules and equipment based on feedback to improve gameplay.

(*Continued*)

Table 6.4 (Continued)

Step	Art: Designing a Collaborative Mural	Music: Composing a School Anthem	Physical Education: Developing a New Team Sport
H: Highlight and Fix	Test paint combinations, adjust placement of elements for balance, and refine small details based on peer feedback.	Perform the anthem for peers to gather feedback and make revisions to lyrics, melody, or harmony based on suggestions.	Organize a "trial match" for the new sport, observing how players interact. Refine rules, timing, or team size based on observed challenges and group feedback.
L: Launch	Paint and unveil the mural for the school community, highlighting its themes and meaning in a presentation or celebration.	Perform the final version of the anthem at a school event and share a recording online to promote school pride.	Host a school-wide tournament or demonstration day for the new sport, encouraging broad participation and inviting students to share reflections on the experience.

ALLITERATION

Alliteration is a literary device where two or more words in close proximity begin with the same consonant sound. This technique is often used to create rhythm, mood, or emphasis in writing. For example, in the phrase "whispering winds", the repetition of the "w" sound not only draws attention to the phrase but also evokes a soft and calming imagery that mirrors the action described. Alliteration can enhance writing by adding rhythm and flow, making it engaging and memorable. Its musical quality is particularly effective in poetry, speeches, and marketing. Writers also use alliteration to focus attention on specific ideas or themes.

The choice of consonant sounds in alliteration can evoke mood and imagery, with soft sounds like "s" and "l" creating a soothing effect, while harsher ones like "b" and "k" add intensity. For instance, "silent shadows slid slowly" conjures an eerie, mysterious atmosphere. This device also improves retention, helping readers remember key ideas or themes, which explains its frequent use in branding (e.g., Coca-Cola, Dunkin' Donuts). Additionally, alliteration can introduce a playful or humorous tone making it particularly effective in children's literature and lighthearted writing.

By incorporating alliteration, students learn how to elaborate on their ideas by focusing on the sound and rhythm of their language, which helps them craft writing that is more engaging and precise. Alliteration encourages students to think carefully about word choice and how repeated sounds can emphasize particular ideas or evoke emotions. This process teaches them to expand basic descriptions into more vivid, memorable expressions, such as transforming "a brave warrior" into "a boldly brave warrior". Experimenting with alliteration helps students explore tone and mood, enabling them to create nuanced, layered writing. Alliteration equips students with a powerful tool to add depth and creativity to their work.

- *Example*: "The sweet, soft scent of summer filled the space as we sat silently, savoring the moment."
- *Memoir context*: Describing a peaceful moment spent on a porch during summer vacation.

ONOMATOPOEIA

Onomatopoeia is a literary device where a word mimics or imitates the natural sound it describes. These words are auditory in nature, helping readers hear the action they represent, such as "buzz", "crash", "sizzle", or "roar". Onomatopoeia brings sensory details to writing, making it more immersive and vivid by replicating the actual sounds of an experience. Words like "boom" for thunder or "pitter-patter" for rain allow readers to "hear" the scene, bringing it to life. This device can also evoke emotional responses, with sounds such as "crack" conveying tension or danger, while softer sounds like "chirp" suggest calmness and cheer. By replicating real-world sounds, onomatopoeia adds energy and pacing to action scenes, making moments like battles feel dynamic and intense with words such as "clang" and "thud".

Its auditory nature makes onomatopoeic words memorable, as they go beyond description to directly connect with the reader's sense of hearing. This is especially effective in children's literature, where playful words like "pop" or "snap" add fun and excitement, fostering phonetic awareness while entertaining young readers. In poetry, onomatopoeia deepens the auditory experience by enhancing rhythm and sound, as seen in Edgar Allan Poe's *The Bells*, where phrases like "tinkle, tinkle, tinkle" mimic the ringing of bells.

By incorporating onomatopoeia, students can elaborate on their ideas by transforming abstract or static descriptions into dynamic and engaging scenes. Instead of merely stating that a door closed, students can describe the "slam" of the door, which adds emotional weight and immerses the reader in the moment. This encourages students to think critically about how sounds affect tone and mood, helping them convey complex ideas more vividly. Onomatopoeia also

113

teaches students to use precise language to enhance their writing, creating a richer and more sensory experience for their audience. Through this, they learn to make their descriptions more detailed, memorable, and impactful.

- *Example*: "The bees buzzed lazily around the blooming flowers, while the ice in my glass clinked against the sides."
- *Memoir context*: A memory of relaxing in a garden on a warm afternoon.

SIMILE

A simile is a literary device that compares two unlike things using the words "like" or "as" to highlight a shared characteristic or quality. For example, "her smile was as bright as the sun" or "he ran like a cheetah" creates vivid imagery by linking the subject to a familiar concept. Similes simplify complex ideas and make them more relatable and vivid for the reader. By comparing a forest to "a dark cave" or love to "a rollercoaster", similes help readers visualize abstract or complex concepts, making them tangible and relatable.

Similes can also add emotional depth and resonance, allowing readers to connect with characters and experiences on a personal level. For example, "His heart felt as heavy as a stone" conveys sorrow in a way that feels poignant. Similes can clarify complicated ideas, such as describing an atom as "like a tiny solar system", making difficult subjects more accessible. Well-crafted similes are memorable, adding originality and creating lasting impressions, as in "She floated through the crowd like a leaf on the wind".

By using similes, students learn how to elaborate on their ideas by making abstract concepts more concrete and engaging. Similes encourage students to think creatively, find connections between different ideas, and describe their thoughts in vivid detail. Instead of simply stating that a character is sad or a forest is dark, students can expand their descriptions with relatable comparisons providing more clarity. This process helps them develop more expressive and imaginative language, improving their ability to explain, evoke, and connect with their audience. Similes can empower students to communicate complex ideas in ways that are both impactful and memorable.

- *Example*: "The sun sank behind the hills like a ball of molten gold melting into the horizon."
- *Memoir context*: Recalling a beautiful sunset during a camping trip.

METAPHOR

A metaphor is a figure of speech that directly compares two unrelated things without using "like" or "as", implying that one thing is another. For example, "time is a thief" suggests that time takes away moments of life, much like a thief steals possessions. Metaphors are used to add depth, meaning, and creativity to writing, helping readers see the subject in a new and imaginative way.

Metaphors elevate writing by transforming abstract ideas into vivid, tangible imagery, making concepts more relatable and engaging. For example, describing a difficult situation as "a storm on the horizon" creates a strong visual and emotional connection. Metaphors can also simplify complex ideas, such as likening the human mind to "a labyrinth", making intricate concepts accessible and easier to grasp. They evoke powerful emotional responses by linking feelings to universally understood images, as in "her words were daggers", which conveys the sting of harsh comments. They also reveal character perspectives, as seen in "I'm trapped in a cage of expectations", which communicates internal conflict and frustration.

By fostering creativity and originality, metaphors challenge writers and readers to think outside the box, making writing dynamic and memorable. Phrases like "her laughter was the music of raindrops" transform simple ideas into poetic expressions. They can also encourage reader engagement by inviting interpretation and reflection, such as "hope is a fragile bird", which sparks imagination and interaction. Metaphors contribute to the flow and cohesion of a piece, tying together disparate ideas and reinforcing central themes through recurring motifs.

For students, metaphors are invaluable tools for elaboration, helping them express complex thoughts and emotions in a concise yet impactful way. By encouraging creative comparisons, metaphors push students to think critically about their ideas and how to communicate them effectively. Instead of stating an idea plainly, students learn to expand their descriptions, making their writing more vivid and engaging. For example, transforming "I felt nervous" into "my stomach was a coiled spring ready to snap" adds depth and specificity, drawing readers into the experience. This practice develops their ability to craft language that resonates emotionally and intellectually, ensuring their writing leaves a lasting impression.

- *Example*: "My heart was a wild bird, trapped and fluttering frantically, as I waited for the test results."
- *Memoir context*: Capturing the anxiety of waiting for important news.

SENSORY IMAGES

Sensory imagery is a literary device that uses vivid and descriptive language to engage a reader's five senses – sight, sound, touch, taste, and smell. By creating mental pictures and invoking sensory experiences, writers can immerse their audience in the world of the story or message. For example, instead of saying, "it was a sunny day", sensory imagery might describe, "the golden rays of sunlight warmed my skin as the faint scent of blooming jasmine filled the air". Descriptions such as "the crackle of dry leaves underfoot" or "the tangy sweetness of freshly picked oranges" engage the senses, allowing readers to experience the moment as if they were there. Sensory imagery strengthens the connection between reader and text by helping readers empathize with characters, such as through a description like "the icy wind sliced through her coat", which creates a sense of shared experience.

In addition to building emotional engagement, sensory imagery is essential for setting the atmosphere and mood of a piece. Eerie descriptions like "the distant wail of an unseen creature" build suspense, while cozy imagery such as "the warm glow of the fire" creates comfort. Sensory details also reinforce themes, such as how decaying fruit can symbolize wasted potential. They make the writing more memorable by appealing to primal human experiences, leaving lasting impressions with specific descriptions like "the velvet softness of rose petals".

For students, sensory imagery is an invaluable tool for elaboration because it helps them transform simple ideas into richly detailed experiences. By using sensory details, students can expand their descriptions, making their writing more dynamic and engaging. For example, instead of writing "the food was delicious", they can describe how "the buttery, flaky crust melted on my tongue", which provides a clearer, more immersive experience. Sensory imagery encourages students to think creatively about how to convey emotions and actions through sensory details, enhancing their ability to elaborate on their ideas. This process allows them to create more vivid, memorable writing that resonates with readers and builds a stronger emotional connection to the story.

- **Smell**: "The aroma of freshly baked bread wafted through the air, warm and inviting, like a hug from the kitchen."
- **Taste**: "The lemonade was tart, sharp as a slap, but with a sweetness that lingered on my tongue."
- **Touch**: "The sand was gritty and warm beneath my fingers, slipping away with each wave that lapped at the shore."
- **Sound**: "The crackle of the bonfire echoed in the night, mingling with the low murmur of friends sharing stories."
- **See**: "The sky was painted with streaks of pink and purple, as if a watercolor artist had dipped their brush in the sunset."

ALLUSIONS

An allusion is a literary device that refers to a person, place, event, or idea from history, literature, religion, mythology, or popular culture. Allusions rely on the audience's familiarity with the reference to convey additional meaning, evoke emotions, or deepen understanding. Using allusions allows writers to add depth and complexity to their work without lengthy explanations. By referencing well-known cultural, historical, or literary figures and events, allusions create resonance by connecting the current narrative to something familiar and meaningful. For example, referring to "Pandora's Box" immediately conveys the concept of unintended consequences. Allusions also strengthen themes as seen when a reference to *Romeo and Juliet* emphasizes the passion and tragedy of young love.

Allusions can add layers of meaning to a story, providing subtle insights without explicitly stating them. Describing someone as having a "Midas touch" not only suggests success but hints at the dangers of greed. They also help establish tone or atmosphere. For students, using allusions is an excellent tool for elaboration because it encourages them to incorporate existing cultural knowledge into their writing, adding richness and nuance to their ideas. Instead of simply describing a situation, students can draw on familiar references to amplify their message, making their writing more layered and sophisticated. Allusions prompt students to think critically about the connections they make between their ideas and the wider world. This can help create more engaging and thought-provoking work.

- **Historical**: "The excitement in the air felt like a modern-day Woodstock, as if everyone was buzzing with the same sense of freedom and possibility."
- **Pop Culture**: "She danced with the carefree energy of a character straight out of a Taylor Swift song, twirling and laughing under the stars."
- **Literary**: "He was like Gatsby, throwing extravagant parties, but always standing apart, watching from the sidelines with a wistful smile."
- **Spiritual**:
  - *Religious*: "The church bells rang, calling us to gather like sheep flocking to a shepherd."
  - *Nature*: "The forest was a cathedral, each tree a pillar holding up a canopy of green."
  - *Bible*: "I felt like Jonah in the belly of the whale, trapped and waiting for a chance to escape."
  - *Mythological*: "The mountain loomed ahead, a Herculean task that seemed impossible to conquer."

DIALOGUE

Dialogue is a written or spoken exchange between two or more characters in a narrative. It is used to convey information, reveal personalities, and advance the plot while imitating natural conversation. Dialogue is a powerful tool in writing that brings stories to life, deepens character development, and propels the plot forward. By revealing a character's personality, emotions, and relationships through their tone, word choice, and rhythm, dialogue offers readers critical insight into who characters are. For instance, short, blunt sentences might suggest impatience, while elaborate phrases could indicate intellectualism. Dialogue also advances the plot, providing key information, revealing conflicts, or foreshadowing events. It creates realism by mirroring natural conversation, drawing readers into the world of the story.

For students, the use of dialogue is a way to elaborate on their ideas and develop their writing. Dialogue offers them a dynamic way to expand on character traits, relationships, and themes without lengthy explanations. Instead of directly describing a character's feelings, students can use dialogue to show those emotions through words and interactions. This approach allows for deeper exploration of subtext and adds richness to their narratives, providing multiple layers of meaning.

- *Example*:
  - **Friend**: "You can't give up now. You've come this far."
  - **Me**: "But what if I fail? What if this was all for nothing?"
- *Memoir context*: Reflecting on a conversation with a friend during a difficult time.

ARGUMENTS

Arguments in writing refer to a structured and reasoned presentation of ideas, opinions, or claims aimed at persuading or informing an audience. An argument is typically supported by evidence, examples, and logical reasoning to build a convincing case around a particular viewpoint. Arguments are an essential element of persuasive and analytical writing. They provide writers with the tools to influence opinions, spark critical thinking, and provoke meaningful discussions. Through well-constructed arguments, writers can persuade readers to adopt new beliefs or take action, presenting compelling evidence to support their claims. Structuring these arguments clearly and logically helps ensure that the audience can follow the reasoning, making the writer's message more impactful.

Arguments encourage readers to critically assess evidence, question assumptions, and engage with different perspectives, sharpening their analytical skills. By presenting sound reasoning and credible evidence, writers build their credibility and establish trust with their audience. Arguments also allow writers to explore complex issues, presenting diverse viewpoints and encouraging readers to consider the nuances of a topic. This complexity challenges readers to think more deeply and avoids simplistic answers. For students, mastering the art of argumentation is an excellent way to elaborate on ideas. Writing strong arguments forces students to organize their thoughts, clarify their reasoning, and present evidence in a structured and persuasive manner. This process helps them to articulate their ideas more effectively and to connect those ideas with broader themes or debates.

- Ethical Argument:
  Requiring homework can create unnecessary stress for students, leaving little time for family, rest, or personal growth. A no-homework policy supports student well-being and ensures a healthier work-life balance, which is essential for their overall development.
- Logical Argument:
  Research shows that excessive homework doesn't significantly improve academic performance, especially in younger students. Class time can be used more effectively for learning, while students can use after-school hours for rest, hobbies, and pursuing interests that develop creativity and critical thinking.
- Emotional Argument:
  Many students feel overwhelmed and burned out by homework, which can lead to frustration and disengagement. Removing homework would allow us to come to school refreshed and more focused, creating a more positive and productive learning environment.

WHO, WHAT, WHERE, HOW, WHY

Specific details in writing refer to vivid, precise, and concrete information that answers key questions such as "Who, What, Where, How, and Why". These details paint a clear picture for readers, making the writing more engaging, credible, and memorable. Specific details are essential in writing because they enhance imagery, clarify ideas, and create a stronger emotional and sensory connection with the reader. Rather than relying on vague descriptions, specific details make writing more vivid and engaging by allowing readers to visualize characters, settings, and actions. For example, describing a girl as "tiptoeing into a dimly lit room, her hands trembling as she clutched a crumpled letter" makes the scene more immersive than simply stating, "the girl walked into the room". These details engage the senses, allowing readers to feel, see, hear, taste, or smell the scene, making the narrative compelling and multidimensional.

In addition to enhancing sensory experiences, specific details help clarify ideas and reinforce the writer's intent. They provide context and reasoning that helps the reader understand the narrative or argument more clearly. Details also add depth and authenticity, grounding the story in realistic, relatable elements. For example, describing a town as having "a single gas station and a diner that closed by 7 p.m." adds specificity and makes the setting more believable. These details help readers connect emotionally with the characters and the situation, as when describing a character's grief with "tears streamed down her face as she clutched the old photo album, unable to bear the memory of losing her father".

For students, incorporating specific details is crucial for elaborating on ideas. These details allow students to go beyond general statements, enhancing their writing by providing concrete examples and sensory descriptions. The process of adding details challenges students to think more deeply about the "Who, What, Where, When, and Why" of their stories, making them more effective in developing complex ideas and emotions. When students master the use of specific details, their writing becomes more engaging, persuasive, and memorable, helping them create work that leaves a lasting impression on readers.

- **Who**: "My grandmother, with her kind eyes and wrinkled hands, was always the one who knew how to make things better, no matter how bad they seemed."
- **What**: "The bike was old and rusty, but to me, it was freedom – a way to escape the small town and see beyond the familiar streets."
- **Where**: "The tiny café on the corner was where we met every Friday, our secret hideaway from the chaos of the world."
- **How**: "She carefully folded the letter, as if each crease would seal away the painful words written inside."
- **Why**: "I took the risk because I needed to prove to myself that I could, that fear wouldn't define my choices anymore."

Symbolism

Memoir Topic: A middle school student reflecting on the challenge of finding their own voice in a big, busy world.
Symbolism Example: The student uses a rainstorm as a symbol throughout the memoir to represent confusion, doubt, and ultimately clarity and self-discovery.

Excerpt

When I started middle school, it felt like walking into a rainstorm without an umbrella. The hallways were loud with chatter, the schedules were like confusing raindrops falling too fast to catch, and I felt small under the weight of it all. I spent weeks trying to blend in, my voice drowned out by everyone else's thunder. But one afternoon, something changed. During the school talent show, I signed up to perform my poem – nervous but determined. As I stood on stage, it was as if the rain stopped. My words filled the room like sunlight breaking through clouds. For the first time, I realized that storms don't last forever, and when you learn to walk through the rain, it can help you find your strength. Now, whenever I hear the patter of raindrops, I smile. It reminds me that even the hardest storms can lead to something beautiful.

HOW THE SYMBOLISM DEVELOPS THE THEME

The rainstorm symbolizes the chaos and self-doubt the student felt in trying to navigate middle school. As the story progresses, the storm shifts from a source of fear to a metaphor for growth and renewal, mirroring the student's journey toward finding their voice and self-confidence. This unique symbolism ties beautifully to the theme of perseverance and self-discovery, showing how challenges can transform into moments of empowerment.

Using symbolism in writing is a powerful way to enhance elaboration because it allows writers to convey deeper meanings and connect abstract concepts with concrete images or objects. Symbolism invites readers to interpret and reflect on these deeper layers, offering more than just a surface-level description or action. This adds complexity and richness to the writing. When writers use symbols, they take something familiar – a physical object, a color, an animal, or even a recurring action – and imbue it with additional significance. For example, in literature, a bird might symbolize freedom, or a storm could represent internal conflict or change. By associating these symbols with themes or emotions, writers provide readers with a more nuanced understanding of the narrative, encouraging them to think critically and explore what the symbols represent.

For students, using symbolism encourages elaboration because it requires them to think about what an object, action, or detail could represent beyond its literal meaning. Instead of simply stating, "she felt trapped", a student might write, "the cage door slammed shut, its cold iron bars a reminder of the weight of her unspoken fears". Here, the cage becomes a symbol of confinement and the character's emotional state, elaborating on the internal conflict in a much more vivid and layered way.

Incorporating symbolism also strengthens the thematic depth of writing. It enables students to go beyond just telling a story or making an argument; they can add multiple layers of meaning that resonate with readers on different levels. By using symbolism to elaborate on ideas or themes, writers can create more complex, impactful, and memorable works. This can help students develop a more sophisticated approach to writing, where they not only describe events or characters but also invite the reader to engage with the deeper significance behind them.

LITERARY DEVICES IN OTHER CONTENT AREAS

The examples below illustrate how each literary element can enrich content by adding depth, emotion, and vivid detail. Once students become familiar with practicing these techniques, they can pick and choose which items would help them investigate topics. These techniques can also be beneficial to explore ideas and elaborate on central concepts. Table 6.5 illustrates how AP Chemistry, AP US History, and AP Psychology can utilize the listed literary devices in unique ways to explore their respective course content.

Table 6.5 Sample Literary Device Elaboration Activities for High School Courses

Literary Device	AP Chemistry	AP US History	AP Psychology
Alliteration	"Sulfur's stinky stench saturates the space" to describe the odor of hydrogen sulfide in chemical reactions.	"Roaring railroads revolutionized regions" to emphasize the industrial impact of railroads in the 19th century.	"Perception pivots on personal perspectives" when discussing theories of sensation and perception.
Onomatopoeia	Use "fizz" and "pop" to describe the reactions in a soda can when opened or chemical reactions involving carbonates.	"Boom!" to illustrate the sound of cannon fire during the Civil War.	"Buzzing" and "humming" to explain the auditory experiences in experiments related to selective attention.
Simile	"Electrons orbit the nucleus like planets around the sun" to explain atomic structure.	"The Great Depression hit the economy like a devastating hurricane" to emphasize its overwhelming impact.	"Memories fade like ink on paper left in the sun" to explain the decay theory of forgetting.
Metaphor	"The periodic table is a map guiding chemists through the elements" to convey its organizational importance.	"The Constitution is the backbone of American democracy" to highlight its foundational role.	"The mind is a labyrinth of interconnected pathways" to explain neural networks in cognitive psychology.
Sensory Imagery	Describe the vibrant colors of flames during a flame test for metal ions: "The copper ions burn a bright green, vivid like a summer meadow."	Describe the physical toll of the Dust Bowl: "The parched land cracked like old leather, and the choking dust clung to every breath."	Describe Pavlov's experiment: "The dogs' mouths watered at the sharp clang of the bell, anticipating the savory scent of meat powder."

(Continued)

Table 6.5 (Continued)

Literary Device	AP Chemistry	AP US History	AP Psychology
Allusions	Reference *Marie Curie* when discussing radioactivity in AP Chemistry.	Reference *Hamilton the musical* when explaining debates over federalism between Hamilton and Jefferson.	Reference *Inside Out (2015)* to explain the interaction of emotions like joy and sadness in psychological development.
Dialogue	A fictional exchange between an atom's protons and electrons: *"You're so negative!"* *"Well, you're always positive!"* to explain atomic charges.	A mock debate between *Andrew Jackson* and *Cherokee leaders* about the Indian Removal Act.	A therapeutic dialogue between a psychologist and a patient discussing cognitive distortions.
Rhetorical Argument	Argue why chemistry is central to life: *"Without the bonds of chemistry, life itself would cease to exist."*	Argue the importance of Reconstruction: *"Was the failure of Reconstruction truly a loss for freedom, or a lesson for future civil rights?"*	Argue the significance of the nature vs. nurture debate: *"Is it not nurture that shapes our very identity, our beliefs, our dreams?"*
Logical Argument	Use the stoichiometric principle: *"If one mole of a substance reacts completely with another, the result must follow the law of conservation of mass."*	Justify the necessity of the New Deal: *"The unemployment rate was unprecedented – government intervention was the logical solution."*	Explain reinforcement schedules: *"Variable-ratio schedules create the strongest responses because of their unpredictability."*

(Continued)

123

Table 6.5 (Continued)

Literary Device	AP Chemistry	AP US History	AP Psychology
Ethical Argument	Discuss the ethics of using fossil fuels: "*Should chemists prioritize progress over the planet? What is our ethical responsibility to the environment?*"	Debate the morality of slavery: "*The institution of slavery was a moral failure despite its economic significance in early America.*"	Address ethical concerns in Milgram's obedience experiment: "*Were the psychological harms justified by the insights into human behavior?*"
Specific Details	*Who*: Dmitri Mendeleev. *What*: Created the periodic table. *Where*: Russia. *When*: 1869. *How*: Organized by atomic mass. *Why*: To predict properties of elements.	*Who*: FDR. *What*: Introduced the New Deal. *Where*: United States. *When*: 1933. *How*: Through federal programs. *Why*: To combat the Great Depression.	*Who*: Sigmund Freud. *What*: Developed psychoanalysis. *Where*: Vienna, Austria. *When*: Early 1900s. *How*: Through free association. *Why*: To explore the unconscious mind.
Symbolism	Use *water* as a symbol of balance in acid-base chemistry, representing neutrality (pH 7).	Use the *Statue of Liberty* as a symbol of hope and immigration during the Gilded Age.	Use a *maze* as a symbol of the complexity of the human mind in cognitive psychology.

Using literary devices in education allows students to explore complex ideas in creative, memorable, and engaging ways. For instance, techniques like similes and metaphors help transform abstract or technical concepts into relatable visuals, making them easier to understand and recall. When electrons are described as "orbiting like planets around the sun", or the Constitution is called the "backbone of American democracy", students form mental connections that bring these concepts to life. Such comparisons not only simplify content but also encourage students to think critically about how ideas relate to broader themes and disciplines.

Incorporating sensory imagery and emotional resonance into learning enhances retention by creating vivid mental pictures tied to course content. Describing the Dust Bowl as "parched land cracking like old leather" helps students visualize the hardships faced during the Great Depression, while discussing the vibrant colors of flames in chemistry fosters curiosity about scientific processes. Similarly, allusions to pop culture, historical events, or literature – like using *Inside Out* to explain emotional development – create bridges between what students already know and what they are learning, fostering a deeper understanding of the material.

Literary devices also teach students to articulate ideas more effectively through critical thinking and structured arguments. Logical and ethical arguments, for example, push students to evaluate evidence, weigh consequences, and defend nuanced positions. Ethical debates, like questioning the environmental impact of fossil fuels, encourage students to consider the societal implications of academic content. By learning to reason persuasively and present ideas compellingly, students gain skills that are essential for problem solving and collaboration.

Literary devices foster engagement by injecting creativity into learning. Dialogue, onomatopoeia, and symbolism transform lessons into dynamic narratives, making topics like historical debates or chemical reactions more interactive. Whether it's a fictional exchange between protons and electrons or a symbolic maze representing the human mind, these techniques spark curiosity and encourage students to explore ideas in depth. By integrating literary devices, students learn not just to understand content but to elaborate on it, think critically, and communicate effectively – skills that extend far beyond the classroom.

SOCIAL AND EMOTIONAL WELL-BEING: USING LAUNCH TO PROMOTE INCLUSIVITY IN THE CLASSROOM

Look: Observe the Problem or Idea Closely

Start by closely observing the dynamics of the classroom to identify where cliques are forming and how they are affecting the social environment. This might involve noticing students who are left out, groups who don't interact with others, or even specific behaviors like exclusive language or actions that create division. Students can be asked to reflect on their experiences and observations, identifying moments where they felt excluded or saw others being excluded.

Understand: Gather Insights and Data to Deepen Comprehension

Next, students can gather insights by discussing their observations in small groups or class discussions. They might survey each other to learn about feelings of exclusion, what it feels like to be on the outside, and the impact of cliques on school life. By gathering data, students gain a deeper understanding of the problem and why it occurs. They could also explore examples of inclusive behavior from other settings or groups that manage to avoid cliques and promote unity.

Ask: Pose Questions that Challenge Assumptions and Explore Possibilities

Now, students should be encouraged to ask themselves key questions: What makes a group feel excluded? What behaviors create cliques? How can we make sure everyone feels included? Students might challenge assumptions about the nature of friendship, like believing that people can only bond with certain individuals. Questions like, "What can we do differently to include people who are new or not part of our regular group?" or "How can we create a space where everyone feels welcome?" help them explore creative solutions to break down cliques.

Navigate: Plan the Path Forward, Identifying Resources and Steps Needed

Once the students have gathered their insights and posed thoughtful questions, they can begin to navigate a path forward. This involves planning actions and identifying what resources or changes will be necessary. For example, students might organize activities that encourage teamwork and interaction among all students, like group games, cooperative projects, or a "buddy system". They could also design posters or host discussions to promote inclusivity in the classroom. Students can create a checklist of actionable steps, such as creating a classroom culture pledge or designing an "inclusion day" where students practice being more welcoming.

Create: Develop the Product or Solution Based on Elaborated Ideas

In this phase, students will implement their plans and create tangible solutions to combat cliques and promote inclusivity. This could include making a list of inclusive behaviors, organizing events where students are mixed together in different groups, or designing activities that encourage everyone to interact. For example, students could create an "inclusion wall" where everyone writes something positive about someone else in the class or post pledges to practice inclusive behavior.

Highlight: Share and Reflect on the Process and Outcomes

Finally, after the students have implemented their solutions, they will highlight and share the process with others, reflecting on how it went. They can discuss what worked well and what could be improved in the future. Students might share their experiences in a group discussion, write about their learnings in a journal, or create a presentation to showcase how inclusivity has improved in the classroom. By reflecting on the impact, they can refine their approach and continue to foster a more inclusive environment.

This LAUNCH technique helps students not only recognize the problem of cliques but actively engage in solving it through creative thinking and teamwork. By following these steps, they can develop a deeper understanding of inclusivity and create practical, effective solutions that build a more cohesive classroom environment.

Spotlight: Inventors Under 18

Erin Smith, a young scientist and innovator, gained widespread recognition for her groundbreaking work in using artificial intelligence (AI) to detect early signs of Parkinson's disease. At just 16 years old, Erin developed a tool called "FacePrint", which leverages machine learning to analyze facial expressions for subtle changes associated with the neurological condition. Her inspiration came from watching videos of Parkinson's patients, where she noticed a common pattern in their facial movements, such as diminished emotional expression or delayed reactions. These observations led her to investigate whether AI could quantify these changes as early biomarkers for the disease.

FacePrint works by analyzing videos of individuals performing specific tasks, such as smiling, blinking, or speaking. The AI tool detects and measures microexpressions – tiny, involuntary facial movements that are often imperceptible to the human eye. Erin's system is unique in its ability to provide non-invasive, low-cost, and highly accurate early detection of Parkinson's disease, which could significantly improve patient outcomes by enabling earlier interventions. The project attracted attention from medical professionals and researchers, who recognized its potential to transform how neurological disorders are diagnosed and monitored.

Erin's work earned her numerous accolades, including recognition as a finalist in the Regeneron Science Talent Search and the Davidson Fellows Scholarship. Her innovative approach to merging AI and healthcare also caught the attention of leading institutions, such as Stanford University, where she was invited to collaborate with researchers to further refine and validate her tool. Erin's journey highlights her perseverance in tackling a complex problem, as she taught herself advanced coding and machine learning techniques to bring her vision to life.

Beyond her technical accomplishments, Erin has become an advocate for the role of youth in driving innovation. She frequently speaks at conferences to inspire other young people to pursue their passions and tackle real-world challenges. Her work underscores the importance of cross-disciplinary approaches, combining technology, neuroscience, and healthcare to address unmet medical needs.

127

CONCLUSION

SCAMPER, 6-3-5 Sketch, LAUNCH, and Literary Device Brainstorming Sessions are valuable frameworks for fostering creative elaboration. These techniques encourage individuals and teams to expand upon their initial ideas, enabling deeper exploration and more nuanced solutions. SCAMPER, for example, helps students think critically by prompting them to substitute, combine, adapt, modify, put to other uses, eliminate, and rearrange elements of their ideas. Similarly, 6-3-5 Sketch engages participants in collaborative ideation, where groups build on one another's contributions to generate diverse and detailed concepts.

Using these approaches, students can practice essential creative thinking skills while discovering innovative ways to engage with content. Through the LAUNCH method, they navigate a structured process that includes observation, inquiry, and creation, ensuring their ideas are thoroughly developed and purposeful. Literary Device Brainstorming Sessions add a unique layer of creativity, as students apply figurative language to expand their thinking and generate imaginative outcomes.

These techniques highlight the importance of elaboration in the creative process, encouraging students to refine and expand their ideas into polished final products. By using such strategies, students not only develop critical problem-solving skills but also gain an appreciation for the iterative nature of creativity. Ultimately, these methods equip learners with the tools to approach challenges with confidence and creativity, paving the way for meaningful innovation.

REFERENCES

Alkaab, S.N.S. (2024). Improving students' creative writing ability through SCAMPER technique. *Theory and Practice in Language Studies*, *14*(5), 1576–1581. https://doi.org/10.17507/tpls.1405.31

Boonpracha, J. (2023). SCAMPER for creativity of students' creative idea creation in product design. *Thinking Skills and Creativity*, *48*, 101282. https://doi.org/10.1016/j.tsc.2023.101282

Buser, J.K., Buser, T.J., Gladding, S.T., & Wilkerson, J. (2011). The creative counselor: Using the SCAMPER model in counselor training. *Journal of Creativity in Mental Health*, *6*(4), 256–273. https://doi.org/10.1080/15401383.2011.631468

Gündoğan, A. (2019). SCAMPER: Improving creative imagination of young children. *Creativity Studies*, *12*(2), 315–326. https://doi.org/10.3846/cs.2019.11201

Ozyaprak, M. (2016). The effectiveness of SCAMPER technique on creative thinking skills. *Journal for the Education of Gifted Young Scientists*, *4*(1), 31–40. Retrieved from https://www.proquest.com/scholarly-journals/effectiveness-scamper-technique-on-creative/docview/2854154895/se-2

Spencer, J., & Juliani, A.J. (2016). *Launch: Using design thinking to boost creativity and bring out the maker in every student*. Dave Burgess Consulting, Incorporated

White, C., Wood, K., & Jensen, D. (2012). From brainstorming to C-sketch to principles of historical innovators: Ideation techniques to enhance student creativity. *Journal of STEM Education, 13*(5), 12.

Chapter 7

Incubation and Struggle

INTRODUCTION

Creativity often emerges not in moments of direct effort but in the spaces between – when the mind is allowed to wander, struggle, and subconsciously work through complex problems. Channa, a chemistry professor researching nanotechnology, biotechnology, and computational chemistry, has found that meditation provides a necessary clearing of the mind during these difficult stages. Rather than forcing a solution, he embraces the quiet space of meditation as a way to allow ideas to incubate, trusting that his subconscious will continue to process problems in the background.

Enrique, the astronomer introduced in Chapter 2, similarly recognizes the power of incubation. While his work involves analyzing vast celestial phenomena, his most profound insights often come during the simplest of activities – doing the dishes. The repetitive, almost meditative act frees his mind from the immediate pressure of problem solving, allowing connections to form naturally. In these moments, he experiences what Guilford described as *incubation* – a stage of creative thought where the mind steps away from a problem yet continues working on it in the subconscious, often leading to unexpected breakthroughs.

For Emma, an outdoor gear designer, the struggle of creative work is best managed through immersion in music. She plays loud music to drown out competing thoughts, allowing herself to focus deeply on a single idea at a time. Her method aligns with Guilford's concept of *struggle*, the necessary cognitive friction that occurs before a breakthrough. By creating an environment that eliminates distractions, she leans into the challenge, pushing her thinking just to the edge of discomfort – a space where creativity thrives.

Tom, introduced in Chapter 1, finds his best moments of creative struggle and incubation while sitting on a riverbank, painting, or carving. For him, the rhythmic flow of water mirrors the natural ebb and flow of thought. Watching its movement, engaging with his hands in creative tasks, he allows ideas to take

DOI: 10.4324/9781003434221-7

shape organically. Guilford's model acknowledges this kind of reflection as essential to creative thinking – giving the mind time and space to form new connections without force.

Each of these individuals illustrates that creativity is not simply about generating ideas on demand. Instead, it requires an acceptance of struggle and an understanding of incubation – letting ideas steep, evolve, and emerge in their own time. Whether through meditation, repetitive tasks, sensory immersion, or the quiet observation of nature, they each embrace the nonlinear process of creative thought, demonstrating that breakthroughs often come when we least expect them.

Incubation and struggle are essential components of the creative problem-solving process because they enable the mind to explore challenges deeply and generate innovative solutions. Incubation refers to the phase when an individual steps back from actively thinking about a problem, allowing the subconscious mind to process it. During this time, the brain continues to work in the background, often leading to sudden "aha!" moments when connections emerge unexpectedly. This phase reduces mental fixation, which can occur when a person becomes stuck in unproductive thought patterns. Stepping away from the problem creates space for creative connections to form between unrelated ideas, a process that has been observed in many historical breakthroughs. Incubation highlights the importance of relaxation or distraction in enabling new insights to surface.

On the other hand, struggle plays a critical role in fostering deep engagement with a problem. While grappling with a challenge may feel uncomfortable, it forces individuals to explore the problem's complexities and constraints, fostering a deeper understanding. Struggle also encourages persistence, which is crucial for overcoming creative blocks and experimenting with alternative approaches. The mental tension created during this phase primes the brain for insight, which often emerges during subsequent periods of incubation. Furthermore, struggling with a problem promotes personal growth by encouraging the refinement of ideas and methods, leading to a greater capacity for innovation.

Together, incubation and struggle create a cyclical process that enhances creativity. Struggle immerses the individual in the problem and generates the tension needed to spark innovative thinking, while incubation allows for the subconscious processing that can lead to breakthroughs. Without struggle, creative problem solving risks lacking depth and perseverance, while without incubation, individuals may experience burnout or remain stuck in unproductive thought patterns. By integrating both phases, the creative mind can achieve its full potential and uncover truly novel solutions.

People often talk about having eureka moments while completing mundane, yet focused tasks such as taking a shower, walking the dog, or gardening (Kluger, 2024). The optimal balance between engagement and disengagement is particularly evident in the shower. John Kounios, a professor of psychology at Drexel

University and co-author of *The Eureka Factor: Aha Moments, Creative Insight, and the Brain* (Kounios & Beeman, 2015), posits that this phenomenon may be explained by the unique conditions of the shower environment. While performing routine tasks such as washing, shampooing, and shaving, individuals remain focused in a purposeful sequence, yet simultaneously experience a degree of sensory isolation. According to Kounios (Kluger, 2024), "There is sensory restriction... white noise... and limited visual stimuli". Moreover, the tactile experience of the shower, with water temperature closely aligning with the body's own, eliminates temperature extremes that might disrupt focus, thereby fostering an immersive environment conducive to creative insight. This combination of cognitive engagement and sensory disengagement appears to facilitate moments of spontaneous creative clarity.

Jonathan Schooler, a professor of psychological and brain sciences at the University of California, Santa Barbara, has extensively studied the role of the hypnagogic state – the transitional phase between wakefulness and sleep – in fostering creative insights. He suggests that this state can significantly enhance creativity (Mehta, 2022). Schooler's research indicates that non-demanding activities, which allow the mind to wander, can facilitate creative thinking. Schooler emphasizes the importance of being comfortable in "liminal spaces", where attention exists at the intersections of various states such as consciousness and unconsciousness, mindfulness and mind-wandering. He believes that these states can illuminate how the curiosities and distractions of the human mind contribute to creativity (Mooneyham & Schooler, 2013). Jonathan Schooler's work underscores the significance of the hypnagogic state and other activities that promote mind-wandering in enhancing creative thinking. By understanding and leveraging these states, individuals can potentially improve their creative problem-solving abilities.

INCUBATION AND STRUGGLE IN EDUCATIONAL MODELS

Incubation and struggle are crucial components in fostering creativity and deeper learning, as various educational models highlight. Lev Vygotsky's Zone of Proximal Development (ZPD) provides a foundational framework for understanding how struggle plays a role in cognitive growth. Vygotsky (1978) suggested that learners encounter tasks within the ZPD – challenging activities that are just beyond their current abilities but can be completed with guidance. This period of struggle is essential for learning, as it forces students to step outside their comfort zones, pushing them to solve problems and gain new insights. Much like incubation in the creative process, the ZPD allows for a transformative struggle where learners internalize new knowledge, often gaining profound understanding after a period of effort and reflection.

Similarly, Constructivism, as articulated by Piaget and Bruner, underscores the value of struggle in the learning process. Piaget (1950) argued that cognitive development occurs when learners encounter disequilibrium – when new information conflicts with existing schemas. This conflict triggers a struggle that, once resolved, leads to accommodation or the creation of new mental structures. Constructivist learning often involves moments of incubation, where students reflect on their experiences and mentally process new information. This process of struggle followed by insight is integral to how students construct knowledge. As students grapple with challenging concepts and work to reconcile their understanding, incubation provides the necessary mental space for creative problem solving and innovation to emerge.

The Creative Problem Solving (CPS) Model by Osborn and Guilford emphasizes that struggle is an inherent part of creativity. The CPS model consists of several stages, including incubation, which occurs after the initial preparation phase. During incubation, individuals unconsciously process the information gathered, often leading to sudden insights or "aha!" moments. Osborn (1953) highlighted that moments of illumination, when solutions suddenly appear, are often preceded by a period of incubation where the subconscious mind continues to work. This model suggests that struggle – particularly the struggle to find a solution to a complex problem – allows for the mental processing needed to generate innovative ideas. In educational settings, encouraging students to embrace these moments of struggle and incubation can help them persevere through creative challenges and emerge with novel solutions.

Inquiry-Based Learning (IBL) builds upon the idea that struggle and incubation are central to the process of discovery. IBL encourages students to ask questions and explore real-world problems, allowing for exploration and uncertainty. The process is inherently challenging and involves periods of incubation as students reflect on their findings and synthesize new information. According to Dewey (1938), problem solving through inquiry requires that students confront ambiguity and engage in moments of struggle that stimulate creative thinking. These struggles provide opportunities for incubation, where students' subconscious minds process the data they have collected. As students refine their questions or theories, the struggle is integral to their ability to think critically and creatively.

Graham Wallas's 4-Stage Creative Process, including the stages of incubation and illumination, provides another valuable lens through which to view the role of struggle and incubation in the creative process. Wallas (1926) described incubation as a period when the mind continues to work on a problem in the background while the individual consciously steps away from it. During this stage, the subconscious mind makes connections that the conscious mind cannot. This is a time of struggle, but it is also where breakthroughs often happen. As Wallas notes, ideas may come to fruition suddenly after a period of mental rest, emphasizing that struggle followed by incubation leads to illumination. For students,

133

understanding this process can help them embrace the challenges they face in problem solving, knowing that the struggle they experience is an important part of the creative process.

The Design Thinking approach, often used in product design and innovation, also emphasizes the importance of incubation and struggle. The ideation phase of Design Thinking encourages divergent thinking, where individuals generate as many ideas as possible, followed by a period of incubation where some ideas are put aside to allow the mind to process and refine them. The struggle in this phase is evident as students wrestle with complex, open-ended problems and narrow down their ideas. The creative process in Design Thinking requires moments of uncertainty and frustration, which can lead to profound breakthroughs after incubation. In classrooms, the Design Thinking approach can help students understand that struggles and setbacks are not barriers but necessary steps toward innovation.

The Zone of Proximal Development, Constructivism, and the Creative Problem-Solving Model highlight the importance of incubation and struggle in fostering creativity and learning. The struggle students face when encountering new and complex tasks is essential for cognitive development, as it requires them to engage with challenging concepts and ideas. This period of struggle, coupled with moments of incubation, allows students to access new insights and develop creative solutions. Moreover, these models emphasize that the creative process is not linear but cyclical, involving reflection, persistence, and a willingness to embrace uncertainty.

INCUBATION AND STRUGGLE DURING THE SONGWRITING PROCESS

In a band where Alex, the guitarist, writes the riffs; Jamie, the drummer, adds the beat; and Sam and Taylor, the vocalists, craft the lyrics, incubation and struggle are vital to their creative process over several months. Each member contributes uniquely, and their journey to the final song reflects a balance of intense effort and reflective downtime.

The process often begins with Alex, who spends hours experimenting with his guitar, trying to nail down a riff that captures the energy of their envisioned song. He goes through periods of frustration, playing the same notes repeatedly, feeling stuck as nothing seems quite right. Eventually, Alex decides to set the guitar down and take a walk. A few days later, while absentmindedly strumming at home, he stumbles upon a variation of the riff that feels fresh and exciting – an idea that only emerged after he gave his brain time to subconsciously process the problem.

Once Alex brings the riff to the band during rehearsal, Jamie dives in to create a beat that matches its tone. This isn't always smooth sailing; Jamie experiments with different rhythms, sometimes clashing with Alex's vision. They debate whether the beat should drive the song forward aggressively or provide a more laid-back groove. This back-and-forth can feel tense at times, but it pushes both of them to think beyond their initial instincts. After several jam sessions and some time away from the practice room, Jamie finds inspiration while listening to an old funk album, sparking an idea for a beat that perfectly complements Alex's riff.

Meanwhile, Sam and Taylor start brainstorming lyrics and melodies to layer on top of the music. This phase is particularly challenging – they want the words to match the song's mood but also convey a deeper story. During practice, Sam throws out a line that doesn't quite land, and Taylor struggles to find a melody that fits the complex timing of Jamie's drum pattern. After a few frustrating sessions, they agree to take a break and revisit it later. Over the next few weeks, the lyrics begin to take shape in unexpected moments – Sam wakes up one morning with a phrase stuck in his head, and Taylor hums a melody while washing dishes that turns out to be perfect. These breakthroughs come during moments of incubation, where stepping away from the song allows their subconscious minds to make the connections they couldn't force in rehearsal.

As the weeks turn into months, the band's process becomes a cycle of struggle and incubation. Each member revisits their contributions with fresh eyes and new ideas, refining and building on what they've created together. Collaborative rehearsals often bring new energy, with Taylor's melody inspiring Jamie to tweak his drum fills or Sam's lyrics prompting Alex to adjust his riff. By the time the band enters the studio to record, their song has evolved into a cohesive, dynamic piece of music – a product of both their effort and the insights gained during moments of rest.

For Alex, Jamie, Sam, and Taylor, the journey to completing the song is as much about navigating struggle as it is about giving themselves space to breathe. The balance between these two elements ensures that their final product is not only polished but also reflects the collective creativity and growth of the entire band.

INCUBATION IN THE CLASSROOM

Incubation often plays a crucial role in the creative process, allowing ideas to percolate in the subconscious while the mind focuses on other tasks. For example, a student working on a short story may feel stuck while trying to develop a compelling climax. Frustrated, they decide to take a walk. As they observe their surroundings – trees swaying, birds chirping, and people chatting – they suddenly imagine the perfect resolution to their story. Similarly, a writer struggling with plotlines may put the project aside for several days, only for an unexpected twist to surface while they're engaged in unrelated tasks like gardening or cooking.

In a math classroom, incubation can help students unlock solutions to challenging problems. A student might find themselves stuck on a complex algebra problem and, rather than forcing a breakthrough, switch to playing a video game or working on another assignment. With their attention elsewhere, the subconscious continues to process the problem, and when they revisit it, the solution feels much clearer. Similarly, mathematicians working on proofs often pause for extended breaks or sleep on the problem, only to wake with a fresh perspective or a key insight into their work.

For visual artists, incubation often fosters creativity in unexpected ways. For instance, a young artist struggling to find inspiration for a painting may set their work aside to play music or journal. Hours later, they feel a sudden spark of creativity and envision a unique concept for their project. Another example could involve a middle school student working on a poster design. They pause to watch their favorite show, and the vibrant colors or patterns on the screen influence a bold, innovative style for their artwork.

In the world of science and engineering, incubation has often sparked innovative solutions. A student working on a science fair project may struggle to design an experiment, so they take a break and go for a run. During the run, they recall an experiment they once saw in a video and adapt it to fit their project. Similarly, a team of engineers brainstorming a product design might shift their focus to a casual board game session. In their relaxed state, one team member notices parallels between the game mechanics and their design challenge, leading to a fresh and promising idea.

Music composition also benefits from moments of incubation. A young musician stuck on a melody might leave the piano to try their hand at drawing. While they doodle, a rhythm suddenly pops into their head that evolves into the missing piece of their composition. Likewise, a composer unable to finalize a chord progression might step away for a walk in nature, where the sounds of rustling leaves and birdsong inspire a new harmony that perfectly fits their work.

Even real-world problem solving benefits from incubation. For instance, a group of students designing a sustainable community garden might pause their brainstorming session and visit a local park. Observing the park's layout and features gives them fresh ideas for organizing their garden's space. Similarly, a teacher struggling to create an engaging lesson plan might find inspiration during a morning commute, when an idea for a hands-on activity suddenly comes to mind. These moments highlight how stepping away and engaging in unrelated activities can unlock originality and propel the creative process forward.

INCUBATION TECHNIQUES

Teachers can purposefully provide opportunities for incubation throughout creative activities or the creative problem-solving process.

Table 7.1 Activities that Allow for Incubation

Strategy	Description	Examples
Scheduled Breaks or Pauses	Build in regular breaks to let students step away from active focus.	Take a five-minute stretch break after brainstorming; silent "think time" before writing ideas.
Engage in Unrelated Activities	Shift focus to unrelated tasks or relaxing activities to encourage subconscious processing.	Use art or music activities, mindfulness exercises, or light stretching to reset their focus.
Provide Opportunities for Play and Exploration	Allow low-stakes creative play and experimentation without judgment.	Encourage doodling, prototyping, or improvisational games to spark ideas.
Incorporate Reflection Time	Create moments for students to reflect on their ideas, both individually and collaboratively.	Journaling unfinished ideas or hosting small-group discussions to exchange thoughts.
Change the Environment	Use physical movement or new settings to stimulate fresh perspectives.	Work in different parts of the room, outside, or at standing desks.
Incorporate Time Gaps	Space tasks over multiple days or encourage students to revisit work after a break.	Assign multi-day projects or encourage students to "sleep on" their ideas overnight.
Use Distractions Intentionally	Let students engage in light distractions to help their minds subconsciously process complex ideas.	Provide puzzles, instrumental music, or organizing tasks as intentional distractions.
Encourage Openness to Inspiration	Promote curiosity and a habit of capturing ideas as they come.	Create an "idea bank" for jotting down thoughts; ask open-ended questions to spark creativity.
Highlight the Value of Downtime	Teach students that incubation is a natural and important part of creativity.	Normalize feeling stuck and celebrate partial progress or small breakthroughs.

INCUBATION MODEL OF TEACHING (IMT)

The Incubation Model of Teaching (IMT) is a dynamic framework designed to engage students in the creative process by guiding them through three key stages: heightening anticipation, deepening expectations, and keeping it going. Each stage builds upon the previous one to foster curiosity, critical thinking, and resilience, helping

137

students develop the skills and mindset needed for creativity. By following this structured approach, educators can create meaningful learning experiences that empower students to explore new ideas and persevere through challenges (Hines et al., 2019).

The first stage, **heightening anticipation**, focuses on capturing students' curiosity and sparking their interest in the task or problem at hand. Teachers employ strategies such as posing thought-provoking questions, presenting intriguing scenarios, or offering real-world contexts that resonate with students. For example, a science teacher might introduce a lesson on ecosystems by asking students, "What would happen if bees disappeared tomorrow?". This stage sets the tone for engagement, encouraging students to enter the learning process with a sense of wonder and excitement.

The second stage, **deepening expectations**, emphasizes guiding students to delve into the topic more thoroughly by exploring multiple perspectives and asking critical questions. At this point, teachers scaffold learning by providing resources, encouraging collaboration, and prompting students to connect their prior knowledge to new concepts. For instance, in an English class, students might analyze various interpretations of a literary theme, examining how different authors express similar ideas. This stage helps students develop a deeper understanding of the subject while fostering their ability to think creatively and critically.

Finally, the stage of **keeping it going** ensures that students remain motivated and resilient, even when they encounter difficulties. Teachers use techniques such as offering constructive feedback, encouraging iterative problem solving, and celebrating small successes to sustain students' momentum. For example, in a math project, students designing a bridge might test their calculations, encounter errors, and refine their designs. Through this iterative process, they not only solve problems but also learn the value of persistence and reflection. By nurturing students' ability to stay engaged, the IMT fosters a growth mindset, equipping them with the tools they need to approach creative challenges confidently and effectively. Here are five examples of how the IMT could be applied to different high school courses.

AP BIOLOGY

- **Heightening Anticipation**: Present a mystery or case study, like a genetic mutation that impacts human health, and ask students to predict what might be causing it.
- **Deepening Expectations**: Guide students through complex experiments and simulations, encouraging them to refine their hypotheses and explore various variables (e.g., enzyme activity, temperature).
- **Keeping It Going**: Provide opportunities for students to revisit their lab results, analyze discrepancies, and iterate on their experimental designs for better outcomes.

PHYSICS

- **Heightening Anticipation**: Pose a real-world problem, such as how cars behave in a crash, and ask students to predict the forces involved.
- **Deepening Expectations**: After initial exploration, have students apply Newton's laws to solve problems involving various forces, providing a deeper theoretical understanding.
- **Keeping It Going**: Give students the chance to continuously modify and refine their models, apply simulations, or test their understanding in new, more complex scenarios.

THEATER: PLAY – *MACBETH* BY WILLIAM SHAKESPEARE

- **Heightening Anticipation**: In *Macbeth*, students are initially introduced to the dark and complex themes of ambition, fate, and power. Students read the witches' prophecy and speculate about how Macbeth's ambition might unfold.
- **Deepening Expectations**: Students analyze Macbeth's psychological descent and its impact on others, asking students to explore various interpretations of his actions.
- **Keeping It Going**: Students revisit key scenes to refine their character portrayal and decision-making as they practice and perform the play.

ART: STYLE – SURREALISM

- **Heightening Anticipation**: In a surrealist art project, students would first explore key artists like Salvador Dalí and René Magritte, whose works depict dream-like imagery and unexpected juxtapositions. Students brainstorm concepts that blend reality and fantasy.
- **Deepening Expectations**: Students are encouraged to incorporate symbolic imagery and dream-like sequences while experimenting with techniques such as collage or distorted proportions.
- **Keeping It Going**: Students refine their ideas and create multiple iterations of their work, allowing their creative ideas to evolve.

MUSIC: SONGS – "BOHEMIAN RHAPSODY" BY QUEEN, "IMAGINE" BY JOHN LENNON, AND "TAKE FIVE" BY DAVE BRUBECK

- **Heightening Anticipation**: Students explore how each song challenges traditional song structures, such as "Bohemian Rhapsody"'s operatic segments or "Take Five"'s unique time signature.

- **Deepening Expectations**: Students analyze the songs for themes (e.g., peace in "Imagine") or musical complexity (e.g., improvisation in "Take Five").
- **Keeping It Going**: Students practice specific sections or even compose a piece inspired by the songs, refining their understanding of musical techniques and thematic interpretations over time.

AP HUMAN GEOGRAPHY

Table 7.2 incorporates the use of GIS and mapping tools into a unit plan for the AP Human Geography classroom.

Subject: AP Human Geography

Unit Title: *Designing the Ideal Global City: Balancing Culture, Economy, and Sustainability*

Table 7.2 Unit Plan Using the Incubation Model of Teaching (IMT) in an AP Classroom

Stage	Objective	Day(s)	Activities and Strategies	Expected Outcomes
Heightening Anticipation	Engage students in the idea of creating a city that reflects the challenges and opportunities of globalization.	Day 1–2	– Present a case study of a global city like Tokyo or Dubai and discuss its strengths and weaknesses. – Ask: "What would a city look like if you could design it to solve today's global challenges?" – Facilitate a brainstorming session to identify the key features of a thriving global city (e.g., infrastructure, culture, economy, sustainability). – **GIS Introduction**: Demonstrate GIS software (ArcGIS, Google Earth, or QGIS) to explore global cities and identify spatial patterns (e.g., population density, transportation networks).	Students will identify the characteristics of global cities and start imagining what an ideal city might include. They will also develop curiosity about how GIS can inform city planning.

(Continued)

Table 7.2 (Continued)

Stage	Objective	Day(s)	Activities and Strategies	Expected Outcomes
Deepening Expectations	Help students explore key human geography concepts, such as urbanization, migration, and cultural landscapes.	Day 3–6	– Teach core concepts such as population density, spatial organization, and cultural diffusion. – Assign small groups to research one aspect of city design (e.g., housing, transportation, economic zones, or cultural integration). – Provide case studies for inspiration, such as how cities like Singapore or Amsterdam tackle urban challenges. – **GIS Application**: Train students to use GIS or mapping tools to analyze real-world data related to their urban planning challenges (e.g., land use, transportation routes, and population demographics). – **Group Work**: Students gather data and insights from GIS to incorporate into their city design.	Students will analyze global trends and case studies, deepening their understanding of urban systems and cultural dynamics. They will begin using GIS tools to map out key urban features and develop city models.

(*Continued*)

Table 7.2 (Continued)

Stage	Objective	Day(s)	Activities and Strategies	Expected Outcomes
Deepening Expectations	Encourage students to apply their knowledge creatively to design their ideal global city.	Day 7–9	– Groups create maps and models of their city, incorporating geographic tools and principles. – Use GIS software (ArcGIS, Google Earth, or QGIS) to map residential areas, industrial zones, and public spaces. – Teach students to calculate distances and areas using GIS tools and apply spatial data to optimize their city layout (e.g., transportation efficiency, proximity to green spaces). – Conduct peer critiques to refine ideas and ensure they address cultural, economic, and environmental considerations.	Students will create detailed and realistic city models using GIS tools, incorporating human geography concepts and geographic data into their designs.
Keeping It Going	Motivate students to finalize and present their projects, reflecting on their learning process.	Day 10–12	– Groups finalize their city plans, focusing on how their designs solve real-world problems like urban sprawl or cultural integration. – Host a "City Expo" where groups present their GIS maps and physical or digital models to peers, teachers, and possibly local urban planners or city officials. – Use rubrics to evaluate creativity, feasibility, and application of human geography concepts.	Students will present innovative and realistic city solutions, demonstrating the integration of GIS technology and human geography principles.

Key Highlights of the Unit

1. **Real-World Connection**: The unit addresses real-world urban planning challenges, helping students understand the role of human geography in solving global problems.
2. **Hands-On Product**: Students create tangible outputs like city models and maps, fostering deeper engagement and practical application.
3. **Collaboration and Reflection**: Group work and iterative feedback encourage sustained engagement and originality in problem solving.
4. **Integration of Technology**: Using GIS software helps students gain technical skills while applying geographic concepts to their projects.

Technology Recommendations

1. **ArcGIS Online** (Free for schools with an education license).

    • Use for mapping layers, analyzing geographic data, and creating interactive maps.
2. **Google Earth** (Free).

    • Use to visualize 3D city layouts and explore global examples.
3. **QGIS** (Free, open-source).

    • Use advanced mapping and spatial analysis tools.

City Design Project Rubric

AP Human Geography: Designing the Ideal Global City
    Criteria: Creativity, Feasibility, and Application of Human Geography Concepts
    Table 7.3 provides details for the City Design Project Rubric.

SOCIAL AND EMOTIONAL WELL-BEING

Understanding incubation during the creative process can significantly contribute to social and emotional well-being by fostering a healthier relationship with creativity, problem solving, and stress. By recognizing incubation as a natural and necessary part of generating ideas, individuals can reduce pressure, build resilience, and enhance self-awareness.

Acknowledging the importance of taking breaks during creative tasks can alleviate the pressure to produce immediate results. When individuals understand that stepping away from a problem or project is not a failure but a constructive step in the process, they are less likely to feel overwhelmed or frustrated.

143

Table 7.3 City Design Project Rubric

Criteria	Excellent (4)	Good (3)	Satisfactory (2)	Needs Improvement (1)
Creativity	The city design demonstrates a highly original and imaginative approach to solving urban challenges. Unique, unconventional solutions are presented for key issues like transportation, housing, and sustainability, making the city stand out as innovative.	The design is original, with several creative elements that add significant value to the project. These elements reflect new ways of thinking about urban issues, though not all aspects are entirely novel.	The design includes basic solutions that are commonly used in urban planning. Although functional, the city layout and solutions lack distinctiveness or a creative edge.	The design lacks originality. The solutions presented are generic and show little effort to think outside conventional urban planning practices.
Feasibility	The city design is highly realistic, with carefully considered plans for all aspects of urban life, including transportation, housing, energy, and waste management. Data and evidence are used effectively to demonstrate that the design can be realistically implemented.	The city design is feasible, and practical solutions for major urban challenges are clearly outlined. While the design is plausible, a few aspects may not be fully thought out or lack sufficient supporting data.	The design includes feasible ideas for some urban issues, but certain components are either underdeveloped or unrealistic. The city plan may overlook key aspects of urban life or present impractical solutions.	The design is not feasible, with major inconsistencies in the planning. Key components of urban life are poorly addressed, and the plan includes ideas that are either impractical or entirely unrealistic.

(Continued)

Table 7.3 (Continued)

Criteria	Excellent (4)	Good (3)	Satisfactory (2)	Needs Improvement (1)
Application of Human Geography Concepts	The design integrates human geography concepts such as population density, migration, cultural landscapes, urbanization, and sustainability in a highly thoughtful and coherent manner. These concepts are applied to specific features of the city (e.g., zoning, infrastructure, cultural integration).	The design applies human geography concepts correctly, and these concepts are clearly incorporated into the city design. Concepts like population density, migration, and sustainability are integrated into the project, though they may not be fully explored in all areas.	The design includes basic applications of human geography concepts. These concepts are mentioned but may not be fully developed or clearly linked to the urban design's key features.	The design demonstrates little to no understanding of human geography concepts. Concepts are applied incorrectly or omitted entirely, and their relevance to the city design is unclear.
Use of GIS/Mapping Tools	GIS and mapping tools are used to create a highly detailed and accurate city model. Layers are effectively applied to show land use, transportation, and other critical elements. The use of GIS data adds depth to the city's design and enhances its functionality.	GIS and mapping tools are used to create a clear and effective city layout. Relevant data, such as land use and transportation routes, is incorporated into the design, though some layers may lack detailed data or full utilization of GIS features.	GIS and mapping tools are used, but the application is basic. The city layout includes a few GIS elements, but many features are either underused or lack detailed data. The map may be incomplete or poorly integrated into the overall design.	GIS and mapping tools are either not used or applied incorrectly. The city design lacks key GIS elements, or the map is not informative or relevant to the design.

(Continued)

Table 7.3 (Continued)

Criteria	Excellent (4)	Good (3)	Satisfactory (2)	Needs Improvement (1)
Presentation and Communication	The presentation is professional, well-organized, and compelling. Students clearly explain their design choices, demonstrating deep knowledge of human geography and the reasoning behind their decisions. Answers to questions are thoughtful and confident.	The presentation is clear and organized, with a good explanation of the design. The reasoning behind design choices is explained adequately, though the answers to some questions may lack depth or clarity.	The presentation is somewhat disorganized, and the explanation of design choices is unclear in places. Students are able to answer basic questions, but struggle to provide detailed explanations for their choices.	The presentation is unclear or poorly structured. The explanation of the design is lacking or confusing. Students struggle to provide coherent answers to questions and fail to justify key design decisions.

For instance, students or professionals who embrace incubation as a strategy can avoid burnout by giving themselves permission to rest, knowing that their subconscious mind continues to work in the background. This shift in mindset reduces stress and encourages patience with themselves and their progress.

The incubation process teaches individuals that solutions often emerge from persistence combined with strategic rest. When someone hits a creative or intellectual roadblock, knowing that stepping away can lead to breakthroughs helps them view challenges as temporary and surmountable. This builds resilience, as they learn to approach difficulties with confidence rather than despair. For example, a student struggling with a project might find inspiration while doing something unrelated, reinforcing the idea that challenges can be overcome with time and flexibility.

Incubation often requires moments of stillness, relaxation, or engagement in non-demanding activities like walking, journaling, or listening to music. These activities not only provide the mental space for ideas to form but also encourage self-awareness and mindfulness. By engaging in these reflective practices, individuals can develop a deeper understanding of their emotions, triggers, and thought patterns. This enhances their emotional intelligence and helps them navigate both personal and interpersonal challenges more effectively.

Understanding incubation also fosters empathy and collaboration in social settings. When working in groups, recognizing that each individual processes information differently – and that some may need time away to think – can improve teamwork and reduce conflict. Encouraging breaks during collaborative projects can lead to fresher ideas and more productive conversations when the group reconvenes. This shared understanding promotes patience and respect for diverse creative processes, which strengthens relationships and fosters a supportive environment.

By valuing incubation as part of creativity, individuals can develop healthier coping mechanisms, improve their emotional regulation, and strengthen their ability to work collaboratively. This understanding ultimately cultivates a sense of balance and well-being, helping people thrive both creatively and emotionally.

SPOTLIGHT: INVENTORS UNDER 18

Xóchitl Guadalupe Cruz López, a young scientist from Chiapas, Mexico, has made remarkable contributions to environmental sustainability and innovation at an early age. At just eight years old, Xóchitl developed a solar-powered water heater made entirely from recycled materials. Her invention was inspired by a desire to help underprivileged families in her community who lacked access to affordable hot water. By using readily available items such as glass, plastic bottles, and hoses, she created an environmentally friendly solution that reduces reliance on electricity or firewood, both of which can be costly and harmful to the environment.

Her ingenuity garnered widespread recognition when, in 2018, she became the first child to receive the prestigious Reconocimiento ICN, an award from the National Autonomous University of Mexico's Institute of Nuclear Sciences. This acknowledgment celebrated her innovative approach to addressing a common issue with a sustainable, community-centered solution. Her invention demonstrates not only creativity but also a profound understanding of environmental and social challenges.

Xóchitl's invention has a broader impact, promoting awareness of renewable energy and sustainable practices. Her work serves as an example of how young people can contribute to solving global challenges through simple yet effective solutions. By focusing on accessible and affordable materials, Xóchitl's water heater can be replicated in other under-resourced communities, extending its impact beyond her local area. Her dedication to using science for social good has made her a role model for young innovators worldwide.

Xóchitl's story highlights the importance of encouraging children to engage in STEM (Science, Technology, Engineering, and Mathematics) from an early age. Her success is a testament to how creativity, combined with practical problem-solving skills, can lead to meaningful inventions. As she continues her journey, Xóchitl is paving the way for other young scientists to think critically about the challenges their communities face and to develop innovative solutions that promote equity and sustainability.

CONCLUSION

Teaching techniques that emphasize the importance of incubation and struggle during the creative process are essential for fostering well-rounded and resilient K–12 students. When students understand that creativity involves moments of uncertainty, frustration, and the need for reflection, they are better equipped to persevere through challenges. By introducing incubation as a natural and necessary part of problem solving, educators can help students realize that stepping away from a task or taking time to process information doesn't mean failure – it's an intentional strategy for achieving breakthroughs. This understanding reduces the pressure for immediate perfection and helps students approach creative tasks with confidence and patience.

Incorporating these techniques also prepares students with critical life skills, such as adaptability and emotional regulation. When students learn to embrace struggle as a productive part of learning, they develop a growth mindset that views obstacles as opportunities for growth rather than barriers to success. The concept of incubation further reinforces the value of reflection and balance, teaching students to pause, reset, and allow ideas to emerge naturally. These habits not only enhance creativity but also improve social and emotional well-being, making students more resilient and self-aware as they navigate academic and personal challenges.

Finally, teaching students about incubation and productive struggle equips them to handle real-world problems with greater originality and collaboration. Whether working on a group project, solving a complex math problem, or designing a creative solution to a community issue, students will understand that solutions often come from persistence and moments of intentional rest. By fostering an environment that celebrates the creative process in its entirety – including its struggles – educators empower students to think critically, innovate effectively, and develop a lifelong appreciation for creativity and problem solving. These skills are foundational not only for academic success but also for becoming adaptable, thoughtful contributors to society.

REFERENCES

Dewey, J. (1938). *Experience and education*. New York, NY: Macmillan.

Hines, M.E., Catalana, S. M., & Anderson, B. N. (2019). When learning sinks in: Using the incubation model of teaching to guide students through the creative thinking process. *Gifted Child Today Magazine, 42*(1), 36–45. https://doi.org/10.1177/1076217518804858 https://go.exlibris.link/TGP8k5jg

Kluger, J. (2024). *Why you get your best ideas in the shower*. Time. https://time.com/6999592/shower-thoughts-best-ideas/

Kounios, J., & Beeman, M. (2015). *The eureka factor: Aha moments, creative insight, and the brain*. New York, NY: Random House.

Mehta, R., Henriksen, D., Richardson, C., Gruber, N., & Mishra, P. (2022). Creativity & the mindful wanderings of Dr. Jonathan Schooler. *Techtrends, 66*(4), 571–577. https://doi.org/10.1007/s11528-022-00747-4

Mooneyham, B.W., & Schooler, J.W. (2013). The costs and benefits of mind-wandering: A review. *Canadian Journal of Experimental Psychology, 67*(1), 11–18. https://doi.org/10.1037/a0031569

Osborn, A.F. (1953). *Applied imagination: Principles and procedures of creative thinking* (3rd ed.). New York, NY: Charles Scribner's Sons.

Piaget, J. (1950). *The psychology of intelligence*. London, UK: Routledge.

Vygotsky, L.S. (1978). *Mind in society: The development of higher psychological processes*. Cambridge, MA: Harvard University Press.

Wallas, G. (1926). *The art of thought*. New York, NY: Harcourt, Brace & Company.

Chapter 8

Evaluation

Assessing Ideas and Solutions

INTRODUCTION

Samantha, the owner of a hair salon, evaluates her creative process by first considering the needs and preferences of her clients. When she comes up with new hairstyle ideas or plans for salon modifications, she reflects on how these ideas align with her customers' desires and the latest trends. She frequently gathers feedback from clients, asking them for their opinions on the styles she offers and whether they would recommend them to others. This direct feedback helps her determine if the new style or change to the salon environment is viable in her specific market.

In addition to client feedback, Samantha evaluates her ideas by considering the practicality and resources required to implement them. For example, when introducing a new coloring technique or hairstyle, she assesses whether the salon's team has the necessary skills, time, and equipment to carry it out effectively. Similarly, when considering modifications to the salon, such as updating the décor, rearranging stations for better flow, or adding new services like a relaxation area, she evaluates if these changes are feasible within her budget and the available space. She also takes into account how these modifications will improve customer experience and satisfaction.

Samantha also looks at the long-term potential of her ideas and modifications by considering how they might evolve over time. She assesses if the new style, service, or salon layout could be a passing trend or something that could have lasting appeal. For instance, when introducing more eco-friendly products or offering a new hair treatment, she evaluates the sustainability of these changes, considering factors like demand, environmental impact, and costs. By tracking customer satisfaction and analyzing booking trends, Samantha can measure how well the new idea or modification performs and decide whether it has the potential for success.

Ultimately, Samantha's goal is to offer innovative yet sustainable services and a welcoming environment that reflect both her creativity and the needs of

DOI: 10.4324/9781003434221-8

her clients. By balancing creativity with practicality and customer feedback, she ensures that her salon stays competitive and provides an experience that clients want to return to.

Evaluation is the process of assessing ideas and solutions during the creative problem-solving process. While a multitude of research studies focus on fluency or originality to assess creative abilities, the role of evaluation has often been misunderstood or overlooked (Boldt, 2019). Evaluation allows individuals to critically analyze their ideas, considering aspects such as quality, feasibility, and overall effectiveness. This process is vital in narrowing down options, refining concepts, and ultimately improving outcomes. Without evaluation, the creative process may lack focus, leaving innovative ideas underdeveloped or misaligned with goals.

The evaluation process requires clarity regarding goals, standards, and requirements. These elements ensure that ideas and products align with the assignment or project. Evaluation acts as a bridge between the brainstorming phase and implementation, helping individuals determine which ideas are worth pursuing and which ones may need modification or elimination. By identifying the most promising ideas, this process facilitates a smoother transition to the development and application phases of creativity.

The ability to navigate the evaluation process effectively is influenced by creative mindsets (Cummiskey, 2021). These attitudes and beliefs are tied to the work of Karwowski (2014) and Dweck (2006), who emphasize the importance of growth-oriented thinking in creative endeavors. A flexible and open mindset allows individuals to view evaluation as an opportunity for improvement rather than a threat to creativity. This perspective fosters resilience and adaptability, enabling individuals to refine their ideas constructively while maintaining their creative momentum.

Assessing the feasibility and viability of ideas involves considering factors such as resources, time, cost, and technical practicality. Each of these components must be thoroughly examined and compared to alternatives to identify the most workable solution. This evaluative process not only enhances the quality of the final product but also ensures that creative efforts are aligned with practical constraints. By incorporating evaluation as an integral part of the creative process, individuals can strike a balance between innovation and functionality.

EVALUATION AND ASSESSMENT IN THE CLASSROOM

On the *Shark Tank*, the investors watch inventors or designers pitch their products and describe their financial journey bringing the idea to fruition, along with future predictions for gathering resources, creating products, advertising, and bringing their items to stores or through online sales. Teachers can provide similar opportunities for students in a unit of study focused on argumentative writing and persuasion. Offer 5–10 minutes at the beginning of each class period for students to consider inventions that would be beneficial. Throughout the unit, study the forms of rhetoric and techniques involved in persuasion such as logical, emotional, and ethical arguments. At the end of the unit, allow students to design a prototype either hand-drawn, with a computer program, or three-dimensional. Then provide the opportunity for students to give a pitch to a group of "sharks" consisting of school personnel or parents. The "sharks" can offer insights about practicality and suggestions for subsequent designs. The following outline describes how this process might play out in the classroom.

DAY 1: BRAINSTORMING AND EVALUATION OF IDEAS

On the first day, Anna begins by brainstorming potential ideas for her product. She writes down a variety of ideas, from simple study aids to more complex tech-based products. As she brainstorms, she constantly evaluates each idea, asking herself questions like, "Will this really help students?" or "How could this be improved?". After some thought, she narrows it down to the VR Study Aid – a product that would allow students to virtually experience history or science. Anna evaluates this idea by considering her own experiences in school, reflecting on how difficult it is to fully understand abstract concepts without a hands-on experience. She checks if the product idea aligns with her goal of making learning more interactive and accessible. Her self-reflection and evaluation of the idea help her make an informed choice about what direction to take.

Goal for the Day: Brainstorm and evaluate ideas to select the most promising one for further development.

DAY 2: RESEARCH AND EVALUATION OF MARKET POTENTIAL

On Day 2, Anna begins researching the feasibility of her VR Study Aid. She wants to understand if VR technology is already being used in education and how her product might stand out. As she digs into the topic, she evaluates different educational VR apps currently on the market and identifies any gaps in the existing products. Anna looks into whether schools are adopting VR technology and the types of subjects that are being targeted for VR experiences. She evaluates the strengths and weaknesses of these existing products, asking herself, "What can I do differently?" or "How can I make my product more useful?". She also checks if there are any financial or logistical challenges, such as the cost of VR headsets or the time required for schools to integrate them into the curriculum. This research helps Anna refine her product and ensure it addresses a real need in the education market, setting the stage for a successful pitch.

Goal for the Day: Conduct research to evaluate market needs and existing competition to refine the product's potential.

DAY 3: STUDYING RHETORIC AND EVALUATING THE ARGUMENT

As Anna begins to learn about persuasive techniques, she realizes that evaluation plays a critical role not just in the design of her product, but in shaping how she'll pitch it. She evaluates how she can make the argument for her VR Study Aid compelling and convincing. She uses logical reasoning (logos) to explain the educational value of VR, evaluating studies and evidence that support its benefits. For emotional appeal (pathos), she reflects on how students might feel more engaged in class if they could experience historical events or scientific phenomena firsthand. Anna also evaluates the ethical considerations of her product, making sure it will be inclusive and accessible to all students. She practices creating her argument and evaluates whether her points are clear, persuasive, and relevant. The act of evaluation here ensures that her pitch will be well-rounded and convincing to the "sharks".

Goal for the Day: Evaluate the effectiveness of persuasive arguments and refine the pitch to make it stronger.

DAY 4: PEER FEEDBACK AND EVALUATION OF PROTOTYPE

On Day 4, Anna shares her initial prototype ideas with a few classmates and asks for their feedback. She presents her sketches of the VR headset and app interface, explaining how she envisions students interacting with the product. Her classmates provide suggestions on how the app interface could be more user-friendly, such as adding color coding for different subjects or providing an easier navigation system. Anna also receives feedback on the VR headset design, with some classmates recommending making the headset more adjustable to fit different head sizes. She evaluates their input carefully, weighing their suggestions against her own vision for the product. This peer evaluation helps Anna refine her prototype, and she makes adjustments based on their ideas to improve the overall design and functionality.

Goal for the Day: Collect peer feedback to evaluate the prototype design and refine it for usability and appeal.

DAY 5: PROTOTYPE EVALUATION AND REFINEMENT

By Day 5, Anna has a clearer vision of what her VR Study Aid will look like. She begins refining her prototype, making decisions about the headset design, app interface, and other key features. During this stage, evaluation is crucial. Anna constantly asks herself questions: "Is this design comfortable for users?", "How user-friendly is the app?", "Will students find this immersive and engaging?". She tests the design on paper, evaluating if it's practical for her target audience – students who need both educational value and ease of use. She might also ask her classmates for their feedback and make improvements based on their suggestions. This self-assessment and feedback collection allow her to make continuous refinements, ensuring that the final design is functional and effective.

Goal for the Day: Evaluate the prototype's design and user experience, and refine based on feedback.

DAY 6: EVALUATING THE FINANCIAL FEASIBILITY AND MARKETING STRATEGY

On Day 6, Anna turns her attention to evaluating the financial side of her VR Study Aid. She starts to consider the cost of producing the VR headsets and developing the app. She also looks into potential funding options, such as grants for educational technology or partnerships with tech companies. Anna evaluates the feasibility of bringing the product to market, considering how much it might cost schools to purchase the product and how she could make it affordable while still turning a profit. She also begins to think about the marketing strategy for her product. Who would be the target audience? How could she effectively communicate the educational benefits of her product to teachers and school administrators? Anna researches effective marketing strategies for educational products and evaluates how she could apply these ideas to her own product, thinking about how to best position it in the market.

Goal for the Day: Evaluate the financial and marketing feasibility of the product, considering cost, funding, and audience.

DAY 7: REHEARSING AND EVALUATING THE PITCH

As the day of the pitch approaches, Anna rehearses her presentation in front of her peers. Evaluation is key during this stage, as Anna watches herself and listens to her classmates' feedback on her delivery and content. She evaluates her performance by asking questions like, "Did I speak clearly?", "Did I address potential questions and concerns?", and "Did I make the product seem exciting and necessary?". Through this process, Anna fine-tunes her pitch, ensuring that she's confident in her delivery and that her argument for the VR Study Aid is persuasive and clear. She may even time herself to ensure her pitch fits within the allotted time. The process of self-evaluation, as well as evaluation from her peers, allows her to identify areas for improvement and perfect her presentation skills before the real pitch.

Goal for the Day: Evaluate and refine the pitch delivery based on feedback from peers.

DAY 8: EVALUATING FINAL PITCH AND ANTICIPATING QUESTIONS

On Day 8, Anna prepares for her final pitch to the "sharks". She focuses on evaluating her entire presentation, considering how well she has communicated the value and feasibility of her VR Study Aid. Anna goes over the key points she wants to make: the educational benefits, the unique features of her product, and its potential impact on student engagement. She anticipates questions the sharks might ask, such as, "How will you scale this product?" or "What are the costs associated with production?". Anna rehearses answering these questions confidently, evaluating her ability to respond with clarity and authority. She also evaluates her body language and tone of voice, making sure she comes across as confident and knowledgeable. This day is focused on fine-tuning her pitch, ensuring she can effectively address any concerns and present her idea persuasively.

Goal for the Day: Evaluate the final pitch and practice answering anticipated questions to ensure a strong, confident presentation.

DAY 9: THE SHARK TANK PITCH AND FEEDBACK EVALUATION

When the day of the pitch arrives, Anna presents her VR Study Aid to the panel of "sharks" with confidence. The sharks ask probing questions, and Anna listens closely, evaluating their feedback and suggestions. She receives questions about pricing, usability, and how the product could be scaled for larger use in schools. Anna evaluates their feedback carefully, noting areas where her product could be improved, such as making the VR headset more affordable or adding customizable features for different subjects. The evaluation process here is not just about assessing her own work but also learning how to take constructive criticism and use it to improve her product. The feedback she receives from the sharks will help Anna understand how to refine her product for real-world application.

Goal for the Day: Receive and evaluate feedback from the sharks to identify areas for future improvement.

Throughout this project, Anna learns that evaluation is a key part of the creative process. From the initial brainstorming to refining her design and pitching her product, constant self-evaluation and feedback from others help her develop a better product and improve her ability to persuade and present. The act of evaluation helps Anna refine her ideas, address weaknesses, and make her product more appealing to her target audience. By the end of the unit, Anna has not only developed a unique and innovative product but also honed her skills in critical thinking and reflection, learning how to incorporate feedback into the creative process to achieve the best possible outcome.

STRATEGY: HITS AND HOT SPOTS

"Hits and Hot Spots" is a technique that involves identifying promising ideas (Hits) that could lead to creative breakthroughs and areas that are most intriguing or have the most potential (Hot Spots) where ideas seem to generate energy, converge, or overlap (Firestien & Treffinger, 1983). The creative exploration can be intensified which can lead to new insights or innovative solutions. The process prioritizes ideas that stand out while ensuring a focus on those with the highest potential.

USING HITS AND HOT SPOTS IN A HIGH SCHOOL CLASSROOM: DESIGNING A SUSTAINABLE WATER BOTTLE

For this project, students are instructed to design a new water bottle that is sustainable, encourages eco-friendly practices, and reduces plastic waste. During the brainstorming component, students might compile a list of items such as the following: A collapsible water bottle, a bottle made from biodegradable materials, a water bottle with a built-in filter for purifying tap water, a water bottle that tracks your daily intake using a connected app, a bottle with a detachable compartment for carrying snacks, or a bottle with eco-friendly skins that can be changed.

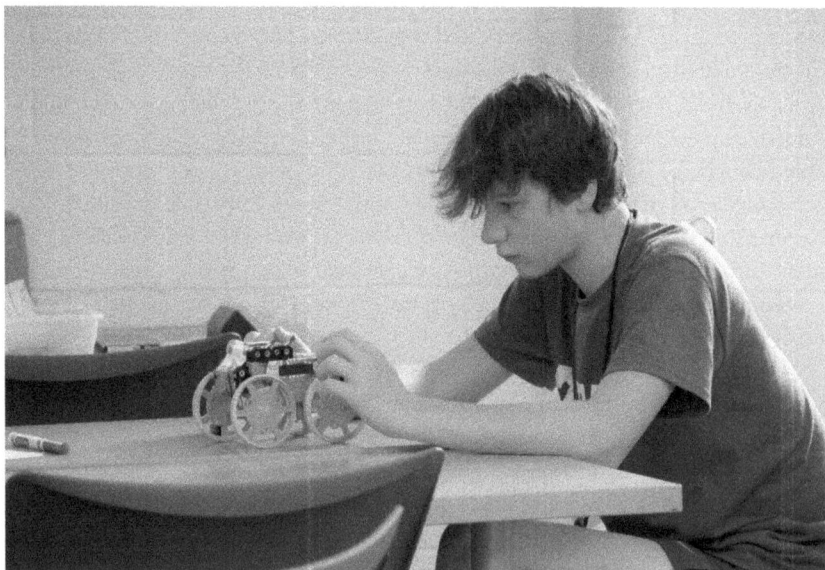

Figure 8.1 A Student Examines his Design before Making Modifications during Rocket to Creativity, a Field Experience for Teachers Earning MAED or AIG Licensure at Western Carolina University.

Identifying Hits from this list might include recognizing the most promising, practical, or innovative ideas. The idea of the collapsible bottle and biodegradable water bottle shows promise due to it addressing sustainability and portability. In addition, the built-in filter promotes eco-friendly behavior as people can use tap water or other sources instead of purchasing bottled water.

The Hot Spots include areas that show promise or generate excitement with overlap where connections can be established. An outcome could be the combination of several ideas to finalize the process leading to a stronger final product. For example, the idea of collapsible design coupled with a biodegradable bottle shows promise. However, it might need further development or exploration as to how compact the item can be, which would depend upon the material from which it is constructed. The idea of a built-in filter has strong potential, but certain aspects would need to be addressed such as the filter's effectiveness and how often it would need to be replaced. The cost factor could also be prohibitive. Finally, the customizable skins might be appealing to certain populations, but the material would need to be further researched to ensure it is eco-friendly and sturdy for reuse. Combining the filter idea with the skins could be beneficial as the marketability could make the cost acceptable for the consumer.

Table 8.1 offers examples of how students can use Hits and Hot Spots in high school classrooms. Hits and Hot Spots technique as a way to select promising possibilities (Hits) and organize or categorize them meaningfully (Hot Spots).

STRATEGY: PAIRED COMPARISON ANALYSIS MATRIX

The Paired Comparison Analysis is a technique that allows an individual to compare a pair of items to judge which one is preferred or has a greater attribute. It is especially useful in projects where the criteria are subjective or complex. The decision-making is broken down into smaller, more manageable comparisons in order to determine an overall selection.

The following is an example of how the Paired Comparison Analysis strategy can be used to evaluate ideas. Middle school students are asked to choose a new school club activity. They have several options in mind and want to find an activity that will be both beneficial and popular. They make a list of ideas that include: Organizing a school talent show, starting a community service project, planning a movie night, hosting a game tournament, or setting up a book club. Next, they set their evaluation criteria which includes how enjoyable the activity will be, how many students will likely participate, what positive effects the club will have on the school community, and how expensive it will be to organize.

The students can design a comparison matrix to compare each activity and each category. Focusing on the fun factor, each club will be assessed as compared to the other clubs. For example, Talent Show vs. Community Service, Movie Night, Game Tournament, and Book Club. The students may all agree that the

Table 8.1 Example of the Hits and Hot Spots Technique in High School Courses

Subject	Course Type	Standard Being Addressed	Activity Example Using Hits and Hot Spots
English Language Arts	General Education	CCSS.ELA-LITERACY.W.9-10.2: Write informative/explanatory texts to examine and convey complex ideas.	While brainstorming essays on *Of Mice and Men*, students identify "hits" (strong symbolic themes like loneliness) and cluster them into "hot spots" (grouped themes like isolation and connection).
	AP English Literature	AP English Literature CED: Analyze how authors use narrative techniques to create meaning.	Students highlight "hits" (key literary devices, such as irony or imagery) in a passage from *The Great Gatsby*, then organize "hot spots" (related devices) to deepen their interpretation of symbolism.
Mathematics	General Education	CCSS.MATH.CONTENT.HSF. IF.C.7: Graph functions expressed symbolically and show key features.	During graphing activities, students identify "hits" (accurate plots of critical points) and create "hot spots" by categorizing graphs based on features such as maxima, minima, and symmetry.
	AP Calculus AB	AP Calculus AB CED: Analyze functions and their derivatives to solve problems.	In analyzing function behaviors, students identify "hits" (accurate derivative interpretations) and group "hot spots" (related problem types, like optimization or rate of change).
Science	General Education	NGSS.HS-PS1-1: Use models to predict relationships between systems or components.	Students evaluate a chemical reaction and identify "hits" (key observations, like temperature changes), then group "hot spots" (clusters of related trends, such as energy transfer).
	AP Biology	AP Biology CED: Explain cellular processes, such as energy transfer, using data and models.	During a photosynthesis lab, students identify "hits" (data trends like increased oxygen output) and organize "hot spots" (clusters related to light intensity or temperature effects).

(Continued)

Table 8.1 (Continued)

Subject	Course Type	Standard Being Addressed	Activity Example Using Hits and Hot Spots
History/Social Studies	General Education	CCSS.ELA-LITERACY. RH.11-12.6: Evaluate differing perspectives on a historical event.	Students identify "hits" (prominent perspectives in Civil Rights Movement sources) and organize "hot spots" by clustering them into broader themes like economic or social equality.
	AP US History	AP US History CED: Develop an argument supported by historical evidence.	While reviewing DBQs, students pick "hits" (strong primary source evidence) and create "hot spots" by grouping sources supporting similar arguments or themes.
World Languages	General Education	ACTFL Standard: Presentational Communication: Write and present information on familiar topics.	In a group discussion, students identify "hits" (effective phrases and vocabulary used) and create "hot spots" (clusters of related expressions for themes like family or school life).
	AP Spanish Language	AP Spanish Language CED: Make comparisons between cultural practices, products, and perspectives.	Students identify "hits" (specific cultural examples) in their essays, then cluster "hot spots" by comparing products, practices, or perspectives from the target culture to their own.
Art	General Education	National Core Arts Standards: VA:Cr3.1.HSI: Apply criteria to evaluate and refine artistic work.	Students critique class projects, identifying "hits" (successful elements like perspective or color use) and categorizing "hot spots" (recurring themes or areas needing adjustment).
Computer Science	AP Computer Science A	AP CS A CED: Implement algorithms in a program and evaluate correctness.	During debugging, students identify "hits" (working sections of code) and cluster "hot spots" (problematic sections needing optimization or troubleshooting).

Talent Show will be the most fun with people laughing, dancing, clapping, and working to support others. It would earn four points for beating all of the others. Next, students will pair Community Service against the remaining three, then Movie Night against the remaining two until all have matched up against each other in the category for the activities the students think will be the most fun.

Table 8.2 includes each comparison and each category. Students can work individually or in small groups to make their decisions. Each category must be carefully considered because the details will matter for how the club is organized or designed. For instance, the cost factor for the book club could vary depending on how students will access the book – online free copy, paperback copy, or hardback copy. This also will happen with the game tournament. Will the games need to be purchased? Are they items the school already owns?

Table 8.2 Paired Comparison Analysis Matrix for School Activities

	Entertaining	Number of Students	Positive Effects	Cost
Talent Show (TS) vs. Community Service (CS)	TS	TS	CS	CS
Talent Show (TS) vs. Movie Night (MN)	TS	MN	TS	TS
Talent Show (TS) vs. Game Tournament (GT)	TS	TS	TS	TS
Talent Show (TS) vs. Book Club (BC)	TS	TS	BC	TS
Community Service (CS) vs. Movie Night (MN)	MN	MN	CS	CS
Community Service (CS) vs. Game Tournament (GT)	GT	CS	CS	CS
Community Service (CS) vs. Book Club (BC)	BC	CS	BC	CS
Movie Night (MN) vs. Game Tournament (GT)	GT	MN	GT	MN
Movie Night (MN) vs. Book Club (BC)	BC	MN	BC	MN
Game Tournament (GT) vs. Book Club (BC)	BC	BC	BC	BC

Total Points

Talent Show: 12 points
Community Service: 9 points
Book Club: 9 points
Movie Night: 7 points

By using the Paired Comparison Analysis Matrix, students are able to evaluate each option and gather data in order to quantify their final decision. The process encourages engagement and informed decision-making. If there is still debate about the solution, students might consider changing their evaluation factors to meet the needs of what the group is hoping to accomplish.

STRATEGY: ALOU

The ALoU strategy is a technique that involves assessing the **A**dvantages, **L**imitations, ways to **O**vercome Limitations, and **U**nique qualities of an idea (Isaksen, Dorval, & Treffinger, 1994). It allows for the reviewer to analyze the positive aspects, areas that will need to be addressed along with ways to do so, and the distinctive aspects in order to enhance them (Treffinger, 2007). The following lesson plan describes how students can use ALoU in a middle school math classroom.

DESIGNING CANDY PACKAGES USING MATH CONCEPTS AND THE ALOU PROCESS

Grade Level: 7th – 9th Grade; **Subject**: Mathematics – Geometry (Surface Area and Volume); **Duration**: 3–4 class periods (45–60 minutes each); **Objectives**: Students will solve real-world mathematical problems involving area, volume, and surface area of 2- and 3-dimensional objects. They will use formulas for cones, cylinders, and spheres. Students will use the ALoU process to assess and improve their packaging designs.
Materials Needed: Graph paper, plain paper, rulers, scissors, tape, glue, calculators, colored pencils or markers, example packaging (e.g., candy boxes, tubes, and bags), computer access (optional, for digital design), worksheets for calculating surface area and volume of 3D shapes.

Introduction (10 min)

Begin by showing different types of candy packages (boxes, cylinders, bags) and ask students to describe what makes each package unique. Explain that they will be designing their own candy package using math concepts to ensure it is functional, attractive, and efficient.

Lesson on Surface Area and Volume (20 min)

Review formulas for calculating surface area and volume of different 3D shapes:

Rectangular Prism:

Volume $= l \times w \times h$ Surface Area $= 2lw + 2lh + 2wh$

Cylinder:

Volume $= \pi r^2 h$ Surface Area $= 2\pi r(h + r)$

Provide a few practice problems to ensure understanding.

Brainstorm Design Ideas (15 min)

In pairs or small groups, have students start brainstorming ideas for their candy package designs. Encourage them to think about the shape of their package, the type of candy it will hold, and how it should be structured.

Initial Design and Calculations (35 min)

Students start by sketching their package design on graph paper. They will choose a shape (e.g., rectangular prism, cylinder, etc.) and determine the dimensions. Students will calculate the volume of their package to ensure it is appropriately sized for their candy product. Next, they will calculate the surface area to determine how much packaging material would be needed. Students will finish the initial design sketches and calculations for surface area and volume and prepare to present their designs and calculations to the class in the next session.

Introduction to ALoU (15 min)

Explain the **ALoU** process and how it can be used to assess their designs.

1. **Advantages**: What is good about the design?
2. **Limitations**: What are the possible drawbacks or challenges?
3. **Overcoming Limitations**: How can the design be improved to address these challenges?
4. **Unique Features**: What makes the design stand out?

Applying ALoU to Design (20 min)

In pairs or small groups, students will present their designs to each other. Each group will evaluate the designs using the ALoU process, discussing the advantages and limitations, brainstorming ways to improve the designs, and identifying any unique features that could be enhanced. Students should take notes on feedback and suggestions.

Student's Package Idea Example

The student designed a cylindrical package for a new type of chocolate-covered almonds. The package is tall and slim, with a colorful design and a clear plastic window on the side to see the candy inside.

ALoU Feedback

1. **Advantages**:
   a. **Attractive Design**: The cylindrical shape is sleek and visually appealing, which might make the product stand out on store shelves. The colorful design with a clear window allows customers to see the product, which can attract buyers.
   b. **Compact and Portable**: The package is easy to hold and can fit in a backpack or purse, making it convenient for on-the-go snacking.
   c. **Efficient Use of Material**: The cylindrical shape provides a good balance between surface area and volume, which means less material is needed compared to a rectangular box for the same volume.
2. **Limitations**:
   a. **Stability Issues**: Since the package is tall and slim, it might tip over easily, especially when there is less candy inside.
   b. **Limited Volume**: The narrow design limits how many almonds can fit inside, which might not be ideal for customers who want more product.
   c. **Plastic Window Concerns**: The clear plastic window is a nice feature, but it adds extra material, which might increase costs and be less eco-friendly.
3. **Overcoming Limitations**:
   a. **Stability**: Consider widening the base of the package slightly or adding a small, flat ring at the bottom to make it more stable. This would help prevent it from tipping over.
   b. **Volume**: If the package needs to hold more almonds, you could either make the cylinder slightly wider or offer two size options – a small and

        a larger version.

    c. **Eco-Friendly Alternative**: Explore the possibility of using a bio-degradable or recyclable material for the clear window, or consider eliminating it and printing an image of the almonds instead.

4. **Unique Features**:

    a. **Clear Window**: The window is a great way for customers to see the product and feel more confident about their purchase.

    b. **Colorful, Bold Graphics**: The vibrant design makes the product eye-catching and easy to recognize.

    c. **Tall, Slim Design**: The unique shape differentiates it from typical candy boxes or bags, making it stand out.

Redesign Based on Feedback (15 min)

Students return to their designs and make adjustments based on the feedback from the ALoU assessment. Encourage them to recalculate surface area and volume if their designs change significantly.

Final Design Adjustments (60 min)

Allow students a short period to finish any adjustments to their designs and calculations.

Presentations (25 min)

Each student (or group) will present their final candy package design, including:

1. Sketches and calculations (surface area and volume).
2. How they used the ALoU process to improve their design.
3. Any unique features or elements that make their design effective or attractive.

Reflection and Wrap-Up (10 min)

As a class, discuss what students learned from the design process and how math concepts like surface area and volume are used in real-world scenarios. Reflect on the importance of feedback (as used in the ALoU process) in improving a design.

SOCIAL AND EMOTIONAL WELL-BEING

These evaluation strategies can also be used when seeking out ideas and potential solutions to social and emotional issues students might be facing. By teaching the technique explicitly and using it frequently with students, they can learn to use the technique themselves to assess their ideas. Establishing personal goals can set the foundation. For example, students can consider ways for managing anxiety using the ALoU method by helping individuals assess their thoughts, strategies, and coping mechanisms in a structured way. Here is how it can be applied.

ALOU ASSESSMENT: MINDFULNESS FOR ANXIETY

After working with children on mindfulness techniques, it can be advantageous to allow them time to evaluate the process in order to consider strengths and weaknesses of the approaches so that they can continue to gain results.

Step One: Consider Advantages

Focus: Identify what is working well with the use of mindfulness techniques.
  Guiding Questions:
  What benefits has the student noticed from practicing mindfulness?
  How does mindfulness help in managing anxiety?
  Example:
  "The student feels more relaxed and focused after practicing mindfulness exercises like deep breathing and guided meditation."
  "Mindfulness helps them calm down quickly when they start to feel anxious, especially before exams or class presentations."

Step Two: Consider Limitations

Focus: Consider any challenges or drawbacks to the student's current mindfulness practice.
  Guiding Questions:
  Are there times when mindfulness doesn't seem to help?
  What obstacles does the student face in using these techniques?
  Example:
  "The student struggles to stay focused during meditation, especially when their anxiety is very high."
  "Mindfulness exercises are harder to practice in noisy or distracting environments, like during school breaks or in crowded classrooms."

Step Three: Consider Opportunities

Focus: Look for areas where mindfulness practice can be improved or expanded.
  Guiding Questions:
  What new mindfulness strategies could the student try?

How can the student make their practice more consistent or effective?

Example:

"The student could try shorter, more frequent mindfulness sessions throughout the day to maintain a sense of calm."

"Incorporating mindful movement (like yoga or stretching) might help on days when sitting still is challenging."

"Using mindfulness apps or guided meditations tailored for teens could offer more engaging, structured practices."

Step Four: Investigate Unique Considerations

Focus: Think about any personal factors that might affect the student's use of mindfulness techniques.

Guiding Questions:

Are there specific times or situations where mindfulness is particularly effective or ineffective?

Does the student have unique strengths or challenges that influence their ability to use mindfulness?

Example:

"The student's anxiety tends to peak in the mornings before school, so a quick mindfulness routine right after waking up might be especially beneficial."

"They are particularly sensitive to sound, so using noise-canceling headphones during meditation might improve their focus."

CHALLENGES IN THE EVALUATION PROCESS

When using evaluation techniques in the creative process, it is crucial to consider potential issues that may arise. One challenge is the possibility of favoritism when evaluating ideas within a group setting. This can lead to certain individuals' ideas being prioritized over others, potentially discouraging participation or stifling diverse perspectives. Additionally, resistance to new ideas can emerge, especially if group members are reluctant to accept unconventional approaches. These dynamics can hinder the free flow of creative thought and limit the potential for innovation.

Another concern is ensuring a proper balance between evaluation and creativity. While evaluation plays a key role in assessing the feasibility and quality of ideas, it should not overshadow the creative process itself. If the evaluation process is too rigid or premature, it can suppress the generation of bold, out-of-the-box ideas that are essential for creativity. Therefore, it is important that evaluation occurs at the right stage, after creative ideas have had the opportunity to develop.

At the same time, evaluation serves an essential function in balancing creativity with real-world constraints. Creativity is often about imagining possibilities that break free from traditional norms, but these ideas must be realistic and workable in practical contexts. Evaluation provides the necessary feedback to guide ideas toward solutions that are not only innovative but also viable. Without evaluation, ideas might remain disconnected from real-world applications, limiting their impact.

Maintaining a balance between evaluation and creativity is key to achieving productive outcomes in the creative process. Evaluation should be used strategically to refine ideas without stifling the creative exploration that precedes it. By addressing issues like favoritism and resistance to new ideas, and ensuring evaluation supports, rather than restricts, creativity, individuals and teams can develop innovative and practical solutions.

Spotlight: Inventors Under 18

Neil Deshmukh, a teenage inventor from Pennsylvania, has earned recognition for his groundbreaking work in artificial intelligence and its applications to solve global challenges. His journey into innovation began at age 14 when he built a device to distinguish between his face and his brother's, unlocking his door only for him – a clever way to keep his younger sibling out of his room and away from his Nintendo DS. This early invention showcased Neil's knack for problem solving and his ability to turn everyday frustrations into creative solutions.

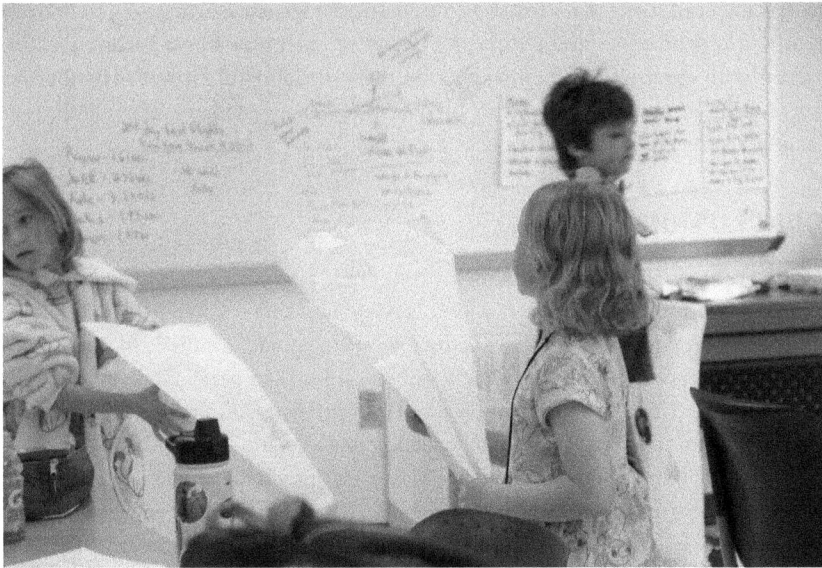

Figure 8.2 Students Evaluate Prototypes of their Airplane Designs during Rocket to Creativity at Western Carolina University.

Since then, he has expanded his focus to address larger societal issues, including agriculture and accessibility, through AI-powered tools. One of his most notable inventions is "PlantumAI", an app designed to diagnose plant diseases and provide farmers with real-time solutions. Inspired by the struggles of farmers in rural India, this tool uses AI to analyze plant images and offer actionable insights, helping farmers improve productivity and reduce losses.

Neil's ingenuity extends beyond agriculture. He also developed "Vibe", an AI-based app designed to assist individuals with visual or hearing impairments. By leveraging machine learning, the app interprets audio and visual input to provide real-time descriptions of the user's surroundings. This empowers people with disabilities to navigate their environments with greater independence. Both inventions reflect Neil's commitment to using technology to create inclusive and impactful solutions, demonstrating his belief in addressing societal needs through innovation.

What makes Neil's approach particularly remarkable is his emphasis on accessibility. He ensured that his tools are affordable and functional even in areas with limited internet connectivity, incorporating offline capabilities to serve users in remote locations. This attention to detail highlights his deep understanding of the challenges faced by underserved communities, as well as his determination to design solutions that are both practical and scalable.

Neil's work has earned him numerous accolades, including recognition from institutions like MIT and the Lemelson-MIT Program. As a high school student, he has inspired many with his ability to harness advanced technology to address real-world problems. Neil's story is a powerful example of how technical skills, paired with creativity and empathy, can drive meaningful change. His journey serves as an inspiration for aspiring inventors and changemakers, proving that age is no barrier to innovation.

CONCLUSION

Using evaluation strategies provides a systematic approach to assessing ideas and solutions, offering a structured way to review and refine concepts. By applying clear criteria, these methods help reduce subjectivity and minimize bias, ensuring that all ideas are considered on their merits rather than personal preferences or assumptions. This impartial approach promotes fairness in decision-making and supports the development of strong, well-rounded solutions.

When students collaborate and evaluate each other's ideas, they create a space for open dialogue and constructive feedback. This collaborative process encourages a diversity of perspectives and ensures that all voices are heard. Through the exchange of ideas, students can refine their thinking, challenge assumptions, and explore alternative solutions they might not have considered on their own.

The act of sharing and evaluating ideas fosters a more inclusive and participatory learning environment.

The evaluation process can be a catalyst for innovation and creative problem solving. As students critically assess each other's ideas, they are prompted to think more deeply and develop more effective solutions. By continuously evaluating and refining their work, students can identify weaknesses, improve their concepts, and ultimately produce more creative and functional outcomes. This iterative process encourages students to view challenges as opportunities for growth, enhancing their critical thinking and problem-solving abilities.

REFERENCES

Boldt, G. (2019). Artistic creativity beyond divergent thinking: Analysing sequences in creative subprocesses. *Thinking Skills and Creativity*, *34*, 100606. https://doi.org/10.1016/j.tsc.2019.100606

Cummiskey, B.M. (2021). *Process information and creative mindsets: An examination of their role in the evaluation of creativity* (Order No. 28963223). Available from ProQuest Central. (2621038319). Retrieved from https://www.proquest.com/dissertations-theses/process-information-creative-mindsets-examination/docview/2621038319/se-2

Dweck, C.S. (2006). *Mindset: The new psychology of success* (1st ed.). New York, NY: Random House.

Firestien, R.L., & Treffinger, D.J. (1983). Creative problem solving: Guidelines and resources for effective facilitation. *Gifted Child Today*, *6*(1), 2–10. https://doi.org/10.1177/107621758300600101

Isaksen, S., Dorval, K., & Treffinger, D. (1994). *Creative approaches to problem solving.* Dubuque, Iowa: Kendall/Hunt.

Karwowski, M. (2014). Creative mindsets: Measurement, correlates, consequences. *Psychology of Aesthetics, Creativity, and the Arts*, *8*(1), 62–70. https://doi.org/10.1037/a0034898

Treffinger, D.J. (2007). Creative Problem Solving (CPS): Powerful tools for managing change and developing talent. *Gifted and Talented International*, *22*(2), 8–18.

Chapter 9

Instructional Practices that Promote Opportunities for Creative and Critical Thinking Skills

INTRODUCTION

Inquiry-based instruction encourages students to pursue individual research driven by their own interests. In this approach, students choose a topic to investigate, while the teacher acts as a facilitator, guiding them through the learning process. Both Problem-Based Learning (PBL) and Project-Based Learning (PjBL) are closely connected to this method. In PBL, teachers present an open-ended problem for students to explore and assign them stakeholder roles to adopt during their investigation (Gallagher, 2012; Gallagher, 2015). In PjBL, students produce tangible projects to demonstrate what they have learned throughout a unit. Across all three methods, instructors provide structure through regular check-ins to ensure students develop a strong understanding of the topic.

Although Problem-Based Learning (PBL) and Project-Based Learning (PjBL) share similarities, each method has distinct characteristics (Benoit, 2000; BIE, n.d.; Esch, 1998; Hung, 2011). PBL begins with a problem that students must solve or explore, whereas PjBL starts with an envisioned end product or "artifact". The problems in PBL are intentionally unstructured to reflect the complexities of real-life situations, while PjBL focuses on a production model that mirrors real-world project creation. In PjBL, the final product drives the process, whereas in PBL, the defined problem serves as the central focus. While students in PBL present conclusions based on their problem solving, they do not always create a tangible product. In contrast, PjBL emphasizes the skills and knowledge gained during the creation process, which are crucial for completing the final product successfully.

Both PBL and PjBL are forms of inquiry-based learning, rooted in constructivist theories developed by Piaget, Dewey, and Vygotsky (Dewey, 1997; Ginsburg & Opper, 1987; Vygotsky, 1962). Inquiry learning involves generating questions, conducting research to address those questions, analyzing data, and developing potential solutions (Bell, Urhahne, Schanze, & Ploetzner, 2010; Wilhelm

        DOI: 10.4324/9781003434221-9

& Wilhelm, 2010). In both PBL and PjBL, teachers act as facilitators or coaches rather than providers of information. With guidance from the teacher, students select authentic problems or challenges, research them, and collaborate on solutions for real-world audiences over an extended time frame (Barron & Darling-Hammond, 2008; BIE, n.d.; Savery, 2006; Thomas, 2000). This approach integrates the curriculum across subject areas, enabling students to acquire cross-disciplinary skills and apply knowledge flexibly (Papert, 2001).

A critical component of both methods is student choice, which boosts motivation as students plan their learning and organize their research to solve real-world problems (Bell, 2010). This process helps students build essential 21st-century skills, including problem solving, information evaluation, effective collaboration, technology use, and the creation of innovative ideas and products (Bell, 2010; BIE, n.d.; Darling-Hammond, 2010; The Secretary's Commission on Achieving Necessary Skills, 1991; Wagner, 2012; Zhao, 2012). Moreover, PBL and PjBL foster deeper learning, incorporating content mastery, critical thinking, communication, self-direction, and academic perseverance (Hewlett Foundation, n.d.). Students are more likely to retain knowledge when they are engaged and see its real-world applications. Additionally, fostering growth mindsets – where students believe in their abilities and persist through challenges – further enhances their learning outcomes (Dweck, Walton, & Cohen, 2014; Farrington, 2013).

As teaching strategies evolve, so do teacher-student dynamics. Teachers in various studies reported that using PBL and PjBL led to more positive classroom climates and stronger relationships with students. These findings align with research on inquiry-based learning, which promotes student-centered instruction, cooperation, and interdependence. For instance, Haney, Jing, Keil, and Zoffel (2007) found that implementing PBL in environmental science classrooms over two years improved both classroom climate and teacher-student relationships. Similarly, Johnson and Johnson (2009) documented substantial evidence that educational practices like PBL and PjBL, which emphasize peer interdependence, positively influence student effort, interpersonal relationships, and psychological well-being.

PROJECT-BASED LEARNING (PJBL)

Project-Based Learning (PjBL) is a process that allows students to design projects to accompany a task or assignment. The project can be situated so that it runs throughout a unit of study or one that is launched to demonstrate understanding toward the end of the project. The products are often real-world in nature so that they can be presented to an authentic audience, but they might also be fanciful and playful, intended to demonstrate understanding through unique avenues. At its core, PjBL allows for hands-on learning where students are active and engaged, while demonstrating critical thinking.

PjBL is situated at the top of Bloom's Taxonomy, where participants are creating or designing based on a complex challenge. The six levels of Bloom's include: Remember, understand, apply, analyze, evaluate, and create. PjBL allows students to have ownership of their learning depending on how the instructor designs the process. Students can be offered choices with the topic, product, process, or presentation style. In addition, instructors can include collaborative components or require interdisciplinary aspects combining various subject areas to help students make connections between topics.

Example of PjBL

The following example of a Project-Based Learning (PjBL) project is geared toward middle school students across different subject areas. The project integrates information throughout the learning process, allowing students to build knowledge progressively and apply it meaningfully.

LIVING HISTORY: COMMUNITY STORIES PROJECT

For this project, students are given the objective to explore historical events and their impact by researching and recording stories from community members. The core assignment is to document a historical event. Students first brainstorm historical events such as local civil rights movements, immigration stories, or technological advances and decide the format for presenting the stories, such as podcast, video documentary, website, or written anthology. Students can choose to interview a relative or request assistance from the instructor. Local retirement communities can be a great resource, especially if the instructor implements this project on a yearly basis.

Before launching the project, students will conduct research about the historical time period, documenting the causes and effects of the historical event. It can be beneficial to also assess the prior causes and further effects. Using a graphic organizer can help students document their ideas. The instructor can provide lessons on research methods, historical inquiry, and interviewing techniques. After conducting interviews, students will create their final products and share them at the retirement community.

Problem-Based Learning (PBL)

Problem-Based Learning (PBL) is a learner-centered approach where students are given a complex problem that serves as the foundation for investigating a topic of study. Typically, the problems are real-world in nature. The approach requires students to apply knowledge in practical ways, seek out information to answer questions, and problem solve using information gained throughout the learning experience. Instructional support is provided at stages throughout the process or at specific intervals when students demonstrate the need for specific mini-lessons to cover key topics. The experience is typically built on student interests and experiences, where a variety of answers are encouraged. The instructor serves as a facilitator during the process, allowing the students to take ownership of their learning. Teachers provide resources and guidance.

The process typically follows several stages, which help guide students through inquiry and discovery beginning with the presentation of the problem. Next, students analyze the problem and identify issues associated with the topic, what they will need to know, and what they will want to learn. Afterward, students conduct research. This may involve contacting experts about the topic or conducting interviews with those who can provide support or insights. Students will design a solution to the problem based on their research, present their findings, and reflect upon the learning objectives.

PBL Example – Designing Delivery Box Packaging: A Real-World Math Project

This project engages middle school students in applying math concepts to a practical challenge of redesigning delivery box packaging to be more efficient, cost-effective, and sustainable. Students will assume the role of product designers tasked with redesigning the packaging for materials shipped to houses.

STANDARDS ADDRESSED

Geometry

- Understand and calculate the surface area and volume of 3D shapes.
- Identify and use properties of geometric shapes to solve design problems.
- Apply concepts of scale and proportion to design.

Measurement and Data

- Convert units of measurement (e.g., square inches to square centimeters).
- Analyze and interpret data related to material use and environmental impact.

Expressions and Equations

- Write and solve equations to calculate costs and optimize designs.
- Use ratios and percentages to analyze packaging efficiency.

173

Problem Solving and Reasoning

- Apply problem-solving skills to real-world scenarios.
- Use logical reasoning to evaluate the feasibility of designs.

Students begin by analyzing the dimensions and materials of existing packaging by calculating its surface area, volume, and space efficiency. Students identify problems as they discuss the weaknesses of current packaging in terms of wasted space, excessive material, or unappealing design. Next, they brainstorm new designs and explore different shapes, such as cylinders, prisms, or hexagons.

Next, they use geometry to calculate and compare the efficiency of their proposed designs. They will need to calculate the surface area and volume of their proposed designs to ensure products will fit efficiently. Students can research the environmental impact of various materials such as plastic, cardboard, or biodegradable materials. The instructor can assign costs for materials, and through cost analysis, students determine the financial impact of their packaging materials. In addition, they can explore environmentally friendly options and incorporate sustainability into their solutions. They will compare their designs to the original packaging using ratios to determine space efficiency and cost.

Once the designs are finalized, students create prototypes using physical materials such as cardstock and cardboard, or 3D modeling software to create prototypes of their new packaging. They will label their prototypes with dimensions, material costs, and space efficiency calculations. The project culminates in presentations where students showcase their designs and mathematical calculations. Students will present their designs to the class or a panel acting as the shipping company's leadership team.

ASSESSMENT CRITERIA

Extensions

- **Interdisciplinary Connection**: Collaborate with an art class to create a marketing campaign for the new packaging.
- **Technology Integration**: Use software like Tinkercad or Canva to create digital designs.
- **Community Engagement**: Partner with a local business or organization to present their designs and receive feedback.

Table 9.1 Criteria for Assessing Math and Design for Shipping Product Package

Category	Points	Description
Mathematical Accuracy	20	Correct calculations of surface area, volume, and cost.
Design Feasibility	20	The proposed design is functional, realistic, and meets the project goals.
Creativity	15	Innovative and original ideas for the new packaging.
Sustainability	15	Demonstrated effort to consider environmental impact and use sustainable materials.
Presentation Quality	20	Clear and professional explanation of the design process, supported by calculations and visual aids.
Reflection	10	Thoughtful discussion of challenges, successes, and connections between math and design.

COMPARING PROJECT-BASED LEARNING (PJBL) AND PROBLEM-BASED LEARNING (PBL)

The main distinction between **PjBL** and **PBL** is that **PjBL** revolves around producing a final product (e.g., models, presentations, or campaigns), while **PBL** centers on solving a real-world problem through inquiry and exploration. Both methods encourage collaboration, critical thinking, and real-world application, but their starting points and end goals differ. See Table 9.2 for PBL/PjBL Comparisons.

CREATIVE PROBLEM SOLVING (CPS)

Creative Problem Solving (CPS) is a structured approach emphasizing creativity and critical thinking to find innovative solutions to problems. First designed by Dr. Alex F. Osborn in the 1940s and elaborated upon by Dr. Sidney J. Parnes in the 1950s, it is a precursor to many methods used in business today. The process enables individuals or groups to consider various perspectives to create or design original ideas and products. The model is represented in several different formats, but all address the following four stages: Clarify, ideate, develop, and implement.

During the initial stage, the goal is to understand the task or problem. Individuals seek clarity about the problem or task while seeking resources, collecting data, and posing questions to explore. Next, they move to idea generation where open-mindedness is emphasized, and the goal is to gather a multitude of potential ideas. This is not a place to seek solutions. In the next stage, development, an idea is chosen for investigation to seek further elaboration.

Table 9.2 Comparisons between PjBL and PBL

Aspect	Project-Based Learning (PjBL)	Problem-Based Learning (PBL)
1. Environmental Awareness	**PjBL Example:** Students create a public awareness campaign, including posters and videos, to reduce single-use plastics.	**PBL Example:** Students explore the question, "What are the main barriers to reducing plastic waste in our community?"
2. Historical Research	**PjBL Example:** Students create a museum exhibit showcasing artifacts and stories from the Civil Rights Movement.	**PBL Example:** Students investigate, "Why did certain events in the Civil Rights Movement spark national change?"
3. Community Improvement	**PjBL Example:** Students design a blueprint for a new community park, including landscaping and features.	**PBL Example:** Students address, "What challenges prevent people in our community from accessing outdoor spaces?"
4. Engineering Challenge	**PjBL Example:** Students build a model bridge and test it for strength using specific engineering constraints.	**PBL Example:** Students investigate, "Why do some bridges collapse, and how can we design safer structures?"
5. Health Education	**PjBL Example:** Students create an informational brochure to teach peers about the benefits of healthy eating.	**PBL Example:** Students explore, "Why is there a rise in childhood obesity, and how can we address it?"
6. Space Exploration	**PjBL Example:** Students design a 3D model of a Mars colony that could support human life.	**PBL Example:** Students investigate, "What are the biggest challenges to sustaining life on Mars?"
7. Business and Economics	**PjBL Example:** Students create and pitch a business plan for a fictional company, including a budget and marketing strategy.	**PBL Example:** Students analyze, "Why do some small businesses fail while others succeed?"
8. Literature and Storytelling	**PjBL Example:** Students write and publish a book of short stories inspired by classic fairy tales.	**PBL Example:** Students explore, "What elements of a story make it timeless across different cultures?"

(*Continued*)

Table 9.2 (Continued)

Aspect	Project-Based Learning (PjBL)	Problem-Based Learning (PBL)
9. Renewable Energy	**PjBL Example:** Students construct a working wind turbine model and present their findings about its efficiency.	**PBL Example:** Students investigate, "What factors affect the adoption of renewable energy sources in rural areas?"
10. Local History	**PjBL Example:** Students create a walking tour of historic landmarks in their town, complete with maps and recorded narrations.	**PBL Example:** Students address, "How can we preserve the history of our town while making room for modernization?"

There is an emphasis at this stage to look for opportunities to improve, not negate the concept. In the final realm, implementation, the steps for making the plan a reality are put into place, including resources and responsibilities.

The process requires a combination of both divergent thinking, where a number of ideas and solutions are generated, as well as convergent thinking, where individuals narrow down ideas to identify a solution and support that solution with scaffolding to make sure it is effective and can be implemented. Allowing students to problem solve using the CPS process can allow them to retain the steps for being a problem solver (Baer, 1988).

In the following example, students move through the CPS process to create an inclusive school sports program. The teacher provides the overall objective that the program should include students of all abilities, backgrounds, and interests, promoting a culture of acceptance, teamwork, and physical well-being.

This CPS model encourages students to design an inclusive sports program that respects diverse interests and abilities, promoting community and physical activity within a supportive school environment. The CPS process can be used by children to explore innovation and critical thinking. It can be a powerful process for community groups and organizations to address local issues or social needs. On a personal level, individuals can find this process beneficial as they problem-solve personal issues and make informed decisions in their lives. See Table 9.3 for CPS examples.

GENIUS HOUR

Inquiry-based instruction serves as the foundation for educational programs like Genius Hour, Passion Projects, and 20% Time, which have gained popularity in recent years (Krebs & Zvi, 2016). These initiatives encourage educators to allocate dedicated class time for students to engage in research on self-selected topics (Katrein, 2016; Krebs & Zvi, 2016; Rush, 2015; Simos, 2015). During

Table 9.3 Steps for the Creative Problem Solving Process

Stage	Steps	Examples of Solutions
Clarify the Problem	– **Define the Challenge**: Explore what inclusivity means in school sports. Discuss questions like, "What barriers prevent some students from participating in sports?", and "Why do students opt out or feel excluded?". – **Research Existing Programs**: Examine current school sports programs through interviews, discussions with teachers, and data review. – **Identify Key Needs**: Create a list of needs for excluded groups (e.g., students with disabilities, beginners, or those preferring non-competitive activities).	– Interview students to understand reasons for non-participation, such as lack of interest, physical limitations, or fear of judgment.
Generate Ideas	– **Brainstorm Solutions**: Facilitate brainstorming for inclusive sports activities, such as: – Teams focused on fun, not competition. – Mixed-ability teams with mentorship. – A variety of activities, including non-traditional games or fitness classes. – **Encourage Diverse Thinking**: Use prompts like, "What if everyone had a place in sports?". – **Prioritize Ideas**: Vote on ideas with the greatest potential and feasibility.	– Brainstorm a variety of activities catering to different interests, like team sports, individual challenges, or creative movement classes.
Develop Solutions	– **Select Top Ideas**: Choose 2–3 solutions for deeper exploration. – **Create Prototypes/Designs**: Develop detailed blueprints for programs like: – Unified sports programs with mixed-ability teams. – Non-traditional events (e.g., dodgeball tournaments, dance challenges). – Inclusive fitness classes. – **Map Logistics**: Consider resources, obstacles, and create checklists for implementation.	– Create an outline for an "Activity Sampler" where students try various sports weekly to discover their interests.

(Continued)

Table 9.3 (Continued)

Stage	Steps	Examples of Solutions
Implement Solutions	– **Develop an Action Plan**: Outline steps, assign roles, and set a timeline. – **Promotion and Awareness**: Plan campaigns like posters, announcements, or classroom presentations. – **Recruitment Strategies**: Encourage participation via open sign-ups or partnerships. – **Training for Coaches**: Provide workshops on inclusivity. – **Launch a Pilot**: Propose a small-scale activity for feedback and adjustments.	– Assign a schedule for a pilot "Inclusive Game Day" with low-stakes, fun games open to everyone.
Evaluate Outcomes	– **Gather Feedback**: Collect participant and facilitator input through surveys or interviews. – **Analyze Participation Data**: Use metrics (e.g., participation rates, attendance) to evaluate success. – **Reflect and Adjust**: Based on feedback, make changes (e.g., adjust times, add activities, or provide extra support). – **Share Results**: Present outcomes, lessons, and recommendations. Plan for sustainability with committees or funding proposals.	– Survey participants after an event for feedback and suggestions, then adjust the program as needed. – Use data to refine and expand the initiative.

this process, students gather information from multiple sources, analyze their findings, and create a final product to demonstrate their learning.

Genius Hour typically consists of a designated period during the school week (often one hour) where students can engage in self-directed projects that foster creativity, innovation, and independent learning. This concept is inspired by Google's "20% time" initiative, where employees were encouraged to spend a portion of their workweek on projects they are passionate about pursuing. Students choose a topic, conduct research, create meaningful products, and give presentations at the culmination of the project.

Several components contribute to the effectiveness of Genius Hour, including student choice, which provides autonomy, offering the opportunity to increase motivation and engagement. Students can express themselves, experiment, take risks, and innovate beyond what is typically allowed in traditional classroom environments. Throughout the process, students are asked to reflect on the process and identify where they need support to complete the project. At the end of the Genius Hour project, students often present their findings or creations to their peers, teachers, or even the broader community. This aspect enhances communication skills and builds confidence.

The Genius Hour process typically involves several stages. First, students select a topic or question they are passionate about investigating. This can be anything from exploring a hobby, solving a community problem, or investigating a scientific phenomenon.

The following is a list of driving questions (Doss, 2018) from a 13-week Genius Hour project conducted in an 8th grade classroom.

Driving Question / Project Description

- How do you build a house?
- How can I create a two-dimensional platform (video game)?
- What type of instrument do people enjoy the most after listening to the chorus of a song on each one?
- How can I create videos for a YouTube channel?
- What causes sleep disorders?
- How do you design an animation?
- How can I learn Greco-Roman style wrestling?
- How can I learn to play a song on the guitar?
- How do head injuries impact the brain and personality?
- How can I create a better habitat for my pet bird?
- How can I help others in need?
- Is climate change real?
- How can I create an app about football teams?
- What is the best airplane design?
- Which coconut water is the best?
- How can I design something using aeronautical engineering?
- What benefits are there to knitting?
- What is the Mandela Effect (alternative universes and time travel)?
- How is power balanced in our government?
- Is dance a sport?
- How can we improve the environment?
- How can we improve public schools?
- How can I design and market my artwork-inspirational Bible quotes on canvases?
- How can I learn about graphic design?
- How can I write a short story about the human mind?
- How can I learn to take professional-style pictures?
- Why were Burr and Hamilton enemies?

- Is Common Core Math better than prior math methods?
- How can I create my own cook book?
- How do I launch my own YouTube channel?

The next stage involves the students planning their process, which includes conducting interviews and gathering research. Creating a timeline can help to provide structure. Students will develop a product throughout the unit, which can be a presentation, a physical prototype, a video, a performance, or a written report. For example, the student exploring climate change might build a small solar-powered device or create an informative video explaining the benefits of renewable energy.

Throughout the process, students reflect on their learning experience, discussing what they are discovering, the challenges they encounter, and how they are overcoming them. The instructor can conduct surveys to monitor the students' experiences. The following are examples of questions that can be used throughout the process (Doss, 2018).

Genius Hour Survey Questions:

1. How well do you understand the Genius Hour Project?
2. How many high-quality, reliable, helpful resources do you have?
3. How well do you understand what makes a source high quality, reliable, and helpful?
4. Where do you get your sources?
5. Do you understand what a database is?
6. Do you have notes (from sources) that are helping you to answer your driving questions?
7. Do you know exactly what you are working towards doing/learning/creating?
8. What are you working towards (what is your product, outcome, impact)?
9. What will your digital element be? Check all options that you are interested in using during this process. (Google Form, Prezi, Google Slides, YouTube, Pictochart/Other Infographics, Haiku Deck, other.)
10. Do you have a clear, solid plan for how to present your final project?
11. Do you have a bibliography?
12. How creative do you believe your project is?
13. Have you encountered any challenges? What did you do to overcome them?
14. Have you experienced flow while working on your project? (Flow is a feeling of energized focus, full involvement, and enjoyment in the process of the activity.)
15. How well are you accepting feedback and willing to make adjustments as a result?
16. How much do you feel you are learning/growing as a result of Genius Hour?
17. What mini-lessons would be helpful to you at this stage? Check all that apply. (Creating a driving question, Using databases, Evaluating sources,

Note-taking, Making a bibliography, Using a specific digital tool, Writing skills, Presentation skills, Organization, Time Management, other.)
18. Any final questions? Comments? Concerns?

The final component should allow the students to showcase their products to an authentic audience. Inviting parents and community members offers the students the opportunity to demonstrate their learning and make connections that could be beneficial for the future.

Toward the end of the study, instructors can provide a lesson on how to complete an annotated bibliography and process paper. In the process paper, students can address the following questions:

1. How/why you created the driving question/project. How did you come up with your idea? What was your outcome/impact? Why was it important/interesting to you?
2. Explain your research process. What did you research? How did you find trustworthy, relevant, and useful sources? What did you learn about databases and bibliographies? What methods did you use to take notes and organize information? Did you collect any data?
3. Reflect on the obstacles, problems, and challenges you encountered. What parts of the process were the most difficult/confusing? What did you do when you felt stuck? Did you quit, adjust, change course, overcome, problem solve? Why? How?
4. Share your learning, insights, and the lasting effects. What lessons did you learn? How will this experience help you in the future? Consider academics as well as life lessons and skills.
5. Offer recommendations, suggestions, and advice to future 8th graders. How can you be successful? Consider what you would do differently or change about your own experience.

Genius Hour is an innovative educational practice that empowers students to explore their passions, develop critical skills, and engage in meaningful learning experiences. By providing a structured framework for self-directed inquiry, Genius Hour fosters creativity, independence, and a lifelong love of learning. Despite potential challenges, the benefits it offers in promoting student engagement and personalized learning make it a valuable addition to educational settings.

MAKERSPACES

Makerspaces are collaborative workspaces that provide students with the resources, tools, and environment to create, invent, and explore. These spaces can blend physical and digital tools depending on the intention of the instructors. The space can allow for open-ended experimentation or experiments with parameters that allow students to understand scientific concepts. Items can be purchased from companies or they can be collected as part of a school-wide recycling campaign. Technology components might include 3D printers, laser cutters, computers, and electronics. Recycled items might include crafting supplies, cardboard, paper, scissors, glue, tape, pens, pencils, safety pins, paint, markers, and other tangible products.

Makerspaces are designed to accommodate different types of projects and collaborative work, providing areas for individual work, group collaboration, and instruction. Instructors can provide mentors to help guide students through projects, help troubleshoot issues, and share knowledge. The process of engaging in a Makerspace typically involves several stages, beginning with brainstorming ideas or identifying problems to solve. This can be structured or unstructured depending on the overall objectives. For example, the task could be to design a product that could be marketed to peers, to create a prototype for a new type of plant watering system, or to design an item from a historical time period. Students can then sketch out their ideas, develop plans, and decide on the tools and materials they will need. They will need to spend time looking at items available in the Makerspace in order to create their design. This process often involves trial and error, experimentation, and iteration. The instructor might choose to focus on the role of feedback and a growth mindset during the different phases. They could also discuss the stages of creativity so that students can apply the process to other projects in the future. Next, they will need to assess how their products function or if improvements can be made to aesthetic aspects. The final component would be to share the results with others, such as parents, classes, or the community.

Makerspace experiences allow students to develop practical skills and deepen their understanding of concepts. They can provide an avenue for blending subjects together for interdisciplinary learning through STEAM (science, technology, engineering, art, and math) activities. In addition, students can learn from one another, share ideas, and collaborate on projects as they engage in problem solving.

EXAMPLES OF MAKERSPACE PROJECTS

- **Robotics**: Students design and build robots using kits or 3D-printed components, programming them to complete specific tasks or navigate obstacles.
- **Art and Design**: Users create artworks or crafts using various materials, such as woodworking, sewing, or digital design software.
- **Product Prototyping**: Students develop prototypes for products or solutions to real-world problems, such as creating a device to assist individuals with disabilities.
- **Community Projects**: Users collaborate on projects that benefit the community, such as building benches for public parks or creating educational resources for local schools.

183

DESIGN THINKING

Design thinking is a human-centered, iterative process used to solve complex problems and create innovative solutions. The foundation is built upon investigating the needs and experiences of users, which promotes empathy, creativity, and collaboration. The problem-solving process is used in businesses, by product designers, and for social innovations. The process is structured to develop solutions for complex, real-world challenges and problems.

Design thinking is human-centered with a focus on understanding the perspectives, emotions, and experiences of users. Rubenstein et al. (2019) found that when students assessed stakeholders' perspectives, they demonstrated more fluency and flexibility while producing more useful and original responses with more elaboration. Exploring perspectives encourages empathy as students investigate the underlying problems and needs. The process depends upon iteration with feedback and refinement of ideas through prototypes and testing. Examining diverse perspectives and collaborating with others are essential to the process.

The design thinking process typically consists of five stages, although these stages can be revisited and repeated as needed. Stage one involves the designer or student empathizing by conducting observations, interviews, or immersing themselves in the situation. The outcome is to understand the users' experiences, challenges, and desires. For stage two, the designer or student uses the insights gained from stage one to define the problem by synthesizing the information. They should be able to articulate a clear problem statement in a concise manner. Stage three involves brainstorming to generate a broad range of ideas. Fluency and flexibility activities can be beneficial for this stage. Stage four requires the designer or student to create a prototype. This can take the form of a model, sketch, or digital representation. These items should be low-fidelity. Fidelity refers to how much the prototype resembles the actual product, which includes visual characteristics, content, and the ability to interact with the product. Stage five includes testing the prototype for feedback, seeking out strengths and weaknesses in order to refine the product or solution.

EXAMPLES OF DESIGN THINKING FOR HIGH SCHOOL FOR MATH, ART, AND PE CLASSES

Math

Students will use mathematical concepts and skills to analyze a school system dilemma. They will collect data such as transition times, crowd density, or bottlenecks. They will create mathematical models to propose optimized schedules or processes. Instructors can require data analysis, graphing, charting, and the use of probability.

Art

Students will create public art that reflects their school or community identity. They will explore various techniques and cultural themes in order to develop aesthetic and practical skills. The goal is to encourage a growth mindset throughout the iterative process and show how art can convey shared values.

Physical Education

Students will design a personalized fitness challenge tailored to their peers' needs and preferences. Using technology like digital trackers, gamification, or even virtual reality, they will encourage sustained engagement in fitness. The overall goal of the project is to promote motivation for health and wellness. See Table 9.4 for the stages in the design thinking process.

Table 9.4 Stages in the Design Thinking Process

Stage	Math Example	Art Example	Physical Education Example
Empathize	Talk to students, teachers, and administrators to identify inefficiencies in the school's schedule (e.g., lunch lines, bus schedules, or class transitions).	Talk to peers and community members about how they connect with public art and how it can represent community values.	Interview students about challenges they face with staying motivated during physical education, such as lack of variety or fitness goals.
Define	Define the challenge: "How might we use math to optimize the school's schedule and improve daily efficiency?"	Define the challenge: "How might we create a mural or sculpture that reflects the identity of our school or community?"	Define the problem: "How might we design a personalized fitness challenge that keeps students engaged and motivated throughout the year?"
Ideate	Brainstorm solutions such as redesigning the bell schedule, creating a flowchart for traffic in hallways, or developing algorithms to reduce wait times in lunch lines.	Generate ideas for the mural or sculpture, including themes, colors, and placement. Explore styles that reflect community history or values.	Brainstorm engaging fitness ideas, such as gamified fitness programs, virtual reality (VR)-based workouts, or an interactive fitness scavenger hunt.

(Continued)

Table 9.4 (Continued)

Stage	Math Example	Art Example	Physical Education Example
Prototype	Build a mathematical model or use software to simulate the proposed schedule or traffic flow changes. Test the model with sample data.	Create a draft sketch of the mural or build a small model of the sculpture using clay or other materials.	Design the fitness challenge, including digital trackers, game rules, or VR mock-ups. Run a small trial with a few students.
Test	Test the redesigned schedule or traffic flow with feedback from peers and staff. Gather data on time savings or reduced bottlenecks.	Share the mural sketch or sculpture model with peers and community members to gather opinions and suggestions.	Implement the fitness challenge in a PE class or after-school program. Collect feedback on engagement, enjoyment, and fitness improvements.

PERSONALIZED LEARNING

Personalized learning involves student choice and voice through a differentiated instructional experience. It is an educational approach that tailors instruction, resources, and learning experiences to meet the individual needs, preferences, and interests of each student. This learner-centered model recognizes that students have diverse learning profiles and aims to provide customized pathways to enhance engagement and academic achievement.

Personalized learning involves learner agency where students set personal goals, select topics of interest, and choose pathways for the learning process or how they demonstrate their learning. There is dedication to tailored learning with the understanding that each student has individual needs, strengths, and challenges. Modifications can take the form of differentiated instruction and varied instructional techniques. The learning environment is often flexible, with opportunites for collaboration, exploration, and creativity. At some levels, there might be the opportunity for hybrid instruction, with some experiences taking place in-person and other aspects online. The instructor should offer timely feedback that is constructive and targets the next learning opportunity. In some cases, students might have a personalized learning plan to meet specific objectives.

Designing personalized learning experiences requires several steps beginning with a pre-assessment for not only content but also for personal interests and learning strategies. This can take the form of observations, interviews, surveys, and content assessments. Based on these results, students can work individually or in collaboration with the instructor to set learning goals. As is often suggested with goal-setting, these goals should be SMART (specific, measurable, achievable, relevant, and time-bound). The instructor can work with the student to help determine the pathway or the process by selecting appropriate activities and resources to help the student accomplish their goals. Students should be able to make decisions about this process, such as working independently or with others. The instructor can monitor progress and offer constructive feedback. When items need elucidation or reinforcement, the instructor can provide mini-lessons and exercises about important concepts. These check-ins can include evaluations, surveys, quizzes, or observations. Students can reflect upon their progress and make adjustments.

The goals for personalized learning are for students to increase engagement by providing the opportunity to pursue topics of interest. In addition, students can achieve at their own pace and make key decisions, allowing for self-directed learning. They can develop self-regulation and executive functioning skills as a result of the goal-setting process. This method provides the opportunity for equity and inclusion, as all abilities are included in the learning experiences. As a final benefit, instructors can build rapport with students as they create a team to design the learning experiences. See Table 9.5 for examples of personalized learning. It provides three examples of the steps involved in personalized learning.

Table 9.5 Examples of Personalized Learning

Steps for Personalized Learning	Math Example	Science Example	Language Arts Example
Pre-Assessment	A math pre-test covering proportions, ratios, and scaling problems.	A KWL chart (what students Know, Want to know, and Learned) about ecosystems and interactions.	A brief writing diagnostic where students write about a personal passion, showcasing current writing skills and styles.
Student Choice	Students choose a favorite dish to adjust recipes for different group sizes.	Students select a biome based on personal interest for game development.	Students choose a personal interest or passion to write about in their blog.
Goal Setting	Define the project goals (e.g., adjusting the recipe for ten people).	Define game objectives and rules to reflect the ecosystem dynamics.	Define the type of content for each blog post (e.g., persuasive, expository, narrative).

(*Continued*)

187

Table 9.5 (Continued)

Steps for Personalized Learning	Math Example	Science Example	Language Arts Example
Research	Gather data on ingredients, costs, and proportions.	Investigate key ecosystem components (food web, abiotic/biotic factors, threats).	Use credible sources to gather supporting evidence for blog content.
Mini-Lesson 1	**Proportions and Ratios Basics**: Use visual aids (e.g., bar models) to demonstrate how to calculate proportions.	**Food Webs**: Create a diagram of a biome's food web and analyze energy flow.	**Crafting Strong Introductions**: Teach how to hook readers with compelling questions or statistics.
Mini-Lesson 2	**Unit Price Analysis**: Calculate unit prices using grocery store examples.	**Abiotic vs. Biotic Factors**: Teach how these influence ecosystems.	**Finding Credible Sources**: Show how to evaluate online sources for credibility and bias.
Mini-Lesson 3	**Graphing Costs**: Guide students to create graphs showing cost changes with serving size.	**Human Impact on Ecosystems**: Explore case studies showing deforestation or pollution effects on ecosystems.	**Integrating Multimedia**: Demonstrate embedding videos or images to enhance blog posts effectively.
Collaboration	Work in pairs or individually to adjust recipes and solve scaling problems.	Test games with peers to identify areas for improvement.	Share drafts with peers and receive constructive feedback.
Application	Create a presentation explaining the math involved in recipe scaling.	Design game rules, cards, or pieces reflecting the biome's characteristics.	Write and edit blog posts, incorporating multimedia elements like images or videos.
Assessment Check-Ins	A short quiz where students solve ratio problems and scale recipes to test comprehension.	A research log check where students show progress on biome research and draft game components.	Blog check-ins where students share drafts for one blog post type (e.g., persuasive or expository).

(Continued)

Table 9.5 (Continued)

Steps for Personalized Learning	Math Example	Science Example	Language Arts Example
Teacher Feedback	"Your calculations are accurate, but try to explain the steps more clearly in your presentation."	"You've included key abiotic factors, but consider how human activities like deforestation might influence this biome."	"Your argument is strong, but include more evidence to support your main points."
Final Product	Create a written or digital presentation explaining recipe scaling and ingredient costs.	Complete a polished version of the game and present it to classmates.	Publish the blog on a classroom platform and reflect on the experience in a final review.
Reflection	Share the project and reflect on challenges and learning outcomes.	Reflect on how the game represents ecosystem dynamics and areas for improvement.	Reflect on feedback received and lessons learned from creating the blog.

PLAY-BASED LEARNING

Play-based learning uses play to promote children's development in learning, creativity, problem solving, social skills, and critical thinking. The methods encourage children to engage with the environment, explore, and experiment in order to develop cognitive, emotional, social, and physical realms. It utilizes structured and unstructured activities that can be adapted for learners of all ages. Learning is driven by the children's curiosity, and the instructor encourages the children to investigate their environment, ask questions, and seek answers through hands-on experiences. Collaboration is encouraged, as is self-expression and creativity. Play-based learning encompasses various types of play.

- **Free Play**: Unstructured play initiated by children that allows them to explore their interests and creativity.
- **Guided Play**: Play that is facilitated by educators who provide scaffolding and support to extend learning opportunities while allowing children to lead the activity.
- **Structured Play**: Collaborative activities with specific objectives or outcomes that incorporate games, challenges, or projects.

- **Pretend Play**: Imaginative play where students take on roles and create scenarios to foster creativity, social skills, and problem solving.

The process of implementing play-based learning typically involves several stages. First, the educator creates a playful environment by providing materials, resources, and activities to stimulate curiosity. For example, this might include blocks, art supplies, books, dramatic play areas, and science exploration stations. Next, the students should be encouraged to explore as the instructor observes and facilitates. Children might choose to build structures with blocks, engage in role-playing in a kitchen area, or experiment with water in a science station. Next, the instructor can ask open-ended questions or join in the play experience to develop different learning scenarios to promote critical thinking and problem solving. For example, while children build with blocks, the instructor might ask, "What happens if we add more blocks to the top?" to encourage experimentation. After the play experience, the instructor can provide the opportunity for students to reflect on the learning experiences by discussing what they learned, the challenges they faced, and the ideas that emerged. For example, the instructor might hold a group discussion where children share their building experiences and problem-solving strategies. Table 9.6 provides examples of all four types of play-based learning.

Spotlight: Inventors Under 18

Riya Karumanchi, a young innovator, has gained recognition for her dedication to improving accessibility and independence for visually impaired individuals. At just 15 years old, Riya invented the SmartCane, a modernized version of the traditional white cane used by visually impaired individuals. The SmartCane incorporates advanced technology, such as ultrasonic sensors, to detect obstacles beyond the reach of a standard cane. It provides audio and haptic feedback to alert users to potential hazards in their path, enhancing their ability to navigate independently and safely. Riya's invention demonstrates her commitment to leveraging technology to solve real-world problems and improve quality of life.

Riya's inspiration for the SmartCane came after visiting a family friend who was visually impaired. Observing the limitations of traditional mobility aids, she recognized the potential to integrate cutting-edge technology into a device that could offer more comprehensive support. Her prototype, developed with the help of mentors and advisors, represents a significant leap forward in assistive technology. Unlike standard canes, which only provide tactile feedback for immediate obstacles, the SmartCane's ultrasonic sensors can detect hazards several feet away, giving users more time to react. The device is also equipped with GPS and voice-assistant capabilities, making it a multifunctional tool for navigation and communication.

Table 9.6 Play-Based Learning Projects

Subject	Project Title	Steps Involved	Category of Play	Developmental Impact
Science	"Mission to Mars: Colonization Challenge"	1. Provide students with materials like modeling clay, LEGO bricks, and recyclables to design a Mars habitat.	Free Play	Cognitive: Deepens understanding of space science, sustainability, and engineering principles.
		2. Encourage students to experiment and create innovative solutions for challenges such as water supply, oxygen, and food.		Social: Builds teamwork as students collaborate and share design ideas.
		3. Facilitate a presentation where students explain how their designs address the unique environment of Mars.		Emotional: Increases confidence and pride in their creativity and problem-solving skills.
Math	"Escape Room: Geometry Edition"	1. Design a math-themed escape room with puzzles involving geometry, like calculating angles, areas, and volumes.	Structured Play	Cognitive: Strengthens problem-solving skills and mastery of geometric concepts through application in an engaging format.
		2. Divide students into teams and give them clues to solve each puzzle to unlock the next step in the escape room.		Social: Fosters collaboration and effective communication in high-pressure, team-based situations.
		3. Debrief with students, discussing the strategies they used and reviewing key geometry concepts.		Emotional: Enhances resilience and persistence as they work through challenging tasks.

(Continued)

Table 9.6 Play-Based Learning Projects

Subject	Project Title	Steps Involved	Category of Play	Developmental Impact
Language Arts	"Alternate Endings: Virtual Reality Literature"	1. Select a novel or short story and provide students with VR tools or craft supplies to create immersive alternate endings.	Pretend Play	Cognitive: Encourages deeper literary analysis by reimagining plotlines and understanding character motivations.
		2. Have students storyboard their ideas and create a prototype of their alternate ending, using VR, stop-motion, or props.		Social: Promotes collaborative storytelling as students work in groups to produce their scenes.
		3. Present the alternate endings to the class and discuss themes, character growth, and creative interpretations.		Emotional: Builds empathy as students explore diverse perspectives and emotions through role-play.
Physical Education	"Medieval Tournament: Fitness Quest"	1. Set up a "medieval" obstacle course with stations inspired by knights' challenges, like archery (bean bag toss), jousting (foam noodles), and castle climbing (wall climbing).	Guided Play	Physical: Develops agility, strength, and coordination through dynamic movement activities.
		2. Divide students into teams and assign roles such as knights, squires, or strategists to complete challenges together.		Social: Encourages leadership and cooperation as teams strategize to win the tournament.
		3. End with a "court ceremony" where students reflect on their teamwork and celebrate achievements.		Emotional: Builds a sense of community and pride in their physical and team efforts.

What sets Riya apart as an innovator is her focus on making the SmartCane accessible and affordable. Recognizing that high costs often limit the adoption of assistive technology, she prioritized creating a cost-effective design. Her efforts have garnered significant attention, earning her accolades and support from the STEM community. Riya's work exemplifies how young innovators can harness their creativity and empathy to address pressing societal challenges and make a tangible impact.

Beyond her technical achievements, Riya is an advocate for STEM education and entrepreneurship among young people. She frequently speaks at conferences and workshops, sharing her journey and encouraging others to pursue their innovative ideas. Her story serves as an inspiration to aspiring changemakers, highlighting the power of combining technical skills with a genuine desire to help others. Through her groundbreaking work and advocacy, Riya Karumanchi is proving that age is no barrier to creating solutions that transform lives.

CONCLUSION

Chapter 9 has explored a variety of problem-solving models and instructional practices that support student learning and development. These models include inquiry-based learning approaches such as Project-Based Learning (PjBL) and Problem-Based Learning (PBL), Creative Problem Solving (CPS), Genius Hour, Makerspaces, design thinking, personalized learning, and play-based learning. Each method offers unique ways to engage students in solving real-world problems, fostering collaboration, creativity, and deep learning. Through these approaches, students are empowered to take ownership of their learning, investigate meaningful challenges, and develop practical solutions that enhance their critical thinking and problem-solving abilities.

The importance of nurturing both creative and critical thinking skills in students cannot be overstated. These skills are essential not only for academic success but also for preparing students to thrive in an increasingly complex and dynamic world. By fostering environments where students can explore, create, and challenge themselves, educators play a pivotal role in shaping the next generation of innovators and thinkers. As educators, it is crucial to incorporate these instructional practices into our classrooms, allowing students to develop the skills they need to navigate challenges, think critically, and embrace their creativity. By embracing these approaches, educators can cultivate an environment of growth and exploration, where students are prepared to tackle the problems of tomorrow.

REFERENCES

Baer, J.M.J. (1988). Long-term effects of creativity training with middle school students. *The Journal of Early Adolescence*, *8*(2), 183–193. https://doi.org/10.1177/0272431688082006

Barron, B., & Darling-Hammond, L. (2008). Teaching for meaningful learning: A review of research on inquiry-based and cooperative learning. *Edutopia*. Retrieved from http://www.edutopia.org/pdfs/edutopia-teaching-for -meaningful-learning.pdf

Bell, T., Urhahne, D., Schanze, S., & Ploetzner, R. (2010). Collaborative inquiry learning: Models, tools, and challenges. *International Journal of Science Education*, *3*(1), 349–377.

Benoit, B. (2000). *Problem based learning*. SCORE History/ Social Science. Retrieved from http://score.rims.k12.ca.us /problearn.html

BIE. (n.d.). *What is project-based learning?* Buck Institute for Education. Retrieved from http://www.bie.org/about/what_pbl

Darling-Hammond, L. (2010). *The flat world and education: How America's commitment to equity will determine our future*. New York, NY: Teachers College, Columbia University.

Dewey, J. (1997). *How we think*. New York, NY: Dover Publications

Doss, K. (2018). Providing opportunities for flow experiences and creative problem solving through inquiry-based instruction. *Global Education Review*, *5*(1), 108–122.

Dweck, C., Walton, G., & Cohen, G. (2014). *Academic tenacity: Mindsets and skills that promote long-term learning*. Seattle, WA: Bill & Melinda Gates Foundation.

Esch, C. (1998). *Project-based and problem-based: The same or different?* San Mateo, CA: San Mateo County Office of Education.

Farrington, C.A. (2013). *Academic mindsets as a critical component of deeper learning*. Chicago, IL: University of Chicago.

Gallagher, S.A. (2012). *Problem-based learning in your classroom*. Unionville, NY: Royal Fireworks Press.

Gallagher, S.A. (2015). The role of problem-based learning in developing creative expertise. *Asia Pacific Education Review*, *16*(2), 225–235.

Ginsburg, H.P., & Opper, S. (1987). *Piaget's theory of intellectual development* (3rd ed.). New York, NY: Pearson.

Haney, J.J., Jing, W., Keil, C., & Zoffel, J. (2007). Enhancing teachers' beliefs and practices through problem-based learning focused on pertinent issues of environmental health science. *Journal of Environmental Education*, *38*(4), 25–33. http://dx.doi.org/10.3200/JOEE.38.4.25-33

Hewlett Foundation. (n.d.). What is deeper learning? The William and Flora Hewlett Foundation. Retrieved from http://www.hewlett.org/programs/education/deeper -learning/what-deeper-learning

Hung, W. (2011). Theory to reality: A few issues in implementing problem-based learning. *Education Technology Research Development*, *59*(4), 529–552. http://dx.doi.org /10.1007/s11423-011-9198-1

Johnson, D.W., & Johnson, R.T. (2009). Educational psychology success story: Social interdependence and theory and cooperative learning. *Educational Researcher*, *38*(5), 365–379. http://dx.doi.org/10.3102/0013189X09339057

Katrein, J. (2016). Inquiry, engagement, passion, and grit: Dispositions for genius hour. *Reading Teacher*, *70*(2), 241. https://doi.org/10.1002/trtr.1496

Krebs, D., & Zvi, G. (2016). *The genius hour guidebook: Fostering passion, wonder, and inquiry in the classroom*. New York, NY: Routledge.

Papert, S. (2001). *Seymour papert: Project-based learning*. Edutopia. Retrieved from http:// www.edutopia.org/seymour -papert-project-based-learning

Rubenstein, L.D., Callan, G.L., Ridgley, L.M., & Henderson, A. (2019). Students' strategic planning and strategy use during creative problem solving: The importance of perspective-taking. *Thinking Skills and Creativity*, *34*, 100556. https://doi.org /10.1016/j.tsc.2019.02.004

Rush, E.B. (2015). Genius hour in the library. *Teacher Librarian*, *43*(2), 26–30.

Savery, J.S. (2006). Overview of PBL: Definitions and distinctions. *Interdisciplinary Journal of Problem-Based Learning*, *1*(1), 9–20. http://dx.doi.org/10.7771/1541 -5015.1002

The Secretary's Commission on Achieving Necessary Skills (SCANS). (1991). *What work requires of schools: A SCANS report for America 2000*. Washington, DC: U.S. Department of Labor. Retrieved from http://wdr.doleta.gov /SCANS/what-work/whatwork.pdf

Simos, E. (2015). Genius hour: Critical inquiry and differentiation. *English Leadership Quarterly*, *38*(1), 2–4.

Thomas, J.W. (2000). *A review of research on project-based learning*. Buck Institute for Education. Retrieved from http://www.bie.org/index.php/site/RE/pbl_ research/29

Vygotsky, L.S. (1962). *Thought and language*. Cambridge, MS: MIT Press.

Wagner, T. (2012). *Creating innovators: The making of young people who will change the world*. New York, NY: Scribner.

Wilhelm, J.G., & Wilhelm, P.J. (2010). Inquiring minds learn to read, write, and think: Reaching all learners through inquiry. *Middle School Journal*, *41*(5), 39–46.

Zhao, Y. (2012). *World class learners: Educating creative and entrepreneurial students*. Thousand Oaks, CA: Corwin.

Chapter 10

Promoting Attitudes and Dispositions that Support the Development of Creative Thinking Skills

INTRODUCTION

Some traditional beliefs about creative and critical thinking assume that such capacities are innate and relatively unchangeable characteristics, but current educational researchers and reformers contend that creativity and critical thinking can and should be nurtured (Beghetto, Kauffman, & Baer, 2015; Couros, 2015; Pfeiffer & Thompson, 2013; Robinson, 2015; Wagner, 2012; Zhao, 2009). Providing opportunities and optimal conditions for creative and critical thinking is key. Pfeiffer and Thompson (2013) identify conditions for nurturing creativity in learning environments as freedom for curiosity, a climate where failure is an option and mistakes are opportunities to learn, provision of appropriate challenges, and application of inquiry-based approaches to learning.

While one could argue that engaging in creative activity is inherently motivating, it might not be the case for all learners, especially those who are performance-driven and/or perfectionistic. Students struggling with perfectionistic tendencies may need direct instruction on how to navigate the creative process in order to understand and appreciate the setbacks and challenges that are necessary to produce an original product. Hence, consideration of motivation is helpful in encouraging learners to think in new and innovative ways.

INTRINSIC MOTIVATION

Experts also contend that intrinsic motivation, fueled by passion, interest, and curiosity, is more conducive to creative and critical thinking than carrot-and-stick approaches that may actually undermine the creative and critical thinking process. Encouraging students to develop and understand intrinsic motivation is especially important as students deal with the stress and pressure of excessive standardized testing. Factors crucial to intrinsic motivation include competence,

196

DOI: 10.4324/9781003434221-10

autonomy, relatedness, and purpose (Ryan & Deci, 2008; Dweck, Walton, & Cohen, 2014). Based on the work of Ryan and Deci's Self Determination Theory, Pink (2011) sheds light on organizations where creativity runs high and brings to the forefront the notion that higher-order thinking tasks, such as creative and critical thinking, are best inspired by organizations that promote mastery, purpose, relatedness, and autonomy in employees.

According to Ryan and Deci (2017) competence, or feeling confident that one can attain mastery in a situation, drives motivation. Similar to and in line with a growth mindset, promoting competence involves an emphasis on goals in the classroom that involve mastery of content or skill, solving a problem, or achieving a milestone as opposed to goals that emphasize grades. Enhancing a sense of competence in the classroom involves having just the right level of difficulty where curiosity is piqued and the problems to be solved are perceived by students as a challenge, albeit an attainable one.

Practices that promote student autonomy involve giving students meaningful choices and allowing opportunity for self-regulation. When students are given meaningful choices in their work and an expectation for self-regulation, it leads to enhanced persistence, effort, and subsequent learning (Patall, Cooper, & Robinson, 2008; Ryan & Deci, 2000). Teachers can help students develop approaches to being successful in these realms through direct instruction and by promoting self-reflection.

Relatedness involves having positive, caring relationships with teachers and other classmates. In a caring environment, students are willing to take risks in their thinking and persist when things become difficult (Niemiec & Ryan, 2009). Creating a classroom that is free from sarcasm and bullying is critical for establishing this type of setting. Equally important is setting norms and expectations, as well as opportunities for collaborative work.

Having a purpose, knowing that work has meaning, relevance or benefit beyond a paycheck, grade or test score, also fuels motivation (Niemiec, Ryan, & Deci, 2009). Students who know the relevance and value of what they are learning or know that they are creating something of purpose or value to others are likely to be more committed to their work. Allowing students to help design projects or problems to investigate can be an avenue for ensuring that students have an authentic, purpose-driven experience.

Taken all together, research on the prime conditions for promoting creativity and motivating learners to think creatively and critically includes: a) development of a growth mindset, b) opportunity and context for engaging in purposeful problem solving in areas of interest and passion, c) development and practice of creative thinking strategies, d) opportunity for collaboration, and e) autonomy support including opportunity for meaningful choice and self-regulation. Creating those conditions is a tall order in light of the current climate of standards-based education and high-stakes assessment.

CREATIVE MINDSETS AND FEEDBACK

Dweck's (2008) research on mindset indicates that traits such as creativity can be improved through a combination of belief, effort, and strategy. Helping learners to develop the mindset that they can become creative can fuel motivation. Learners who adopt a growth mindset are more motivated and willing to take risks, accept challenges, and persist in the face of setbacks in the classroom compared to learners with fixed mindsets (Blackwell, Trzesniewski, & Dweck, 2007). Dweck's research indicates that in addition to promoting a growth mindset, learners need practice, effort, strategy, and a safe environment.

As with developing any new skill or talent, ample opportunity to engage in creative and critical thinking will help learners sharpen that skill. Early behavioral psychologist B.F. Skinner acknowledged that creativity was the result of time spent engaging in creative activity. For example, he acknowledged that "the physical act of writing is the cause, not the effect, of new and original thought" (Skinner, 1968, p. 269). Effort and practice with creative thinking over time will increase learner capacity for creativity. Dweck (2015) explains that in addition to belief, practice, and effort, individuals with a growth mindset seek, learn, and apply strategies. Helping learners develop strategies for creative thinking will enhance their success by making creativity seem more accessible.

Doing something new always feels risky and uncertain. Some learners, especially those with perfectionistic tendencies, don't always appreciate the opportunity to venture from a prescribed program or assignment. Failure avoidance can undermine the creative process (Icekson, Roskes, & Moran, 2014) as fear of earning a low grade overrides a desire to learn and be creative. Hence, some students want to be told exactly what to do and how to do it in order to avoid perceived failure. Promoting a growth mindset involves creating a space where risks are encouraged, mistakes are opportunities to learn, and failures are potential sources of new ideas, projects, and investigations. Teachers can model, demonstrate, and celebrate taking risks and learning from failures.

Creative performance is influenced by multiple factors, including personality and the work environment. Key elements such as self-efficacy, creative identity, creative mindset, and metacognition shape decisions to engage in or avoid creative tasks (Hass, Katz-Buonincontro, & Reiter-Palmon, 2016; Hu, Wang, Yi, & Runco, 2018; Karwowski & Kaufman, 2017). The concept of a creative mindset, coined by Karwowski (2014), refers to an individual's belief in their ability to enhance their creative potential. A mindset, as described by Dweck (2006), represents a way of thinking about the learning process. Individuals with growth mindsets believe that intelligence and creativity are malleable, whereas those with fixed mindsets perceive these traits as static. People with growth mindsets tend to focus on learning rather than external measures such as grades or test scores. Research has shown that adolescents who adopt a growth mindset are more motivated, seek feedback, and outperform their peers academically (Blackwell, Trzesniewski, & Dweck, 2007; Good, Aronson, & Inzlicht, 2003).

Demonstrating a growth mindset involves key characteristics such as believing that talents and intelligence can improve through effort, accepting mistakes as part of the process, and welcoming feedback. These traits are particularly important when navigating the challenges of creative problem solving (Zhao, Zhang, Heng, & Qi, 2021). A growth mindset not only fosters motivation to engage in creative activities (Karwowski, 2014) but also enhances creative self-efficacy (Hass et al., 2016). Additionally, it supports perseverance after setbacks or poor performances (Beghetto & Dilley, 2016).

Research emphasizes that children and youth are significantly influenced by the mindsets they develop (Dweck, 2006). Fixed mindsets can lead individuals to view failure as a defining personal trait and to feel threatened by others' successes. Those with fixed mindsets often avoid challenges, conceal flaws, disregard feedback, or interpret feedback as criticism. Consequently, they may miss opportunities for growth and creative exploration (Dweck, 2006).

The relationship between external evaluation and creativity is complex and influenced by various factors, such as the timing, form, and individual perception of feedback. Beghetto (2007) highlighted the benefits of providing feedback to help learners understand the parameters of a creative task. Feedback can take many forms, including controlling feedback, which aims to modify behavior, and informational feedback, which provides guidance without imposing control (Zhou, 1998). While controlling feedback has been shown to negatively affect creativity (Shalley & Gilson, 2004), informational feedback generally enhances creative performance. Hu et al. (2018) explored different types of feedback, including positive controlling, negative controlling, positive informational, and negative informational. They found that informational feedback improved creativity, whereas controlling feedback, such as criticism emphasizing mistakes (e.g., "You did very poorly. This should not have happened. Remember, you should not repeat the poor performance, or we can't use your data."), diminished creative output. Interestingly, participants in this study displayed higher creativity when given negative informational feedback compared to positive feedback (Hu et al., 2018).

The potential for negative feedback can lead some individuals to avoid or reject feedback altogether (Kohli & Jaworski, 1994). Receiving controlling feedback may also reduce an individual's sense of autonomy, thereby impacting their creative motivation and performance (Deci, Koestner, & Ryan, 1999). However, constructive and positive feedback from experts can bolster creative identity, enhance self-efficacy, and drive creative accomplishments (Bandura, 1997; Lebuda & Csikszentmihalyi, 2017). Yet, individuals with heightened sensitivity to feedback may not experience these benefits in the same way (Sordia & Martskvishvili, 2022).

199

Given the complexities of feedback, Beghetto and Dilley (2016) emphasized the importance of teaching individuals how to receive and utilize honest, supportive feedback to maximize their creative potential. Their work adds to ongoing research into how feedback influences creative tasks, particularly students' willingness to seek and apply constructive criticism. The following table provides examples of negative, controlling, positive, and constructive feedback for middle school assignments in various subject areas.

Subject	Negative Feedback	Controlling Feedback	Positive Feedback	Constructive Feedback
Math	"Your tessellation pattern doesn't fit together properly, and there are gaps. It's hard to see the geometric relationship."	"You must use only triangles and hexagons for your tessellation. Any other shapes won't work."	"Your tessellation has an eye-catching design, and I like how you explored using nontraditional shapes!"	"Your tessellation has an interesting start. To fix the gaps, try adjusting the angles of your shapes so they interlock properly."
Science	"Your eco-friendly water filtration system didn't work well because it failed to remove impurities. Test your materials better next time."	"You need to follow the instructions exactly and use only the materials I listed to build your filter."	"Your idea to use activated charcoal in your water filter was creative, and it showed good problem solving!"	"Your water filter had some innovative ideas. To improve, try experimenting with layering the materials differently for better filtration."
Social Studies	"Your infographic about ancient civilizations is confusing, and some of the data is inaccurate. Double-check your sources."	"You have to use only the templates provided for your infographic, or it won't meet the assignment criteria."	"Your infographic is visually appealing, and I like how you highlighted the role of trade in ancient civilizations!"	"Your infographic has a great design. To improve, double-check the data you included and make sure it clearly explains the connections between the civilizations."

(Continued)

Subject	Negative Feedback	Controlling Feedback	Positive Feedback	Constructive Feedback
Language Arts	"Your short story has an interesting plot, but the grammar mistakes make it hard to read. Proofread it carefully next time."	"Rewrite your short story using only the outline structure we discussed in class. Deviating from it won't work."	"Your short story has a strong beginning, and I enjoyed the twist you added to the ending!"	"Your short story has a lot of potential. To improve, work on sentence structure and punctuation to make it easier to follow."
Music	"Your melody is hard to follow because the notes are too random and don't form a pattern. It needs more structure."	"You have to use the exact rhythm pattern I showed you in class. Any other rhythm is incorrect."	"Your melody is unique, and I like how you included syncopation in your rhythm!"	"Your melody has some interesting elements. To make it more cohesive, try using a repeating motif to create a clearer structure."
Physical Education	"Your circuit training plan isn't balanced – it has too much cardio and no strength exercises. Balance your activities better."	"You need to follow the example circuit training plan exactly, or it won't meet the goals of the assignment."	"Your circuit training plan has some fun and creative exercises, like the agility ladder drills!"	"Your circuit training plan is a good start. To improve, include at least one strength-training exercise for better overall fitness."
Art	"Your 3D sculpture is incomplete, and the pieces don't connect securely. It doesn't look finished."	"Redo your sculpture using only the techniques demonstrated in class. No other methods are acceptable."	"Your 3D sculpture is visually engaging, and I like the way you experimented with texture!"	"Your sculpture shows good effort. To improve, focus on securely attaching the pieces and refining the details for a more polished look."

CURIOSITY – RELEVANCE, PURPOSE, PASSION, AND INTEREST

Curiosity is a powerful driver of learning, innovation, and personal growth. It stems from an innate desire to explore, question, and understand the world, making it a cornerstone of intellectual and emotional development. Relevance is often the first spark of curiosity. When individuals perceive that something directly relates to their lives or goals, they become more eager to engage with the topic. For example, a student may become curious about environmental science after noticing pollution in their local park, realizing the subject's relevance to their community. By highlighting the connections between learning content and real-world applications, educators can foster curiosity and encourage students to take ownership of their learning journey.

Purpose further fuels curiosity by giving exploration a meaningful direction. When individuals understand the "why" behind their pursuits, they are more likely to stay motivated and engaged. A student researching renewable energy may feel a sense of purpose knowing their findings could contribute to creating a sustainable future. Purpose allows learners to see their actions as part of a bigger picture, encouraging them to dig deeper and push through challenges. Teachers and mentors can cultivate this by helping students set goals that align with their values and interests, emphasizing how their efforts can lead to positive change.

Passion, on the other hand, ignites curiosity at an emotional level. When individuals are genuinely excited or fascinated by a subject, they are more likely to delve into it with enthusiasm and persistence. Passionate learners often spend extra time researching, experimenting, and asking questions because they find joy in the process itself. For example, a student passionate about technology might eagerly learn coding languages to create their own app. Educators can nurture this by creating opportunities for students to explore their interests and providing resources to deepen their understanding.

Finally, interest is the seed from which curiosity grows. While passion can be intense and focused, interest is more fluid and exploratory, allowing individuals to dip their toes into various topics before diving deeper. Encouraging students to explore diverse subjects and perspectives helps them discover what truly captivates their minds. For instance, a teacher might introduce students to a wide range of books, experiments, or projects, allowing them to identify areas they find intriguing. By fostering an environment where curiosity is valued and encouraged, educators can inspire learners to seek knowledge with a sense of wonder and excitement. This table describes projects that have relevance and purpose while allowing students to explore their passions and interests.

Subject	Project Title	Objective	Description	Relevance and Purpose	Passion and Interest
Science	**"Biohacking for Better Living"**	Explore biological processes and innovative solutions to improve daily life.	Students design a personal "biohacking experiment" to optimize health or productivity (e.g., changes in sleep, nutrition, exercise). They collect and analyze data, presenting their findings in visual formats.	Applies scientific principles to personal wellness. Emphasizes how science can improve daily life.	Appeals to students interested in health, fitness, or self-improvement. Encourages curiosity about how biology influences their daily habits.
Math	**"Escape Room Architect Challenge"**	Use mathematical problem solving and geometry to design an interactive escape room.	Students design an escape room with puzzles based on algebra, geometry, and probability. They calculate material costs, ensure the room is solvable, and align challenges with mathematical principles.	Shows practical applications of math in real-world problem solving and game design. Reinforces math skills while encouraging creative thinking.	Appeals to students who enjoy puzzles, games, and creative problem solving. Engages those with an interest in design and challenges.
Language Arts	**"Unwritten Chapters of Famous Stories"**	Analyze narrative techniques and create original content.	Students write a new chapter or alternate ending to a classic novel, mimicking the author's style and incorporating historical research.	Encourages deeper engagement with literature while fostering creativity. Promotes critical thinking about storytelling.	Lets students personalize classic stories they've read, engaging them in literary analysis while offering a chance for creative self-expression.

(*Continued*)

Subject	Project Title	Objective	Description	Relevance and Purpose	Passion and Interest
Social Studies	**"Alternate Histories Podcast Series"**	Analyze historical events by exploring alternate outcomes.	Students choose a major historical event and create a podcast episode presenting an alternate history. They research the original event, hypothesize different outcomes, and back their claims with evidence.	Helps students connect history with speculative thinking and storytelling. Promotes critical thinking about history's impact on the present.	Appeals to students interested in history, current events, and creative media formats like podcasts. Fosters imagination and research skills.
Music	**"Soundtrack to My Life"**	Analyze music as a form of personal and cultural expression.	Students curate a personal soundtrack with songs representing pivotal moments in their lives. They write short essays about each song's significance and create an original composition.	Highlights music's emotional and cultural influence. Encourages students to reflect on their personal identity through music.	Encourages exploration of personal music preferences and creative expression. Engages students with a passion for music and storytelling.
Technology and Engineering	**"Designing Assistive Tech for Everyday Challenges"**	Apply engineering principles to improve accessibility.	Students identify a challenge faced by people with disabilities and design a prototype to address the issue. They create 3D models or physical prototypes and present them to the class.	Focuses on real-world problem solving and social impact. Helps students understand the power of design and technology in making a difference.	Appeals to budding engineers, humanitarians, and students passionate about accessibility and social justice.

(Continued)

Subject	Project Title	Objective	Description	Relevance and Purpose	Passion and Interest
Physical Education	**"Sports in Space: Adapt an Athletic Event for Zero Gravity"**	Apply knowledge of physics and biomechanics to design a sport for space.	Students modify or invent a sport that could be played in zero gravity, creating a rulebook, describing equipment, and simulating gameplay.	Combines physical education with STEM concepts like physics and engineering. Promotes interdisciplinary learning and practical application of scientific principles.	Appeals to students curious about space and creative problem solving. Engages those with an interest in space exploration and inventiveness.
Art	**"Sound-to-Color Synesthesia Creations"**	Explore the connection between sensory experiences and visual expression.	Students listen to a curated playlist of diverse sounds and create abstract artwork that captures the mood, rhythm, and energy they perceive. They experiment with different mediums and provide explanations of their work.	Encourages interdisciplinary connections between art and auditory perception. Develops critical thinking and artistic techniques.	Appeals to students who enjoy music, sensory exploration, or abstract expression. Stimulates creativity through multisensory engagement.
Math and Social Studies Integration	**"Budgeting for a Historical Festival"**	Combine financial literacy with historical understanding.	Students plan a community festival based on a historical era (e.g., Renaissance or 1920s Jazz Festival). They calculate costs and incorporate accurate historical elements like music and fashion.	Reinforces budgeting skills while bringing history to life. Encourages financial literacy in practical settings.	Appeals to students interested in event planning, history, and budgeting. Combines learning with fun, hands-on application.

(Continued)

205

Subject	Project Title	Objective	Description	Relevance and Purpose	Passion and Interest
Language Arts and Science Integration	**"Climate Fiction Short Stories"**	Combine creative writing with environmental science concepts.	Students write speculative fiction stories imagining life in a world impacted by climate change, incorporating scientific details and possible solutions.	Raises awareness of climate issues through storytelling. Engages students in learning about climate change and its potential impacts.	Appeals to students interested in science fiction and environmental activism. Encourages creativity while raising awareness of critical global issues.
Social Studies	**"Community Action Projects: Building a Better Tomorrow"**	Explore community issues and propose real-world solutions.	Students research a local issue (e.g., homelessness, access to clean water) and create a community action plan that addresses the problem. They present the plan to the class, complete with an implementation timeline and potential challenges.	Teaches students how to identify social issues and use their voices to make a difference. Fosters civic engagement.	Appeals to students who care about community issues, social justice, and activism. Inspires students to take action for positive change.

(*Continued*)

Subject	Project Title	Objective	Description	Relevance and Purpose	Passion and Interest
PE	**"Design Your Own Adventure Course"**	Apply physical fitness and creativity to design a personalized obstacle course.	Students design an obstacle course using different physical challenges that relate to fitness concepts like agility, endurance, and strength. They then test and refine the course based on peers' feedback.	Encourages students to create fun, fitness-based activities while incorporating physical education principles. Promotes teamwork and problem solving.	Appeals to students who enjoy hands-on learning, physical challenges, and teamwork. Excites those who like to design and test physical challenges.
Math	**"Math in the Real World: Architecture Design"**	Integrate geometry and algebra into architectural design.	Students design a house or building, applying geometry and algebra to calculate dimensions, angles, and cost estimates for materials. They use digital tools or sketches for the design.	Demonstrates how math principles apply to real-world applications like construction and design. Reinforces math skills in creative contexts.	Appeals to students interested in design, architecture, and engineering. Brings real-world context to mathematical learning.
Art	**"Urban Art and Public Space"**	Explore the impact of public art on community identity.	Students create a piece of urban art (e.g., mural, sculpture) that reflects community issues or local history. They design the art and present a proposal for its placement in the community.	Encourages students to think critically about art's role in public spaces and social engagement. Promotes social responsibility and creativity.	Appeals to students interested in art, urban culture, and social activism. Stimulates students' desire to make a meaningful impact through art.

OPEN-MINDEDNESS

Open-mindedness is a key ingredient for creativity because it allows individuals to entertain new ideas, perspectives, and possibilities without immediate judgment. Creativity often thrives in environments where people feel free to explore unconventional paths or challenge traditional ways of thinking. By being open-minded, individuals are more likely to embrace diverse viewpoints, which can lead to richer, more innovative solutions. For example, a student working on a group project might initially resist a teammate's unusual suggestion, but an open-minded approach could reveal its potential to transform the project into something groundbreaking. This willingness to consider alternative approaches fosters a culture of innovation and collaboration.

Another way open-mindedness benefits creativity is by encouraging risk-taking and reducing the fear of failure. Creative endeavors often require individuals to step outside their comfort zones and experiment with ideas that might not work. An open-minded mindset allows people to view mistakes as opportunities to learn and refine their approach rather than as setbacks. This perspective can help students, for instance, when designing an art project or developing a new scientific hypothesis. By staying open to unexpected outcomes, they are more likely to uncover unique insights and solutions that rigid thinking might overlook.

Open-mindedness promotes adaptability, which is essential for navigating the creative process. Creativity rarely follows a linear path; it often involves revising, rethinking, and pivoting in response to new information or challenges. Open-minded individuals are more willing to adapt their thinking, allowing them to integrate feedback, build on ideas, and find innovative ways to solve problems. For instance, an entrepreneur designing a product might initially target one market but, after listening to diverse perspectives, pivot to a different audience with greater success. In this way, open-mindedness not only enhances creativity but also ensures that creative efforts are flexible and responsive to real-world needs. The following table outlines ten activities that either promote open-mindedness or do not promote open-mindedness.

Promoting Open-Mindedness	Not Promoting Open-Mindedness
1. Debating Multiple Perspectives: Students research opposing sides of a controversial issue and argue both sides to understand different viewpoints.	**1. Single-Sided Argument Writing**: Students write an essay supporting only one predetermined perspective without exploring alternatives.
2. Cultural Exchange Projects: Students explore traditions, values, and practices of different cultures through presentations or virtual exchanges.	**2. Focused on One Culture**: Assignments that examine only one culture without any comparison or discussion of other cultural practices.

(Continued)

Promoting Open-Mindedness	Not Promoting Open-Mindedness
3. Brainstorming Without Judgment: Group brainstorming where every idea is encouraged before any critique is allowed.	**3. Limited Brainstorming**: Only accepting ideas that align with a specific solution or perspective.
4. Role-Playing Scenarios: Students assume the roles of different stakeholders in a community issue to explore diverse perspectives.	**4. Limited Role Assignments**: Assigning only roles that reinforce a single, dominant perspective on an issue.
5. Encouraging "What If" Questions: Asking students to explore alternative scenarios or imagine outcomes based on different decisions.	**5. Focus on "Right Answer"**: Emphasizing assignments with one correct answer and discouraging creative or alternative thinking.
6. Open-Ended Projects: Allowing students to choose topics or solutions for a project, fostering exploration of diverse ideas.	**6. Prescriptive Projects**: Assigning the same project with identical solutions or methods for every student.
7. Analyzing Bias: Teaching students to identify and evaluate bias in media, literature, or historical accounts.	**7. Ignoring Bias**: Assigning texts or materials without discussion of bias or varying perspectives.
8. Collaborative Problem Solving: Group activities where students bring different ideas to solve a complex problem.	**8. Teacher-Led Problem Solving**: Only the teacher presents a solution, with no input from students.
9. Literature from Diverse Authors: Reading and discussing books from authors of different backgrounds and worldviews.	**9. Limited Reading List**: Using only texts from one cultural or historical perspective without diversity in voices.
10. Reflective Journaling: Encouraging students to reflect on how their views have changed after exploring new ideas or perspectives.	**10. No Reflection Opportunities**: Skipping discussions or reflections after learning activities, limiting the chance for perspective shifts.

The activities on the left foster open-mindedness by encouraging exploration, multiple perspectives, and critical thinking. In contrast, the activities on the right limit opportunities for students to think broadly, reinforcing narrow viewpoints.

AUTONOMY

Autonomy plays a significant role in fostering creativity because it empowers individuals to take ownership of their creative processes. When people have the freedom to make choices about their work, they are more likely to explore original ideas and take risks. Autonomy removes the constraints of rigid guide-lines, allowing individuals to approach problems from unique angles. For exam-ple, in a classroom setting, when students are given the opportunity to choose their own project topics, they are more likely to engage deeply and produce creative, personalized outcomes. This sense of control fuels intrinsic motivation, which is a critical driver of creative thinking.

In addition to enhancing motivation, autonomy encourages self-directed learning and experimentation. People with the freedom to explore their inter-ests often engage in trial and error, testing different strategies to find the most effective solutions. This process can lead to innovative ideas that may not emerge under strict supervision or heavily prescribed tasks. For instance, in a workplace environment, an employee given the autonomy to design their own workflow might create a more efficient system that benefits the entire team. Autonomy provides the space for individuals to experiment and refine their ideas, leading to more meaningful and innovative results.

Autonomy builds confidence, which is essential for creativity. When individu-als are trusted to make decisions and take charge of their creative processes, they develop a stronger belief in their abilities. This confidence encourages them to push boundaries, tackle complex challenges, and persist through difficulties. For example, an artist creating work without external constraints may feel more empowered to take bold stylistic risks, resulting in a unique and impactful piece. By fostering a sense of independence, autonomy nurtures both the courage and resilience needed to produce truly creative outcomes.

Aspect	Assignments with Autonomy	Assignments without Autonomy
Structure	Flexible guidelines allow students to explore personal interests. For instance, in a science class, students might design an experiment to investigate a self-chosen topic such as plant growth under different lighting.	Rigid instructions provide little room for exploration. For example, students are required to replicate a teacher-provided experiment, like measuring water evaporation rates.
Student Choice	Students have control over task components. In English, they might choose their own book for a literary analysis project.	Teachers make all decisions. For example, assigning every student the same book and essay prompt for analysis.
Engagement	High engagement results from personal relevance. In social studies, students might create a documentary about a historical event tied to their cultural background.	Lower engagement can occur due to lack of connection. For example, writing a report on a historical event chosen by the teacher without room for personalization.

Aspect	Assignments with Autonomy	Assignments without Autonomy
Critical Thinking	Encourages problem solving and innovation. In math, students could apply geometry concepts to design a blueprint for a dream house.	Focuses on following instructions. For instance, solving a set of geometry problems from a textbook with fixed answers.
Creativity	Fosters creativity by allowing students to experiment with ideas. In art, students might create a piece using any medium to represent an emotion of their choice.	Restricts creativity by limiting expression. For example, drawing a still-life with specific materials as directed by the teacher.
Motivation	Intrinsic motivation thrives when students are invested. For example, in a business class, students might pitch a product idea they are passionate about.	Relies on extrinsic motivation, such as grades. For instance, writing a business plan for a generic company type assigned by the teacher.
Learning Outcome	Promotes deeper understanding through exploration. In science, students might research and develop a presentation on an environmental issue affecting their local community.	Focuses on surface-level learning. For example, completing a worksheet on environmental vocabulary without applying the terms to real-world issues.
Feedback Process	Involves peer feedback and iterative improvement. For instance, in a writing class, students share drafts with peers and revise based on their suggestions.	Focuses on teacher-driven feedback. For example, students submit an essay directly to the teacher, with no opportunities for revisions based on peer input.
Real-World Skills	Builds independence and decision-making. For example, in technology, students might create their own app prototype to solve a real-world problem.	Develops adherence to instructions but limits self-direction. For instance, coding an app following a step-by-step tutorial provided by the teacher.

IMAGINATION, MIND-WANDERING, AND OBSERVATION

Nurturing imagination, mind-wandering, and observation play a vital role in fostering creativity in students. When students are given the freedom to let their minds wander and imagine without constraints, they are more likely to think outside the box and explore new possibilities. This unstructured thinking allows

211

them to make connections between seemingly unrelated ideas and concepts, leading to unique solutions and innovative approaches. Imagination encourages them to explore hypothetical scenarios, dream up new ideas, and visualize different outcomes, all of which are essential skills for creative problem solving. Additionally, engaging in activities that support mind-wandering – such as journaling or free-thinking exercises – helps students develop flexibility in their thinking, enhancing their ability to adapt to new challenges and produce creative work.

Observation is also key in the development of creativity. By observing their surroundings more closely, students begin to notice details that others might overlook, sharpening their ability to analyze and interpret the world. When students are encouraged to observe through various lenses – whether through art, science, or storytelling – they are better able to notice patterns, draw insights, and translate their observations into creative expressions. This practice enhances their attention to detail and increases their capacity for generating original ideas. As students nurture these abilities, they begin to think more critically and creatively, which supports their overall cognitive and emotional growth. In turn, this helps them become more effective problem solvers and innovators, capable of bringing fresh perspectives to any field they pursue.

TECHNIQUES TO ENCOURAGE IMAGINATION, MIND-WANDERING, AND OBSERVATION

1. Create "Wonder Walks"

    - Description: Take students on outdoor excursions where they are encouraged to observe their surroundings without distractions. During these walks, students can take notes, sketch, or record anything that captures their attention, whether it's the shape of a leaf, the sound of birds, or how light plays off objects.
    - Encouragement of Imagination: These walks allow students' minds to wander and make connections between seemingly unrelated things. They can ask open-ended questions like, "What could this look like in a different world?" or "What story could this tree tell?".
    - Mind-Wandering: The quiet, unstructured time allows students to daydream, encouraging the exploration of their imagination without constraints.

2. Incorporate Free-Writing or Journaling Time

    - Description: Set aside time for students to free-write or journal daily without worrying about grammar, structure, or other rules. Prompts can be open-ended (e.g., "If you could invent anything, what would it be?" or "Describe an imaginary world you'd want to live in.") or simply allow them to write whatever comes to mind.

- Encouragement of Imagination: Writing freely allows ideas to flow, unlocking imaginative thoughts that may not emerge in structured writing exercises.
- Mind-Wandering: The process of journaling naturally invites mind-wandering, helping students explore their thoughts and ideas in a safe space.

3. Engage with "What If" Scenarios

- Description: Present students with "What If" scenarios that challenge their current thinking. For example, "What if the world was upside down?" or "What if animals could talk?". Have students brainstorm creative answers to these questions through writing, drawing, or group discussion.
- Encouragement of Imagination: These scenarios encourage students to think beyond the present reality and imagine new possibilities.
- Mind-Wandering: They provide space for students to let their minds wander and consider alternate realities, thereby nurturing their creative potential.

4. Incorporate Observation-Based Art Projects

- Description: Have students engage in art projects where the focus is purely on observation. They could sketch, paint, or photograph objects, places, or people in their environment. Instead of focusing on what is "right" or "realistic", encourage students to observe details that others might overlook (like the textures of a rock or the reflection of light).
- Encouragement of Imagination: This practice challenges students to think creatively about what they observe and how they can translate it into a visual form, often leading to surprising interpretations.
- Observation: It helps students hone their observational skills by encouraging them to notice minute details and subtleties.

5. Introduce Creative Play and Storytelling

- Description: Create opportunities for students to engage in creative play, such as role-playing games, improv storytelling, or group narrative-building. For example, students can work together to create a story where each person contributes a sentence or scenario, building off one another's ideas.
- Encouragement of Imagination: Storytelling exercises encourage students to think imaginatively and adapt to new twists in the narrative, challenging them to think quickly and creatively.
- Mind-Wandering: The open-ended nature of these activities invites students' minds to wander into fantastical realms, building scenarios and characters as they go.

By incorporating these strategies into the classroom, students can enhance their imagination, improve their ability to observe their surroundings, and allow their minds to wander in creative and meaningful ways.

SPOTLIGHT: INVENTORS UNDER 18

Bishop Curry V, a young inventor from Texas, made headlines at just ten years old with his invention designed to prevent hot car deaths in children. After hearing about a tragic incident where a baby passed away due to being left in a hot car, Bishop was motivated to create a solution. His invention, called "Oasis", is a device that monitors the temperature inside a car and automatically activates when conditions become dangerously hot. The device is designed to blow cool air into the car and send an alert to parents or emergency services, potentially saving lives.

The idea for Oasis came from Bishop's natural curiosity and problem-solving mindset. Using his knowledge of basic mechanics and technology, he sketched a prototype and began researching how to make it a reality. His invention is simple yet impactful, relying on a combination of temperature sensors, a cooling fan, and communication technology to address a life-threatening issue. Bishop's initiative has sparked a wider conversation about child safety in vehicles and the role of young innovators in solving critical problems.

Bishop's work quickly gained recognition, and he launched a GoFundMe campaign to raise money for patenting his invention and developing a working prototype. The campaign exceeded its initial goal, showing how his idea resonated with people across the country. His efforts earned him national attention, including coverage in major media outlets. The response to his invention highlighted the urgent need for solutions to prevent hot car deaths, and Bishop's creativity demonstrated that even young minds could contribute to solving pressing societal challenges.

Bishop's story is an inspiring example of how empathy and innovation can drive change. His determination to address a real-world problem at such a young age serves as a reminder that creativity and ingenuity are not bound by age. By channeling his ideas into meaningful action, Bishop has shown how children can play a pivotal role in creating solutions that make the world a safer place. Through Oasis, he not only introduced a practical tool but also raised awareness about the importance of child safety and the dangers of leaving children unattended in vehicles.

CONCLUSION

In conclusion, Chapter 10 explored the key attitudes and dispositions that help cultivate creative habits in students. These included intrinsic motivation, which ignites a genuine passion for creativity, and creative mindsets that encourage openness to new ideas and solutions. Curiosity, driven by relevance, purpose, passion, and interest, enhances creative thinking, while open-mindedness allows students to embrace diverse perspectives. Autonomy gives students the freedom to explore and create independently, while imagination, sparked by mind-wandering and keen observation, plays a crucial role in innovation. The chapter provided a detailed exploration of these traits and practical activities and strategies to nurture them. By fostering these dispositions, educators can help students develop creative habits that will support their long-term growth and innovation. The chapter also offered examples, exercises, and guidance on how to integrate these dispositions into everyday classroom practices, helping students unlock their full creative potential.

REFERENCES

Bandura, A. (1997). *Self-efficacy: The exercise of control*. New York, NY: Freeman.

Beghetto, R.A. (2007). Ideational code-switching: Walking the talk about supporting student creativity in the classroom. *Roeper Review*, *29*(4), 265–270. https://doi.org/10.1080/02783190709554421

Beghetto, R.A., Kaufman, J.C., & Baer, J. (2015). Teaching for creativity in the Common Core classroom (Foreword by R.J. Sternberg). New York, NY: Teachers College Press.

Beghetto, R.A., & Dilley, A.E. (2016). Creative aspirations or pipe dreams? toward understanding creative mortification in children and adolescents: Creative aspirations or pipe dreams? *New Directions for Child and Adolescent Development*, *2016*(151), 85–95. https://doi.org/10.1002/cad.20150

Blackwell, L.S., Trzesniewski, K.H., & Dweck, C.S. (2007). Implicit theories of intelligence predict achievement across an adolescent transition: A longitudinal study and an intervention. *Child Development*, *78*(1), 246–263. https://doi.org/10.1111/j.1467-8624.2007.00995.x

Couros, G. (2015). *The innovator's mindset: Empower learning, unleash talent, and lead a culture of creativity*. San Diego, CA: Dave Burgess Consulting.

Deci, E.L., Koestner, R., & Ryan, R.M. (1999). A meta-analytic review of experiments examining the effects of extrinsic rewards on intrinsic motivation. *Psychological Bulletin*, *125*(6), 627–668. https://doi.org/10.1037/0033-2909.125.6.627

Dweck, C.S. (2006). *Mindset: The new psychology of success*. New York, NY: Random House Inc.

Dweck, C.S. (2015). Growth. *British Journal of Educational Psychology*, *85*(2), 242–245. https://doi.org/10.1111/bjep.12072

Dweck, C.S., Walton, G.M., & Cohen, G.L. (2014). Academic tenacity: Mindsets and skills that promote long-term learning. Seattle, WA: Bill & Melinda Gates

Foundation. Retrieved from https://ed.stanford.edu/sites/default/files/manual/dweck-walton-cohen-2014.pdf

Good, C., Aronson, J., & Inzlicht, M. (2003). Improving adolescents' standardized test performance: An intervention to reduce the effects of stereotype threat. *Journal of Applied Developmental Psychology, 24,* 645–662.

Hass, R.W., Katz-Buonincontro, J., & Reiter-Palmon, R. (2016). Disentangling creative mindsets from creative self-efficacy and creative identity: Do people hold fixed and growth theories of creativity? *Psychology of Aesthetics, Creativity, and the Arts, 10*(4), 436–446. https://doi.org/10.1037/aca0000081

Hu, W., Wang, X., Yi, L.Y.X., & Runco, M.A. (2018). Creative self-efficacy as moderator of the influence of evaluation on artistic creativity. *The International Journal of Creativity & Problem Solving, 28*(2), 39–55.

Icekson, T., Roskes, M., & Moran, S. (2014). Effects of optimism on creativity under approach and avoidance motivation. *Frontiers in Human Neuroscience, 8,* Article 105. https://doi.org/10.3389/fnhum.2014.00105

Karwowski, M. (2014). Creative mindsets: Measurement, correlates, consequences. *Psychology of Aesthetics, Creativity, and the Arts, 8*(1), 62–70. https://doi.org/10.1037/a0034898

Karwowski, M., & Kaufman, J.C. (Eds.) (2017). The creative self: Effect of beliefs, self-efficacy, mindset, and identity. San Diego, CA: Academic Press.

Kohli, A., & Jaworski, B. (1994). The influence of coworker feedback on salespeople. *Journal of Marketing, 58*(4), 82–94. https://doi.org/10.1177/002224299405800407

Lebula, I., & Csikszentmihalyi, M. (2017). Me, myself, I, and creativity: Self-concept of eminent creators. In M. Karwowski & J.C. Kaufman (Eds.), *The creative self: Effect of beliefs, self-efficacy, mindset, and identity* (pp. 137–154). Academic Press.

Niemiec, C.P., & Ryan, R.M. (2009). Autonomy, competence and relatedness in the classroom. Applying self-determination theory to education practice. *Theory and Research in Education, 7*(2), 133–144.

Patall, E.A., Cooper, H., & Robinson, J.C. (2008). The effects of choice on intrinsic motivation and related outcomes: A meta-analysis of research findings. *Psychological Bulletin, 134*(2), 270–300. https://doi.org/10.1037/0033-2909.134.2.270

Pink, D.H. (2011). Drive: The surprising truth about what motivates us. New York, NY: Riverhead Books.

Pfeiffer S.I., & Thompson T.L. (2013). Creativity from a talent development perspective. In K.H. Kim, J.C. Kaufman, J. Baer, & B. Sriraman (Eds.), *Creatively gifted students are not like other gifted students. Advances in creativity and giftedness, vol 5.* Rotterdam: Sense Publishers.

Robinson, K, (2015) *Creative schools.* New York, NY: Penguin Random House.

Ryan, R.M., & Deci, E.L. (2000). Self-determination theory and the facilitation of intrinsic motivation, social development, and well-being. American Psychologist, 55(1), 68–78. https://doi.org/10.1037/0003-066X.55.1.68

Ryan, R.M., & Deci, E.L. (2008). Self-determination theory and the role of basic psychological needs in personality and the organization of behavior. In O.P. John, R.W. Robins, & L.A. Pervin (Eds.), Handbook of personality: Theory and research (3rd ed., pp. 654–678). New York, NY: Guilford Press.

Ryan, R.M., & Deci, E.L. (2017). *Self-determination theory: Basic psychological needs in motivation, development, and wellness.* New York, NY: Guilford Publishing.

Shalley, C.E., & Gilson, L.L. (2004). What leaders need to know: A review of social and contextual factors that can foster or hinder creativity. *The Leadership Quarterly*, *15*(1), 33–53. https://doi.org/10.1016/j.leaqua.2003.12.004

Skinner, B.F. (1968). *The technology of teaching.* New York, NY: Appleton-Century-Crofts.

Sordia, N., & Martskvishvili, K. (2022). Creative self and fear of rejection: The role of feedback-related individual characteristics in creativity. *Journal of Individual Differences*, *43*(3), 115–123. https://doi.org/10.1027/1614-0001/a000365

Wagner, T. (2012). *Creating innovators: The making of young people who will change the world.* New York, NY: Scribner.

Zhao, H., Zhang, J., Heng, S., & Qi, C. (2021). Team growth mindset and team scientific creativity of college students: The role of team achievement goal orientation and leader behavioral feedback. *Thinking Skills and Creativity*, *42*, Article 100957. https://doi.org/10.1016/j.tsc.2021.100957

Zhao, Y. (2009). Catching up or leading the way: American education in the age of globalization. Alexandria, VA: ASCD.

Zhou, J. (1998). Feedback valence, feedback style, task autonomy, and achievement orientation: Interactive effects on creative performance. *Journal of Applied Psychology*, *83*(2), 261–276. https://doi.org/10.1037/0021-9010.83.2.261

Creative Collaboration and Learning Environments that Enhance Creativity Thinking

INTRODUCTION

Creative collaboration involves individuals working together to generate new ideas, solve problems, and create innovative solutions. This process can enhance idea generation because diverse perspectives are engaged in the process. With proper structure, individuals are encouraged to take risks and experiment with new methods. In turn, this can promote critical thinking and collective problem solving.

The ability to be a productive team member and to collaborate well with others are necessary 21st-century skills important for motivation, as well as the creative process. The Partnership for 21st Century Learning (2016) identifies collaboration as one of the four C's of essential 21st-century skills ranking high in priority along with critical thinking, creativity, and communication. Learners need strong collaborative skills to be ready for the complexities and challenges of 21st-century work environments where sharing ideas is highly valued and teamwork in problem solving is demanded.

Positive productive working relationships with peers are key to learning and motivation in the classroom (Ryan & Deci, 2017). In a collaborative environment free from sarcasm and ridicule, students are willing to take risks in their thinking and persist when things become difficult (Niemiec & Ryan, 2009). Working in collaborative teams gives learners access to more ideas and more information as each person shares knowledge and ideas gleaned from their own understanding and personal experiences (Paulus & Nijstad, 2003).

Experts recognize how critical diversity, interconnection, and exchange are to creative endeavors (Ashton-James & Chartrand, 2009; Robinson, 2011). Similar minds with similar experiences often see the same solution to a challenge because they have the same ideas. Working collaboratively with people who think differently can spark new ways of looking at and solving problems. Tech tools and web-based programs provide opportunities for rich and diverse experiences with

DOI: 10.4324/9781003434221-11

collaboration by connecting learners to a world of ideas across the classroom and across the globe.

IN THE CLASSROOM

In Mrs. Chapel's class, a dedicated Makerspace provides students with a creative environment to engage with content in a hands-on way. She believes that allowing students to physically create representations of the concepts they are learning helps to solidify understanding. For example, in a unit on ancient civilizations, Mrs. Chapel challenges small teams to demonstrate five differences between major cultures, such as the Egyptians, Mesopotamians, and Greeks, using materials in the Makerspace. These materials range from construction paper and clay to recycled items and simple electronic components. By having students design models, maps, or even interactive displays, they can explore the differences in architecture, art, religion, and governance in a tangible and engaging manner.

While working on the project, students are encouraged to think critically about the cultural features they choose to highlight. They must collaborate as a team to decide which differences to focus on and how to best represent them using the materials at hand. As the students work together, they develop problem-solving skills and deepen their understanding of how these ancient civilizations interacted with their environments and each other. Mrs. Chapel circulates through the room, offering guidance on both the content and the creative aspects of the project, making sure each team is on track. By integrating creativity and content, Mrs. Chapel's Makerspace gives students a unique and memorable way to engage with history.

At the end of the unit, students present their creations to the class. They not only explain the content they learned but also the creative process behind their project. Each group shares how they chose to represent the cultural differences and how working collaboratively helped them come up with new ideas. Mrs. Chapel uses this final presentation to assess both their understanding of the subject matter and their ability to work as a team. Through this hands-on approach, students not only learn about ancient civilizations but also develop valuable skills in creativity, collaboration, and critical thinking.

Mr. Winslow notices that one of his students, Jessica, struggles with perfectionism. Throughout the semester, he has observed that Jessica often works alone to ensure her assignments meet her very high standards. For her upcoming group research project on *The Odyssey*, Mr. Winslow recognizes that Jessica's tendencies might create friction within the group dynamic. Instead of waiting for problems to arise, Mr. Winslow proactively meets with Jessica at the start of the project to discuss her concerns. He listens to her frustrations and helps her realize that each group member has a valuable role to play and that collaborative work doesn't mean compromising on quality, but rather sharing the workload and combining individual strengths.

During their meetings, Mr. Winslow also checks in on how much time Jessica is spending on the project outside of class, as her perfectionism often leads her to devote excessive hours to her work. He encourages her to focus on the project's basic requirements and to delegate tasks to her group members rather than taking on all the responsibility herself. Mr. Winslow helps Jessica understand that teamwork doesn't mean she needs to do everything herself, and that allowing others to contribute is part of the learning experience. By discussing strategies for time management and balancing expectations, Mr. Winslow works to reduce Jessica's anxiety and helps her shift her perspective toward collaboration rather than individual perfection.

As the project progresses, Mr. Winslow continues to meet with Jessica and her group members to ensure everyone is on track. These check-ins help Jessica feel more comfortable with the collaborative process, and she begins to trust that her group will meet the project's high standards. Over time, Jessica learns to embrace teamwork and see the value of others' input, which not only improves the quality of the project but also reduces her stress. Mr. Winslow's guidance helps Jessica realize that it's okay not to be in control of every aspect of the work, and that creative collaboration can produce results that exceed her own expectations.

In Mrs. Roe's STEM class, students are tasked with understanding the complexities of bridge design and the factors that engineers must consider when building structures that withstand environmental challenges. To deepen their understanding, Mrs. Roe incorporates an innovative approach by connecting her students with a bridge engineer in Germany. Through an online platform, her students watch as her friend, an experienced bridge designer, discusses various models he has created over the years. He describes how environmental factors such as wind, water flow, and seismic activity influence the decisions he makes when designing bridges. This real-world connection allows students to see the practical application of geometry and engineering principles in action.

The engineer's explanation of how different materials and designs must be adapted to different climates and geographical locations sparks deep questions and curiosity among the students. They ask about the specific challenges he has faced in designing bridges in various parts of the world. The engineer demonstrates how technology is used to model potential designs and test them against environmental conditions, offering students a glimpse into the cutting-edge tools engineers use to solve complex problems. Mrs. Roe facilitates a discussion where students connect the engineer's insights with their own understanding of geometry, encouraging them to consider how these same factors might apply to the hypothetical bridges they will design as part of the class project.

As the lesson continues, students begin to apply what they have learned about the interplay between geometry and environmental factors to their own bridge designs. Mrs. Roe provides materials for the students to create scaled models of bridges, encouraging them to think about how wind resistance, load-bearing capacity, and environmental conditions will affect their designs. Students use their knowledge of geometry to calculate measurements and ensure their designs are structurally sound. The online session with the bridge engineer brings the theoretical aspects of the lesson to life and empowers students to think creatively and practically about engineering challenges. By integrating expert knowledge from a real-world professional, Mrs. Roe enhances the students' learning experience and shows them how STEM concepts are applied in careers outside of the classroom.

With the real-world examples described above, the teachers have prepared their students well for creative collaborative activities. In addition, they have provided psychologically safe places both physically and virtually to allow for creative expression. These factors are essential to consider when planning lessons and units of study.

PHYSICAL SPACES FOR CREATIVE COLLABORATION

Classroom space can be arranged to be most conducive to collaboration that nurtures creativity. When seating is comfortable, moveable and its arrangement is flexible, students can group and re-group. Tables can be used in the place of desks for small group work, large group work, and presentations. Alternatively, small rugs, carpet squares, or floor mats can designate collaborative meeting areas. Open spaces can be designed so that that it is easy for students to integrate disciplines, for example, science with art. Teachers can provide a stimulating, multicultural environment by incorporating examples of creative products from diverse cultures.

If students have access to technology, it may be important to include areas for computer-supported teamwork on projects or for different types of activities such as a drama, art, or STEM projects. Although these would be separate areas they should still allow for free-flowing interchange. Specific areas in a school where individuals can work through the creative process are important locations for collaboration as well. Teachers can make use of hallways, library nooks, lab space, and so forth.

Makerspaces are spaces designated for hands-on interaction with materials where students can explore, design, create, and learn. These spaces can range from small areas filled with materials for working on small, hands-on projects to large areas where students are able to use tools such as welding materials or 3D-printers. In some cases, Makerspace materials can be stored in portable units so they can be moved from classroom to classroom for easy access among several classes or to be used school-wide.

IN THE CLASSROOM: INVOLVE YOUR STUDENTS IN CLASSROOM DESIGN

Working in small groups, involve your students in re-designing the classroom as a project-based learning activity. Be sure to include students with disabilities in the groups to help identify barriers to accessibility and to facilitate inclusion. The following are suggestions for activities for the groups.

CONDUCT RESEARCH ON THE ELEMENTS OF 21ST-CENTURY CLASSROOMS

Have students consider all of the possibilities that are currently available. Schools around the world have implemented different features they deem important such as the Japanese Kindergarten where the classroom has no walls, but is framed by a garden, and trees grow through the roof, which is one large circle where students are encouraged to run and play. Even though your school may have limited funds, do not skip this process. It is important to explore the possibilities in order to see what other cultures are creating in order to encourage specific outcomes.

COLLECT OR CREATE PHOTOS, IMAGES, AND DRAWINGS OF FUTURISTIC CLASSROOMS

Now, it is time to think the future, and perhaps imagine things that might be silly or absurd. How will life be different in five years, 20 years, or 50 years? Allow students to think about how technology will evolve. Let them be playful as they draw. Perhaps having a slide as a way to enter class would be a great way to exert energy and provide an exciting entrance for their upcoming learning experiences.

Brainstorm ideas on how to connect their classroom activities with classroom design elements. For this activity, students need to think about their favorite classroom activities in order to consider what materials are required and how the workspace is arranged. Within a larger framework, they should investigate how the classroom can be altered in order to make these activities easier to navigate.

After students have completed the brainstorming activities, they can bring their ideas to life. Allow them to decide how to present their ideas to the class.

PSYCHOLOGICAL COMFORT AND EMOTIONAL SAFETY IN CREATIVE COLLABORATION

Providing physical space for creative collaboration is half of the equation. Spaces must also provide for psychological comfort and emotional safety as well. In psychologically safe and comfortable environments, learners are free of ridicule and pressure for perfectionism. Mistakes are welcomed opportunities to learn. In

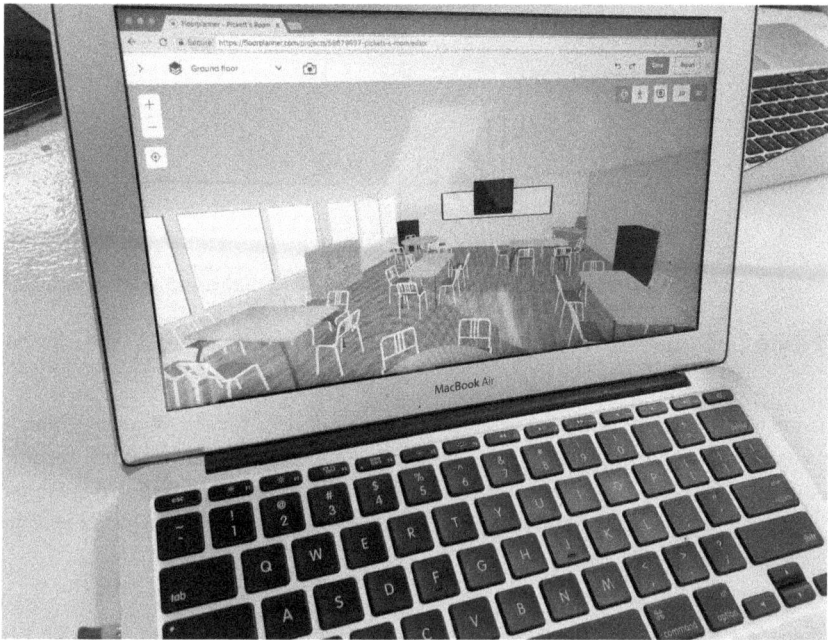

Figure 11.1 A Student-Generated Classroom Layout.

addition, collaboration and teamwork are valued and encouraged. In a school in North Carolina, positive statements about collaboration adorn the halls.

For some students, effective creative collaboration comes naturally, while for others, this might not be the case due to motivation or a lack of specific skills. Establishing roles for students, setting expectations for appropriate behavior during collaborative activities, and addressing dysfunctional group dynamics can ensure that students learn and practice appropriate collaborative skills.

ESTABLISHING ROLES

One strategy that can promote successful collaboration is assigning roles to students. When students have specific duties or responsibilities, they are less likely to feel disengaged or left out. Assigning roles also invites students to take ownership and be accountable for their learning experience. Allowing students to self-select roles can be even more beneficial, as they can choose to take on a role they feel comfortable in or select one where they are seeking to gain strength.

Procedures and roles can enable an effective process, and these will vary depending on group dynamics and learning goals. For some activities, participants can take on a variety of roles such as group leader, notetaker, doodle

223

Figure 11.2 A Positive Message About Collaboration Adorns the School Hallway.

master, questioner, or social leader. Roles are essential for encouraging creative collaboration in group settings, as they help guide the process, establish responsibility, and foster engagement. Here's a breakdown of each role and how it can enable effective collaboration, especially tailored to group dynamics and specific learning goals.

Group Leader

The group leader organizes the group's activities, keeps everyone on task, and ensures the project remains aligned with learning objectives. They act as a facilitator, guiding discussions, clarifying goals, and helping resolve conflicts or misunderstandings. This role is ideal for activities that require strong direction or time management, especially when deadlines are critical.

Notetaker

The notetaker is responsible for documenting discussions, ideas, and decisions. This role is crucial for capturing the group's collective knowledge and ensuring that key points aren't lost in the creative process. For activities with complex or multi-step outcomes, a notetaker can record insights and keep track of progress, which can be essential for later stages of refinement or analysis.

Doodle Master

The doodle master uses visual notes, sketches, or diagrams to represent ideas, concepts, and group discussions. By creating visual representations, they help the group conceptualize abstract ideas, see connections, and think outside the box. This role is especially valuable in activities where innovation and visual thinking are needed, as well as when group members have diverse learning preferences.

Questioner

The questioner challenges the group's assumptions, asks probing questions, and prompts deeper exploration of ideas. By introducing new perspectives, they help the group avoid "groupthink" and consider multiple angles, encouraging critical thinking and ensuring that ideas are well thought out. This role is ideal for groups needing to explore complex topics or where diverse opinions are crucial to the learning goal.

Social Leader

The social leader maintains group morale, manages interpersonal dynamics, and ensures all members feel included. They foster an environment where participants feel comfortable sharing ideas without judgment, contributing to a positive and supportive atmosphere. This role is particularly important for collaborative activities where group cohesion and morale directly impact productivity and creativity.

Timekeeper

The timekeeper monitors the group's pace, ensuring discussions stay on track and deadlines are met. They help prevent digressions and keep the group moving forward, especially in brainstorming sessions or complex tasks that need structure to achieve timely results. This role is ideal for groups that need focused bursts of creativity or are working within strict time constraints.

Encourager

The encourager supports each member's contributions, offering positive reinforcement and recognizing ideas. This role helps create a safe environment where everyone feels valued and motivated to participate, which is especially helpful for more reserved members. The encourager role is particularly useful in groups that benefit from high morale and open expression.

Connector

The connector looks for relationships between ideas, identifying patterns or linking concepts that may not initially seem related. They help synthesize ideas from different members, fostering integrated thinking and new insights. This role is valuable in creative projects where drawing connections across disciplines or perspectives can lead to innovative solutions.

Researcher

The researcher gathers relevant information, data, or resources that can inform and inspire the group's work. They bring external knowledge into the discussion, enriching the group's ideas and helping ground creativity in facts or examples. This role is helpful in projects that require data-driven insights or where informed creativity is needed for problem solving.

Critic (or "Devil's Advocate")

The critic offers constructive criticism, helping the group refine and improve ideas by highlighting potential flaws or challenges. This role encourages thorough examination of ideas and builds resilience by preparing the group to address critiques. The critic is beneficial for activities where vetting and strengthening ideas are as important as generating them.

Resource Manager

The resource manager organizes the tools, materials, or digital assets the group needs to collaborate effectively. They ensure everyone has access to necessary resources, such as shared documents or brainstorming tools, and that materials are used efficiently. This role is ideal for projects that involve multiple resources or require logistical planning.

Synthesizer

The synthesizer pulls together ideas at the end of discussions, summarizing and presenting a cohesive view of the group's progress or decisions. They help clarify the group's direction, ensuring that everyone understands the outcome of each phase. This role is useful in complex projects where clear takeaways are needed to guide the next steps.

"Experts"

Group members can rotate roles depending on the task or adopt multiple roles if the group is small, allowing for adaptation to different projects and group needs. For larger assignments and projects, each group member can be in charge of one of the creative components. The following are examples of roles that can be used with projects:

- Technology expert
- Art and design expert

* Communication expert
* Organizer
* Top researcher
* Interview expert
* Editor or writing expert

Here's how each role can support a creative, collaborative project:

* **Technology Expert**: This person manages any technical needs, from using software to troubleshooting issues and handling digital tools needed for the project. They can guide others in using tech effectively, ensuring smooth project execution.
* **Art and Design Expert**: Responsible for the project's visual elements, such as slides, posters, or other visual aids. This role is ideal for students who want to apply their creative skills to make the project visually appealing and engaging.
* **Communication Expert**: Manages external and internal communication, ensuring the group's ideas are clearly expressed. This student may handle emails, coordinate interviews, and work on delivering the project's presentation.
* **Organizer**: Ensures the project stays on track by managing the timeline and task allocation. They help plan meetings, track progress, and ensure all group members are clear on their tasks, supporting overall project management.
* **Top Researcher**: Focuses on gathering detailed and relevant information for the project. This role involves sourcing credible materials, organizing data, and providing insights that help deepen the project's content.
* **Interview Expert**: Takes the lead on any interviews or information-gathering from outside sources. They craft effective questions, coordinate interview logistics, and ensure that the team gains meaningful insights to enhance the project.
* **Editor or Writing Expert**: Manages all written content, ensuring it is clear, accurate, and well-organized. They review the final drafts, check for consistency, and polish the language, maintaining a professional quality in all written outputs.

These roles empower students to make significant contributions to the project and can build their confidence and skills in both familiar and new areas. Self-selecting roles fosters responsibility and a stronger connection to the project, making the process more personalized and motivating for each student.

GOALS AND PROCEDURES

Certain facets help develop effective collaborative practices including establishing clear goals and procedures. The goals should include shared objectives. These can be generated by the group members and associated with the expected outcomes for the task, assignment, or project.

For example, by the end of the class period, the group will generate three avenues for solving the following math problem: A bakery sells two types of items: cupcakes and cookies. On Saturday, the bakery made a total of $96 from selling 30 items. Each cupcake sells for $3, and each cookie sells for $2.

Question:

How many cupcakes and cookies did the bakery sell?

Solution Approaches:

Method 1: Using Systems of Equations (Substitution)

- Set up a system of equations to represent the situation.
  - Let x be the number of cupcakes.
  - Let y be the number of cookies.
- The system of equations will be:

$$x + y = 30 \text{ (total items)}.$$
$$3x + 2y = 96 \text{ (total revenue)}$$

Steps:

- Solve the first equation for y:y = 30 − x
- Substitute y = 30 − x into the second equation: 3x + 2(30 − x) = 96.
- Simplify and solve for x.
- Substitute x back into y = 30 − x to find y.

Method 2: Using Systems of Equations (Elimination)

Steps:

- Start with the same system of equations:

$$x + y = 30$$
$$3x + 2y = 96$$

- Multiply the first equation by 2 to align the terms with the second equation: $2x + 2y = 60$.
- Subtract this new equation from the second equation to eliminate y: $(3x + 2y) − (2x + 2y) = 96 − 60$.
- Solve for x and then use the value of x in $x + y = 30$ to find y.

Method 3: Logical Reasoning with Guess and Check

Since cupcakes cost $3 and cookies cost $2, reason out some possible combinations that add up to $96 for 30 items.

Steps:

- Start by assuming different quantities of cupcakes (e.g., 10, 15, 20) and calculate the number of cookies needed to reach a total of 30 items.
- For each guess, check if the total revenue adds up to $96.
- Through iteration, find that $x = 12$ cupcakes and $y = 18$ cookies meet both conditions.

By having clear goals, the group can work to create the three pathways for solving the problem by the end of the class period. This task required that groups work on a SMART (specific, measurable, achievable, relevant, time-bound) goal. The outcomes were measurable with three outcomes and time-bound with one class period to complete the challenge. In addition, the task was specific, achievable, and relevant.

SETTING EXPECTATIONS FOR APPROPRIATE COLLABORATIVE BEHAVIORS

Beyond content mastery, there are social and emotional components that should be addressed that help students collaborate effectively. Teachers can lead students in identifying and discussing norms and expectations for successful collaboration. Individual or group goals for learning the behaviors and meeting expectations can be set. For this step, goals should be differentiated to meet individual needs. By observing students working within their teams, teachers can identify increasingly apparent skills that need to be developed to ensure positive group experiences.

DISCUSSION STEMS

In Mrs. House's class, Miley tells her classmate that she respectfully disagrees with the idea presented by another classmate that using yellow lettering on light blue poster board. She describes that the lack in contrast will make the poster difficult to read. Another student comments that he would like to add his thoughts as well. In another group during a brainstorming session, Jonas tells Del that he is not sure he understood Del's idea and asks him to tell more about it. In this classroom, Mrs. House has taught her students appropriate language for disagreeing, questioning, and adding to the discussion. She has sentence stems posted in her room. The talk stems provide learners with respectful and appropriate language to use when they are engaged in creative collaboration.

Stems for appropriate discussion may include:

I respectfully disagree with you because...
I would like to add another idea.
I'm not sure I understand; can you tell me more about your idea...
I'm concerned that this idea may not work because...
What I hear you saying is...
We haven't heard from everyone yet...
I agree with...
What do you mean when you say...
Our team sees this differently because...

There are many traits or behaviors that are important to consider when discussing expectations for collaboration and teamwork that encourage taking responsibility and being a supportive team member. They may include the following:

Volunteering. All group members must take ownership over the learning experience. In its most effective form, individuals can offer to complete tasks in areas which they are skilled or with tasks that may not be appealing.

Taking responsibility. Realizing that a project takes commitment from all group members helps to establish trust. This component is important when establishing the foundation of the group. Teachers may want to designate time for allowing group members to bond and write a brief statement for success.

Communicating effectively. Expressing opinions in a productive way may not be a skill that students possess. One helpful strategy is encouraging students to offer a compliment, make a suggestion, and then follow with a positive statement. For those who may be reluctant to express how they feel because of fear of conflict, the teacher can create time during the day for groups to discuss what is working well and what needs to improve.

Accepting ideas from others. Accepting and using criticism are skills that are not innate for many individuals. It can be helpful to practice and model how to give criticism, how to accept criticism, and how to seek criticism in a healthy way. Have students practice asking others for help by writing specific questions about areas that they would like others to review. Help students to understand that they do not have to take all of the advice given by others, but that they should be thankful for someone taking the time to review their work.

Supporting group members. Students may benefit from explicit instruction on how to help each other during the learning process. Growth Mindset and Grit are popular concepts in educational realms where the focus on instruction relies on determination, perseverance, and the understanding that failure can and should be part of the process.

Relinquishing control. For some students, allowing others to contribute fully means that the work may not meet their standards. The instructor needs to make sure that this does not occur, as it is a critical factor in the success of groups of differing abilities working together as a team. The students need to feel safe that everyone can contribute and their work will not be evaluated as a whole.

Avoiding all-or-none-mentality. When working with other group members, students must be able to compromise. This can be a challenge for individuals who may develop an idea for how the assignment should be completed, for the creative components within the assignment, or for what they envision for the final product. Understanding the importance of compromise is an important idea for teachers to discuss with students and to encourage throughout the group work experience.

Having students self-select collaboration goals can be beneficial for personal growth. They can write their goals in a short paragraph and then self-assess at the end of the lesson or project. The following is an example of a Collaboration and Goal Setting form.

Sample

Collaboration Goal Setting and Review Form

Name:_____.

Group Members:_____.

Project or Assignment Objectives:

_____

_____.

Collaboration Goals

In order for our group work to go well, all members should give 100%. My strengths when working in a group are:

_____

_____.

An area that I am working to improve is _____

I can take the following steps to make this happen:

Step One:_____.

Step Two:_____.

Step Three:_____.

Midpoint Check

My greatest contribution to the group thus far has been:

_____

_____.

Areas that I am struggling with:

_____

_____.

Steps I can take to address these problems:

_____

_____.

Self-Assessment

After completing the group work, I feel like I did ___ or did not ___ improve my collaboration skills. Here is an example of why or how it happened:

_____

_____

_____.

BREAKING DOWN DYSFUNCTIONAL GROUP DYNAMICS

Some behaviors that persist over time may need to be addressed every time collaboration is expected. In addition, requesting time with the school counselor or even encouraging parents to seek therapy in the community may be the best option if situations become debilitating in nature. Talking with prior instructors may provide insights for how students overcame these tendencies in the past.

Students struggling with perfectionistic tendencies tend to hold other group members to their personal expectations. These students need to know that they are not responsible for being the leader or taking on the roles of other group members. They may need boundaries set in order to help them maintain balance and not take on the work required of other classmates.

When working in a group, those who are reluctant to participate fully can cause frustration for others and limit their own success. Helping these students to take small steps to achieve success can be beneficial. In addition, helping them find a voice in the process will encourage authentic engagement. Having these students self-assess engagement on a daily basis can also help them recognize when they disengage. Making sure there are options for choice and authentic outcomes may prompt the student to persevere. Assigning specific roles for students may also be helpful.

FOSTERING FLOW

Once the ground rules and structures for creative collaboration are in place, students can be so engaged in the work of the classroom that they are often disappointed when it's time to leave. This type of engagement is often referred to as *flow*, a state of optimal performance and engagement with a task as defined by Mihaly Csikszentmihalyi (2007). Sawyer (2007) offers the following conditions for group members to reach a place of *flow*: Pursuit of a collective goal, listening closely to others, complete concentration, individual autonomy or feeling in control, blending egos, equal participation, familiarity of group members, constant communication, keeping things moving forward, and the potential for failure.

These conditions can be addressed when teachers design assignments and projects. Allowing for personal choice in topic, role, process, and final product can help provide the opportunity for students to have autonomy and feel in control. Providing time to discuss effective collaboration can help students recognize strengths in others which can help with blending egos. Presenting to authentic audiences or giving a live performance addresses the component of potential for failure which can bring intensity to producing a successful product. Teachers can promote other aspects of flow during creative collaboration by allowing students to think about personal actions that facilitate the creative process such as the following.

Offering Suggestions and Taking Risks

Groups benefit from open, engaging discussions. In some cases, it might feel intimidating to voice an opinion or idea. Students should recognize the importance of contributing ideas.

Building on Others' Ideas, Elaborating on a Topic, or Modifying a Current Idea

Small steps come together in order to produce a strong final product or performance. Allowing students to think about how they added new ideas in incremental but powerful ways reveals that these steps are essential.

Listening Carefully and Encouraging Others

In this realm, it might be helpful to have students understand different personality types. Some people are naturally outgoing, while others can be reserved. Extroverts may need to be reminded to work on listening and letting others contribute, while introverts may need encouragement to share ideas. Promoting the ideas of listening and encouraging others, students can help contribute to a highly productive environment

Building Meaningful Opportunity for Creative Collaboration

Providing social situations in the classroom for students to communicate their own thinking and understand their classmates' thinking is important in the development of critical thinking and collaboration skills. It is also important that students have opportunities to communicate and learn beyond the four walls of the classroom. Opportunities for collaboration can be built into assignments and projects. Digital tools can be used to facilitate collaboration in the process.

Building Creative Collaboration into the Assignment

Teachers may consider designing a project or assignment based on specific final products that students should be able to create as 21st-century learners. Determining the best structure for final products depends on resources and the amount of time designated for the lesson, project, or unit of instruction. In classrooms where technology resources are limited, teachers can make use of low-tech tools such as poster boards and whiteboards. Consider the following ideas for projects in which require both creativity and collaboration.

Websites

Allowing students to create a website provides the opportunity to publish their work to an authentic audience. This platform requires the group to create products, edit, and revise in order to publish work that is professional.

Blogs

Writing a blog requires that students polish their writing and present ideas in an organized, entertaining format. Students can explore personal ideas about different subjects and express their opinions so that others can understand their perspectives. Ideally, blogs can be written online but traditional paper journals provide a reasonable alternative.

Podcasts

Creating a podcast involves a great deal of research about a topic and a heightened focus on providing an entertaining experience for the listener that may use techniques to promote suspense and tension. Podcasts can be created to be posted online or recorded using low-tech tools such as a tape recorder.

Vlogs

Incorporating the use of videos allows students the opportunity to include dramatic performances along with a polished piece of writing. They will need to focus on being able to provide engaging commentary, while also focusing on enunciation, inflection, and tone.

Multimedia Presentations

Students can learn how to convey important information and incorporate music, video clips, and sound effects. With this mode, it is important to understand how to provide details in a concise and visually-pleasing manner.

Graphics

Infographics can be created for different purposes and audiences. The goal may be to inform, to persuade, or to entertain. Incorporating visual features and concise language are essential to ensure that the posters are effective. Students can create their own infographics with poster board or whiteboards but can also use a variety of online tools.

How-To Guides or Videos

In order to demonstrate mastery of material learned, students can design instructional guides or videos to share with others. Students can show others how to build a rocket, use paper maché, or create objects on a 3D-printer.

Tools for Facilitating the Collaborative Process

In order to set the stage for success, it is important to think about the process involved in a lesson plan or unit of study. Digital and low-tech tools are available to help students collaboratively brainstorm, discuss topics, contact experts, and compile data. When designing the process for implementing these tools, instructors must consider the amount of scaffolding needed to completely support each learner.

Brainstorming

Certain platforms allow students to use tools to help brainstorm and also organize the brainstormed ideas. Groups can brainstorm and collaborate on group presentations, create mind maps, or work in virtual spaces to collaborate on boards, documents, and web pages. In addition, there are interactive online whiteboards where students can post ideas in the form of texts, images, or videos to brainstorm and organize ideas.

Discussions

Annotation and discussion platforms allow students to upload and discuss documents. Teachers can create online class communities where students can interact on discussion boards. Students can also interact through teacher-created video discussion networks.

Contacting Experts

Avenues are available that connect teachers and students with industry experts. Students can video chat or voice call anywhere in the world.

Compiling Data

Students can collaborate on the creation and editing of web-based documents, spreadsheets, and slide presentations. Real-time digital workspaces allow for visual collaboration and teamwork where students can keep team chats, meetings,

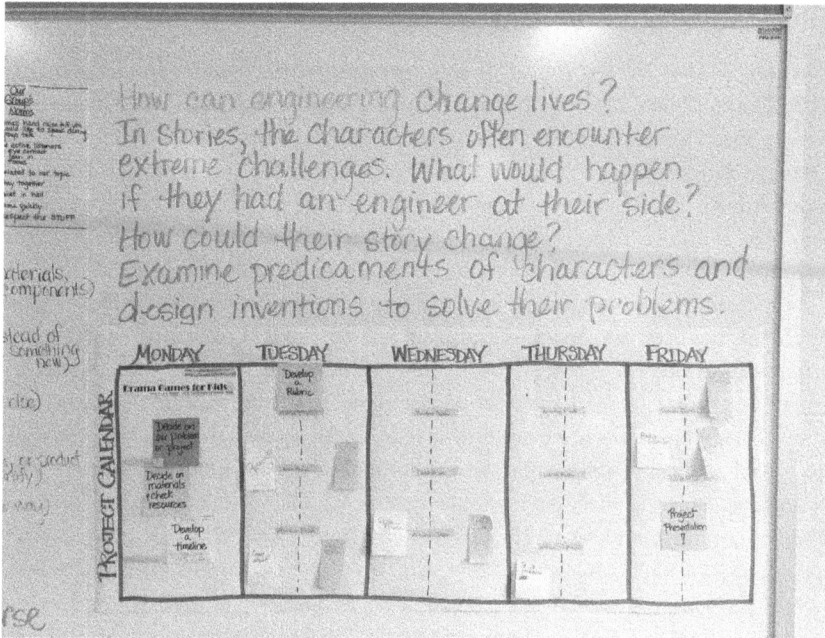

Figure 11.3 Low-Tech Collaboration and Planning Board.

files, and apps together. 3D software design and printing encourages innovation, communication, and collaboration.

Consideration of Online Spaces for Collaboration and Creativity

If one of the main goals of a project is to have students collaborate with other classrooms around the world, instructors might consider using open-source online platforms or global initiative programs. These programs often have assignments and projects that are already aligned to content standards or are easily modified to align with standards where students work together through the creative problem-solving process.

Open Source Learning Platforms

Content-specific platforms have also been created to allow students to communicate and collaborate in realms such as math, music, and writing. These platforms are open-source, where instructors and students can add to the knowledge base pushing forward innovation in the STEM fields and music creation.

Global Initiative Programs

Technology has the power to bring diverse students from around the world together to collaborate on authentic activities. Global Initiative Programs provide a space for students to communicate with each other and follow different frameworks to promote engagement, critical thinking, and mastery of content standards through creative problem solving. Other online platforms offer opportunities for students to discuss topics with other classrooms around the world to promote empathy and understanding while learning about other cultures.

Curiosity is encouraged by having students describe their daily experiences with cuisine, activities and games, culture, environment, family, history, interests, and school experiences. Students communicate through video, personal emails, or online formats such as text responses appearing within the online program. Many programs are geared to help children understand and seek solutions to global or local problems. Students complete activities where they brainstorm questions, work in discussion groups, create a call for action, design steps for implementation, and share their solutions. Along with the student-generated problem-solution features, these programs also offer the opportunity for students to collaborate on specific topics already designed for students to explore, such a sustaining food production around the world. Within these components, content is aligned with instructional standards.

Spotlight: Inventors Under 18

Katelyn Sweeney is a remarkable individual whose journey into the world of engineering and innovation began somewhat serendipitously. Initially interested in theater, she was mistakenly placed in a technology class, which ultimately changed her life. It was in this class that she met a passionate teacher who inspired her to pursue a career in STEM. This newfound interest led her to join the Lemelson-MIT InventTeam, where she and her teammates designed, built, tested, and patented a Search and Rescue Robot, a remote-controlled submersible rescue vehicle for ice divers.

Her passion for engineering and helping others didn't stop there. Katelyn's work with the Natick Fire Department on the Search and Rescue Robot project earned her and her team an invitation to present their invention at a Science Fair at the White House in 2014. This exposure further fueled her desire to make a difference through technology. She went on to work on healthcare engineering projects in Uganda, Kenya, and Ethiopia, demonstrating her commitment to using her skills to improve lives globally.

Katelyn's academic journey took her to the Massachusetts Institute of Technology (MIT), where she graduated with a degree in Mechanical Engineering and a minor in Entrepreneurship and Innovation. Her time at MIT was marked by significant achievements, including an internship with SpaceX, where she gained valuable experience in the aerospace industry. Today, Katelyn works as a mechanical engineer and mentors an all-girl robotics club in Palo Alto, California, continuing to inspire the next generation of female engineers.

In addition to her professional accomplishments, Katelyn Sweeney is also an advocate for STEM education, particularly for young girls. She actively participates in outreach programs and mentors students, sharing her story and encouraging them to pursue careers in science, technology, engineering, and mathematics. Her dedication to innovation and education makes her a role model for aspiring engineers and inventors everywhere.

CONCLUSION

Collaborative skills are crucial for 21st-century learners, as they help students develop the ability to work effectively with others, think creatively, and solve problems together. The physical environment plays a significant role in fostering creativity and collaboration. A safe, supportive space encourages students to explore new ideas without fear of failure, promoting curiosity and open-mindedness. This can include spaces designed for teamwork, such as tables arranged for group work or areas dedicated to brainstorming and sharing ideas. Providing a flexible workspace allows students to collaborate freely, adapt to different tasks, and produce creative projects.

To ensure effective teamwork, it is important to explicitly teach students the expectations and skills necessary for successful collaboration. Teachers can provide examples of creative collaboration, highlighting how diverse perspectives can lead to innovative solutions. Honest discussions about behaviors or mindsets that hinder collaboration, such as dominance or lack of communication, can help students reflect on their actions and improve their collaborative abilities. Additionally, allowing students to assess their own performance and set goals for improvement can encourage self-awareness and accountability in group settings.

Incorporating both digital and low-tech tools can also facilitate the collaborative process. Digital tools, such as online brainstorming platforms or collaborative document editing, allow students to work together even when they are not physically present in the same space. Low-tech tools, like whiteboards or sticky notes, provide tangible ways for groups to map out ideas and track progress in real-time. Combining these tools with a well-designed physical environment and clear teamwork expectations helps create an effective space for creative collaboration.

239

REFERENCES

Ashton-James, C.E., & Chartrand, T.L. (2009). Social cues for creativity: The impact of behavioral mimicry on convergent and divergent thinking. *Journal of Experimental Social Psychology*, *45*(4), 1036–1040. https://doi.org/10.1016/j.jesp.2009.04.030

Csikszentmihalyi, M. (2007). *Creativity*. New York, NY: Harper Collins.

Niemiec, C.P., & Ryan, R.M. (2009). Autonomy, competence and relatedness in the classroom. Applying self-determination theory to education practice. *Theory and Research in Education*, 7(2), 133–144.

Paulus, P.B., & Nijstad, B.A. (2003). *Group creativity: Innovation through collaboration*. New York, NY: Oxford University Press. https://doi.org/10.1093/acprof:oso/9780195147308.001.0001

Robinson, K. (2011). *Out of our minds: Learning to be creative*. Oxford: Capstone.

Ryan, R.M., & Deci, E.L. (2017). *Self-determination theory: Basic psychological needs in motivation, development, and wellness*. New York, NY: Guilford Publishing.

Sawyer, R.K. (2007). *Group genius: The creative power of collaboration*. New York, NY: Basic Books

Chapter 12

Assessing Creative and Critical Thinking Skills

INTRODUCTION

In a data-driven age, educators must advocate for creative thinking and provide avenues to assess growth for their students. To effectively make this happen, educators must establish a clear goal for activities, outcomes, or student behaviors. These three avenues require different forms of assessment. A teacher might provide guidelines with a checklist for activities such as moving through the creative problem-solving process (Brookhart & Nitko, 2019). To evaluate a final product, they could design a rubric to assess the creative process. Behaviors can be monitored during class as students work independently or in small groups. Instructors can choose to design a project to help students grow in different ways such as risk-taking, collaboration, ability to seek feedback, resiliency, persistence, or independence. Performance-based approaches, portfolios, and products have been advocated as avenues for demonstrating the ability to apply and synthesize knowledge (Moon et al., 2005; VanTassel Baske, 2013; VanTassel-Baska & Little, 2017).

ASSESSING CREATIVITY IN THE REAL WORLD

Sophie is an experienced engineer working for a renewable energy company. Sophie frequently takes time to self-assess her creativity in both individual and group projects to improve her problem-solving skills and overall performance. When Sophie works on individual engineering projects, such as designing a new solar panel system, she starts by reflecting on her creative process. She considers how many different solutions she explored before settling on the final design, asking herself, "Did I challenge myself to think outside the box, or did I rely on common solutions?"

Sophie also reviews how innovative her design is compared to industry standards and previous designs. Did she introduce any new materials or methods that could increase efficiency? To gather objective feedback, she often seeks input from a colleague or mentor, ensuring her design ideas are both creative and feasible.

In group projects, Sophie assesses her creative contributions to the team's work. For example, when collaborating on a wind turbine design, Sophie reflects on her ability to generate unique ideas during brainstorming sessions and on how she helped the group move past traditional design concepts. She assesses how well she worked with her teammates, whether she listened to their ideas and expanded on them or if she dominated the conversation. Sophie also evaluates how well she contributed to creating a collaborative and open-minded atmosphere in which all team members felt encouraged to share creative solutions.

Sophie evaluates the success of the project by measuring its outcomes. For an individual project, such as a new battery design, she might assess whether the final product meets the energy output goals and is more cost-effective than existing models. For group projects, Sophie looks at the final design and evaluates how well the team's collaboration led to innovative solutions. Were challenges overcome in a way that promoted creativity? Sophie then sets goals for her future work, such as experimenting with new materials or improving communication strategies to foster even greater creativity in future group efforts. This continuous self-assessment enables Sophie to grow as a creative engineer and stay at the forefront of innovation in her field.

ASSESSING CREATIVITY IN THE CLASSROOM

Alex, a high school junior in his STEM class, has always been interested in engineering but struggles with self-assessing his creative thinking skills, particularly in the areas of fluency, flexibility, originality, elaboration, and evaluation. When tasked with solving complex problems, such as designing a new device or developing a solution for an environmental issue, Alex finds it difficult to measure his creativity. He often feels that he isn't generating enough ideas (fluency) or that his ideas are too conventional. He worries that his approach to the problem lacks originality and that his solutions are not as unique as those of his classmates. Alex often feels frustrated because he cannot clearly identify whether he is coming up with a variety of solutions (flexibility) or exploring enough innovative possibilities. Even though his teachers praise his work, Alex feels unsure about whether he's truly being creative in the ways he needs to be.

In group projects, like developing a model for a new sustainable energy source or creating a robotic system, Alex struggles with evaluating his contributions. He feels that his ideas lack the depth of some of his teammates' suggestions. While his classmates offer elaborate solutions, Alex often feels his own contributions are underdeveloped or less imaginative. He has a hard time expanding on his ideas (elaboration) or thinking of new angles to improve existing designs. When brainstorming with the group, Alex finds himself questioning if he's being flexible enough with his thinking or if he's too focused on one solution. He's aware that creativity often requires looking at problems from multiple perspectives, but he still feels that his ability to adapt his thinking is limited. His self-doubt makes it hard for him to trust his ideas and sometimes prevents him from sharing them with the group.

Alex also struggles with evaluating the success of his ideas. When reviewing his work, he finds it difficult to determine whether his solutions meet the goals of the project or if they align with the creative standards expected in a STEM environment. He has trouble identifying how effective or feasible his ideas are, which leads to uncertainty about how he can improve in future projects. For instance, in designing a prototype for a new product, Alex might question if the product could be enhanced further or if he's missing key aspects of the design process. The lack of clarity in evaluating his work makes it challenging for him to set meaningful goals for growth. Even when receiving feedback from his teacher or peers, Alex struggles to use that information to improve, often feeling that he's too far behind in his creative development.

Despite these challenges, Alex is committed to improving his creative thinking skills. He begins to focus on generating more ideas during brainstorming sessions, pushing himself to think beyond the first solution that comes to mind. To improve fluency, he sets a goal to come up with at least five different design solutions before narrowing them down. To work on flexibility, Alex practices rethinking problems from different angles, challenging his assumptions and asking, "What if we tried something completely different?". For originality and elaboration, he seeks out inspiration from other fields of engineering or technology to spark more innovative ideas. Alex also starts keeping a reflection journal where he evaluates his own solutions, looking at what worked well and what could be improved. By focusing on these areas of creative thinking, Alex gradually gains more confidence in his abilities and begins to see how much room he has for growth in his STEM work.

LEARNER AGENCY

Learner agency involves students taking an active role in their education. They have a voice and the power to make choices about what they are learning and about the process. Ownership is further established through goal-setting and progress monitoring. Students move through the creative problem-solving process as they make decisions about what they learn and how they choose to learn. They sharpen their evaluation techniques as they assess their progress and final products.

An important aspect to consider with learner agency is the option of allowing students to be creative in the way that they express or demonstrate their learning. The instructor might emphasize the key points that should be included in the final product but allow the students to select the mode such as written, video, or artistic representation. By allowing this form of products for final assessment, the teacher is giving the student responsibility in shaping their educational journey.

Allowing students to have a voice in what they want to learn encourages autonomy as they become self-directed learners. Teachers working to personalize learning can provide opportunities for students to select topics they wish to explore. Students can set their own goals and create action plans to achieve these goals. The Autonomous Learning Model (ALM) developed by George Betts and Jolene Kercher provides guidelines for how to structure this type of instruction. The student collaborates with the instructor to identify skills and topics. Together, they can collect resources, determine activities, and define timelines.

Allowing students to self-evaluate and set goals provides the avenue for increased engagement and motivation. Within this process, the student must reflect on what is working in the process and areas where they need to improve. Empowering students to take ownership during this experience is essential. This metacognitive process is beneficial and can be a very useful skill for future academic and professional challenges.

SELF-EVALUATIONS

Self-evaluations can be created in many ways. Journal prompts, conferences, checklists with learning objectives, and surveys are a few formats teachers can use to allow students to reflect on their experiences or on final products. These reflections can enable students to understand their own learning processes and the strengths and weaknesses of the learning outcomes. By developing this self-awareness, students can become prepared to set goals for subsequent learning experiences. Self-evaluating the creative process requires that students assess the stages. These items will vary according to task or assignment. The following stages can be areas to target for having students self-assess their experiences and decisions.

1. Fluency: Brainstorming ideas about the topic, prompt, or problem.
2. Flexibility: Searching for diverse ideas or unique solutions.
3. Preparation: Gathering resources, researching, and understanding the task, problem or challenge.
4. Incubation and Illumination: Allowing ideas to meld, assessing weaknesses, aha moments.
5. Drafting: Writing, drawing, sketching out initial plans.
6. Evaluation: Requesting guidance, seeking insights about ideas or product design.
7. Final Products, Presentations, and Implementation: Completing products, polishing presentations, putting ideas into action.

8. Monitoring Progress: Overcoming obstacles, pivoting when necessary, setting goals.
9. Assessing Experience and Final Products: Evaluating product or solution effectiveness.

Self-reflection journals completed at the end of class can help students catalog their experiences. At the end of the unit of study, students can read through and highlight different phases of the creative process. They can also examine their emotional reactions to various experiences throughout the process. Have them complete the following questions at the end of class each day.

1. What did you complete during class today?
2. Did you face challenges or overcome obstacles?
3. How did your work make you feel?
4. What are your plans for tomorrow?

As students reflect on these questions, they can seek out areas where they may have struggled during the creative process, where they persevered, and where they experienced "aha!" moments that allowed them to overcome challenges along the way. In addition, students can assess different strategies or tools that were helpful. For their emotional responses, students can investigate how they aligned with different stages of the creative process and influenced motivation, creativity, or productivity. Different responses might include excitement, frustration, joy, disappointment, or satisfaction. As a final activity, students can establish three specific goals for their next project or endeavor. This encourages adaptability which can lead to better outcomes in the future.

Self-evaluations completed at the end of a project can help students consider other aspects of the creative process such as collaboration and feedback from peers or mentors. After answering these questions, students can consider avenues for improving this process in the future. Students can answer the following questions.

1. Did you seek out feedback from a classmate or the instructor?
2. Did you ask specific questions or areas that you hoped to revise and edit?
3. How did this process influence your final product?

Self-evaluation should be a continuous cycle that enhances creativity over time. Students can learn techniques that increase their creative capacities. They can improve their adaptability as innovative thinkers which, in turn, may become an integral part of the creative journey.

Figure 12.1 Students Experimenting with Tools and the Marks They Make during a Crime Scene Investigation Activity at Rocket to Creativity, Western Carolina University.

LEARNER-GENERATED GOALS

The process for goal-setting can take many forms. It is important to help students understand how to create goals that are meaningful and empowering. In addition to increasing engagement and motivation, goal-setting can help students with time management, organization, and self-regulation. Goal-setting can take place at the beginning of a class period and be focused on a single aspect of creative behavior or for an assignment or project. One framework for goal-setting uses the SMART acronym.

Specific: Define the goal clearly and precisely.
Measurable: Ensure that you can track your progress and measure the outcome.
Achievable: Set realistic and attainable goals.
Relevant: Make sure the goal aligns with your broader objectives and values.
Time-bound: Set a deadline or time frame for achieving the goal.

Students can follow this process within the containment of a specific project. The teacher can establish an overall framework. For example, students can consider different aspects of creativity involved in an inquiry-based science project about the Laws of Motion.

246

Goal 1: Designing a Unique Experiment

Specific: "I want to creatively design an experiment to demonstrate Newton's Third Law of Motion. My goal is to build a unique setup where two objects interact, such as using magnets, water rockets, or a balloon car, and find a way to measure and illustrate how forces act on both objects."

Measurable: "I will measure my success by developing a clear plan with a hypothesis, materials, procedure, and data collection. I will record how the objects react to different forces and track this over at least three different trials, documenting my results in both a written report and a visual presentation."

Achievable: "I will achieve this goal by researching examples of experiments that demonstrate Newton's Third Law, then brainstorming at least three creative ways to set up my experiment. I'll choose the one I think is most interesting and unique and get feedback from my teacher to refine my idea."

Relevant: "This project is relevant because it will help me understand how forces work in real life, and it allows me to think creatively about designing experiments. Understanding these principles is essential for engineering, robotics, and other areas I'm interested in."

Time-bound: "I will complete my experiment within two weeks. During the first week, I will plan and gather materials. In the second week, I will conduct my experiment, analyze my results, and prepare a visual presentation."

SMART Goal: "Over the next two weeks, I will design and conduct an experiment to demonstrate Newton's Third Law of Motion. I will create a unique experiment setup involving magnets, water, or balloons, collect data over three trials, and present my findings in a visual and written report. This will help me apply creative problem solving and experimentation to a scientific concept."

Goal 2: Creating a Visual Explanation

Specific: "I want to create a creative visual project that explains Newton's Laws of Motion. I plan to use animation or stop-motion video to show how each law works, using everyday objects to make the concepts easier to understand."

Measurable: "My success will be measured by creating a storyboard, script, and final video that clearly explains all three laws, each in a different one-minute segment. I will seek feedback from my classmates and teacher to ensure my visual explanations are clear and engaging."

Achievable: "I will achieve this by using simple, everyday objects in my animations, like toy cars, balls, and marbles. I will research examples of animations that explain scientific concepts and sketch out my ideas before filming. I'll use basic video editing software to put everything together."

Relevant: "This goal is important because visual storytelling can make complex scientific concepts easier to understand. It also allows me to think creatively and find new ways to communicate scientific information."

Time-bound: "I will complete this project over the two-week period. In the first week, I will plan the storyboard and gather materials. In the second week, I will film, edit, and present my final animation."

SMART Goal: "Over the next two weeks, I will create a three-minute animation that explains Newton's Laws of Motion using everyday objects. Each segment will creatively illustrate one of the laws, and I will share the final product with the class to make the concepts clear and memorable. This project will help me combine creative storytelling with scientific understanding."

Goal 3: Developing a Real-World Application

Specific: "I want to creatively solve a real-world problem using Newton's Laws of Motion. My goal is to design a prototype for a device, like a catapult or a model roller coaster, that uses the laws to accomplish a specific task, such as launching an object or transporting a ball through a course."

Measurable: "I will measure my progress by drawing up blueprints, gathering materials, and building a working prototype. I will test it at least three times, documenting how well it works and how Newton's Laws are applied at each stage. I will also include a reflection on how I solved problems during the design process."

Achievable: "I will achieve this goal by brainstorming at least three possible prototypes, selecting one to develop further, and researching examples of similar devices. I will seek help from my teacher and classmates to troubleshoot issues and refine my design."

Relevant: "This project is relevant because it helps me see how Newton's Laws apply in real-world engineering, which is something I'm interested in pursuing. It also lets me practice creative problem solving by figuring out how to design a device that works effectively."

Time-bound: "I will complete this project in two weeks. In the first week, I will brainstorm and finalize my prototype design. In the second week, I will build, test, and refine my prototype, finishing with a presentation to the class."

SMART Goal: "Over the next two weeks, I will design and build a prototype of a device that demonstrates Newton's Laws of Motion, such as a catapult or roller coaster model. I will test and refine it over three trials, document how the laws apply, and present my findings. This project will encourage me to creatively solve problems and explore engineering concepts."

These SMART goals allow students to define their creative behaviors during the project, emphasizing experimentation, visual communication, and real-world problem solving. By setting clear, achievable objectives, students can better integrate creativity with scientific inquiry.

RUBRICS FOR ASSESSING CREATIVITY

In a systematic review of the literature, Long et al. (2022) found that creativity in education is still mainly assessed by divergent thinking or creativity tests, self-report questionnaires, and product-based subjective techniques. These methods can be refined and improved with attention to purpose and intention. Rubrics provide guidelines for expectations for assignments and projects. They allow students to see levels of performance for different indicators of success. Providing clear criteria can establish be beneficial for students, but if not carefully constructed, they can also diminish creativity. Rubrics for assessing creativity can take many forms depending on the subject area and the assignment. They should be designed to provide constructive feedback that promotes growth. Allowing students to participate in designing the rubric and enhance understanding and encourage buy-in.

For some projects, a rubric might focus on creativity in ways that align with definitions for the level of creativity displayed in a final product or creative abilities such as originality, flexibility, elaboration, risk-taking, collaboration, execution, and reflection. Other factors can also be included such as style, value, and marketability if students are designing products for potential consumers. Table 12.1 is a Rubric for Assessing Creativity and includes aspects that assess behaviors during the creative process, as well as components for evaluating the aesthetic quality of the final product.

EXPLANATION OF EACH CATEGORY

1. Originality: Presents concepts that are highly unique and surprising, showing significant creative thinking.
2. Flexibility: Demonstrates seamless adaptability, switching between various strategies or perspectives as needed.
3. Elaboration: Highly detailed and developed ideas, using rich examples and visuals to expand on the concept.
4. Risk-Taking: Proactively takes creative risks, exploring new and unconventional methods, even if outcomes are uncertain.
5. Aesthetic Quality: Work is visually and conceptually compelling, with polished presentation that enhances its appeal.

Table 12.1 Rubric for Assessing Creativity

Category	4 – Exceptional	3 – Proficient	2 – Developing	1 – Emerging
Originality	– Ideas are highly unique and go beyond typical responses, presenting innovative and surprising concepts that are distinct and imaginative.	– Ideas are creative and show originality, introducing fresh concepts or approaches.	– Ideas show originality, yet tend to rely on conventional solutions.	– Ideas are predictable and conventional, lacking distinctiveness.
	– Demonstrates creative thinking by combining unrelated ideas in unexpected ways.	– Presents distinct ideas that suggest thinking beyond typical or obvious solutions.	– Creative thinking is present but often follows predictable paths.	– Displays minimal evidence of creative thinking; follows common patterns and established solutions.
	– Stands out significantly from conventional work in the field.	– Includes innovative elements but may draw on familiar themes or existing patterns.	– Attempts at originality exist but lack the depth or boldness to stand out.	– Concepts do not reflect originality or innovation.
Flexibility	– Easily shifts between multiple approaches, perspectives, or ideas, showing adaptability.	– Demonstrates adaptability by considering different approaches or solutions.	– Shows limited flexibility, often sticking to initial ideas or familiar methods.	– Rigid in approach, adhering strictly to initial ideas without exploring alternatives.
	– Considers various solutions or strategies and selects the most effective one.	– Shifts between perspectives and ideas with guidance or prompting.	– Struggles to explore beyond the first solution, showing reduced adaptability.	– Resists change and shows minimal effort to adapt strategies.

(Continued)

Table 12.1 (Continued)

Category	4 – Exceptional	3 – Proficient	2 – Developing	1 – Emerging
	– Incorporates different viewpoints and adjusts strategies as needed when encountering challenges.	– Generally adapts well to changes in direction or new ideas.	– Occasionally considers other viewpoints but reverts back to comfort zones.	– Avoids considering other perspectives or approaches.
Elaboration	– Ideas are fully developed, with detailed explanations that clarify and expand the concept.	– Ideas are well-developed, with clear supporting details that clarify the main concepts.	– Ideas are partially developed, lacking depth in explanation.	– Ideas are underdeveloped, with minimal explanation or elaboration.
	– Uses rich descriptions, examples, and visuals to add depth, making the work comprehensive and engaging.	– Uses examples and visual elements effectively, though more elaboration could enhance depth.	– Provides basic examples or descriptions, without expanding on key elements.	– Lacks depth, failing to add supporting details that clarify the concept.
	– Each aspect of the concept is well-explored and refined, reflecting thorough thought.	– Most parts of the idea are articulated clearly, with some aspects needing further detail.	Concepts are presented but require more detail and refinement.	The work is incomplete and does not provide sufficient information for full understanding.
Risk-Taking	– Proactively explores unconventional ideas and boldly experiments with new approaches or concepts.	– Engages with creative risks, exploring new ideas or approaches.	– Reluctant to take risks, leaning towards familiar or safe ideas.	– Avoids risk-taking, adhering strictly to safe, predictable approaches.

(Continued)

251

Table 12.1 (Continued)

Category	4 – Exceptional	3 – Proficient	2 – Developing	1 – Emerging
	– Takes creative leaps that enhance the work, pushing beyond standard practices. – Confidently engages with new challenges, seeking out innovative solutions even when uncertain of success.	– Shows a willingness to step beyond comfort zones but may hesitate with more daring ideas. – Experiments with new methods, although often returns to safer approaches.	– Hesitates to explore unconventional approaches, sticking mostly to what has been proven to work. – Occasionally tries new things but defaults back to familiar methods when faced with challenges.	– No evidence of attempting new or unconventional methods. – Unwilling to experiment, remaining confined to known solutions.
Aesthetic Quality	– Work is visually striking or conceptually engaging, showing a strong sense of design and creative flair. – Exceptional attention to detail, ensuring that the presentation is polished and refined. – Effectively engages the audience, creating a memorable impression that enhances the overall work.	– Work is visually or conceptually appealing, with a thoughtful design that adds to the presentation. – Consistent attention to detail, resulting in a clear and cohesive presentation. – Successfully engages the audience, though there may be minor inconsistencies in presentation quality.	– Work is visually or conceptually average, lacking refinement. – Presentation shows inconsistent effort, leading to a less polished result. – Audience engagement is present but lacks strong design elements or cohesion.	– Work is visually or conceptually weak, with minimal attention to design or detail. – Little effort in presentation, resulting in a basic and unengaging outcome. – Fails to effectively engage the audience, with poor design or organization.

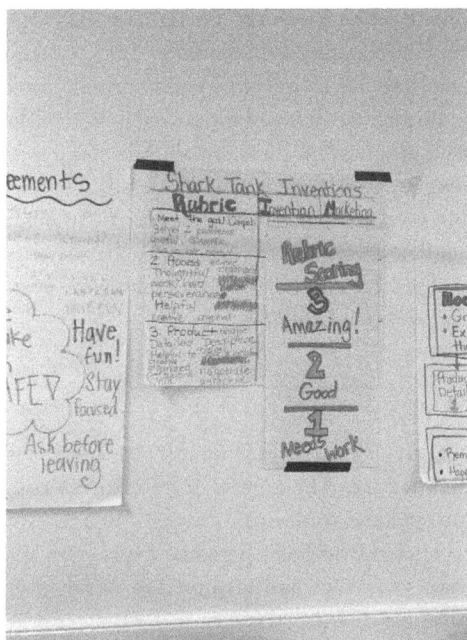

Figure 12.2 Student-Generated Rubric Developed for Shark Tank Group during Rocket to Creativity at Western Carolina University.

STUDENT COLLABORATION

Having students collaborate to design a rubric can be an important first step. For example, a teacher might create a unit of study centered around the concept of change. She could have students read poetry, picture books, and articles about historical events that describe an aspect of change – physical, mental, or emotional. After reading, discussing, and participating in whole group discussions about these pieces, she could have students write a personal memoir where they select a moment in their life where they experienced change, perhaps moving to a new neighborhood, the birth of a sibling, or finding a new hobby or sport.

They could read a sample memoir and look at the characteristics and features of the memoir. Then, the instructor could work with the students to design a rubric for the students to use. The rubric might include items expected in the final product, but it could also include components that focus on the creative process of writing. Categories might include: Brainstorming at least ten ideas, creating ten literary devices that could be used in the memoir, or requesting specific help during the proofreading and revision process such as asking a partner their thoughts on the effectiveness of the dialogue.

Students could also design their own rubric based on individual needs. The student choice allows for authenticity. For example, a student who struggles with finding ideas to write about might select to use a variety of brainstorming tools such as mind maps or journey maps. Another might need tools to help with elaboration. Taking the time to "explode a moment" in their initial draft could help with this aspect. Exploding a moment involves adding sensory details, slowing down time, using dialogue, and using specific details to build a scene. Students can select certain strategies from a generated list or meet with the teacher directly for a conference to discuss options. Table 12.2 is a rubric for examining the creative process of a middle school student writing a memoir.

Explanation of Each Category

1. **Idea Development and Creativity**: Assesses how unique, engaging, and well-developed the ideas and themes are. The highest level involves rich, imaginative storytelling that captivates the reader.
2. **Use of Voice and Style**: Evaluates the author's personal expression and effective use of language. A distinctive voice and creative use of language enhance the memoir's depth and engagement.
3. **Use of Literary Devices and Elaboration**: Looks at the skillful use of literary devices (e.g., metaphors, similes, symbolism) and how well the author elaborates on details to build a vivid narrative. Creativity is shown through effective imagery, figurative language, and dialogue.
4. **Creativity in Structure and Organization**: Evaluates how the memoir is structured. Creative and deliberate choices in the organization, such as non-linear storytelling, show higher creativity.
5. **Engagement and Emotional Impact**: Measures the emotional resonance of the memoir. Strong engagement and the ability to evoke empathy or reflection are key indicators of effective creativity.
6. **Creative Process and Revision**: Focuses on the effort put into the creative process, including drafting, revising, and incorporating feedback. Significant improvement and exploration of ideas show dedication to creativity.

This rubric ensures that students understand the importance of creativity in every aspect of their memoir, from the initial idea generation to the final draft. It encourages them to be expressive, reflective, and engaged in the writing process. Offering specific, actionable feedback on the creative activities and the final product can help the students grow in their writing skills and creative actions. This can be accomplished by including written commentary where the instructor specifically notes passages in the memoir. The rubric can be used for self-assessment, as well as peer assessment. As students assess themselves, they can consider different aspects of the writing process that were beneficial, as well as those that were challenging.

Table 12.2 Middle School Memoir Creativity Rubric

Category	4 – Exceptional	3 – Proficient	2 – Developing	1 – Emerging
Idea Development and Creativity	– The memoir presents a deeply personal, unique, and imaginative perspective, with original ideas and fresh insights.	– The memoir displays a personal and creative approach, with well-chosen themes.	– The memoir demonstrates limited creativity, often relying on conventional or predictable themes.	– The memoir shows minimal originality, using a predictable theme.
	– The topic is engaging and thought-provoking, capturing an event or theme in an unexpected or novel way.	– The topic is interesting and engaging, showing an effort to stand out.	– The topic is relevant but lacks originality; the story does not fully captivate the reader.	– The topic fails to engage, with no evident effort to add creative elements.
	– Rich details and vivid descriptions bring the memoir to life, making it memorable.	– Uses descriptive details to enhance the narrative, though some moments could be expanded.	– Basic descriptions are present but lack vividness and depth.	– Descriptions are vague or absent, making it difficult for readers to connect with the story.
Use of Voice and Style	– The author's voice is distinct and authentic, effectively capturing their personality and emotions.	– The author's voice is clear and genuine, with a consistent tone.	– The voice lacks consistency, making it hard to get a sense of the author's personality.	– The author's voice is inconsistent or difficult to discern, showing little expression of personality.
	– Creative use of language enhances the narrative, showing a strong command of tone, mood, and pacing.	– Language is descriptive and purposeful, though not always varied or dynamic.	– Basic language and limited stylistic choices do not fully capture the emotions or themes.	– Simple or repetitive language fails to enhance the narrative.

(*Continued*)

Table 12.2 (Continued)

Category	4 – Exceptional	3 – Proficient	2 – Developing	1 – Emerging
Use of Literary Devices and Elaboration	– The memoir features skilled use of literary devices (e.g., metaphors, similes, symbolism, personification) to enrich the story. – Elaborate details are woven seamlessly, creating a vivid and immersive experience for the reader. – Creative and thoughtful imagery, figurative language, and dialogue enhance the emotional depth and meaning.	– The memoir includes effective use of literary devices, showing an effort to add depth to the narrative. – Descriptive details are present and provide a clearer picture of events and emotions. – Imagery and figurative language are used, though not always consistently or effectively.	– The memoir shows limited use of literary devices, with occasional attempts that may not fully enhance the narrative. – Details are often brief, with minimal elaboration, leading to a less immersive experience. – Literary elements are used sporadically and do not always connect well with the story.	– The memoir lacks the use of literary devices, resulting in a flat narrative. – Minimal elaboration, making the story feel undeveloped and simplistic. – No attempt to use figurative language or creative expression.
Creativity in Structure and Organization	– The memoir follows a unique and inventive structure that adds to the story's meaning or emotional impact.	– The memoir is well-organized, with a logical sequence of events.	– The structure is basic, with a clear beginning, middle, and end, but lacks creativity.	– The memoir is disorganized, making it difficult to follow.

The style is consistent and adds depth, making the memoir compelling. row:

| | The style is consistent and adds depth, making the memoir compelling. | The style supports the narrative and keeps the reader engaged. | The style often feels flat, leading to sections that do not engage. | The style is disjointed or ineffective, making the memoir difficult to engage with. |

(Continued)

Table 12.2 (Continued)

Category	4 – Exceptional	3 – Proficient	2 – Developing	1 – Emerging
	– The flow of events is smooth and well-thought-out, with clear, deliberate transitions.	– Transitions are clear, and the structure supports the story.	– Transitions are sometimes abrupt or unclear.	– No clear structure or logical flow of events, with confusing or missing transitions.
	– Creative use of non-linear storytelling, flashbacks, or dialogue enhances the narrative.	– Attempts at creative elements in structure (e.g., using dialogue or varying pacing) are present.	– The use of creative structural elements is limited or underdeveloped.	– The structure lacks any creative elements, leading to a flat and predictable narrative.
Engagement and Emotional Impact	– The memoir evokes strong emotions, allowing readers to deeply connect with the author's experiences.	– The memoir is engaging and emotionally relatable, providing insight into the author's experiences.	– The memoir elicits some emotional response, but lacks powerful or memorable moments.	– The memoir fails to evoke emotions or engage the reader.
	– Memorable moments are created through well-chosen details and creative storytelling.	– Effective storytelling is used to highlight key moments, even if not all are deeply moving.	– Occasional engagement, but parts of the memoir may feel disconnected or underdeveloped.	– Lacks key details and storytelling elements that draw the reader in.
	– The narrative encourages reflection or empathy, drawing the reader into the author's world.	– The reader is able to connect with the story on an emotional level.	– The emotional impact is inconsistent, with key moments not fully realized.	– The narrative does not encourage reflection, making it difficult for readers to connect.

(Continued)

Table 12.2 (Continued)

Category	4 – Exceptional	3 – Proficient	2 – Developing	1 – Emerging
Creative Process and Revision	– Demonstrates a strong commitment to the creative process, exploring multiple drafts and refining ideas.	– Engages with the creative process, revising and improving drafts with clear effort.	– Limited engagement with the creative process, with few drafts or revisions.	– Little to no engagement with the creative process; minimal drafting or revision.
	– Consistently seeks feedback, incorporating suggestions to improve the memoir.	– Open to feedback, though some suggestions may not be fully implemented.	– Resistant to incorporating feedback or only makes surface-level changes.	– Resistant to feedback, showing no effort to refine the memoir.
	– Final product reflects significant revision and growth, showing careful consideration of creative elements.	– Final product shows clear progress from earlier drafts, with creative development.	– Final product shows minimal improvement, with creative elements left underdeveloped.	– Final product lacks development, with initial ideas unchanged and creative aspects underexplored.

When students assess their peers, they can find components that they might wish to include in their future writing pieces.

PROGRESS MONITORING

Progress monitoring involves regularly tracking student progress to inform instruction. Collecting student work can show growth over time. Students can compile finished pieces, pictures, videos, and other artifacts to demonstrate growth in understanding and skill development. Portfolios, digital or hard copy, can be used for this purpose. Other avenues for collecting data can take the form of formative assessments or check-ins. The goal of collecting the data is for teachers to design instruction based on their evaluation of the documents.

Teachers can build skills through specific activities and monitor the growth. For instance, students can participate in daily brainstorming activities to build fluency, flexibility, and originality. One technique is to display an item or picture of an item and ask students to consider all the uses for the item. This can be engaging as students study specific topics in language arts, social studies, or science as the items could pertain to key elements in a novel, for a certain historical time period, or within a scientific inquiry. At the end of each session, students can record the number of responses, the flexibility within the responses, and the originality by sharing out with the class to see if any answers are unique.

Goal tracking sheets can allow students to record their objectives, steps they have taken, and achievements. Students can reflect individually, with a peer, in small groups, or with the instructor. At these times, it might be beneficial to break projects into smaller components or to seek support in areas where a student might be struggling. Feedback from peers or the instructor should be specific, avoiding vague comments such as "good work". Instead, return to the initial goal of the task, assignment, or project to look at the purpose. If the goal is for the final product to be marketable, offering specific comments on the aesthetic components would be beneficial. In addition, emphasizing students' strengths and accomplishments should be part of the process.

As teachers work to use the data to design instruction, they can consider implementing instruction through several formats. Specific instruction to targeted populations can offer support or additional rigor. This enables a teacher to provide differentiated instruction to the entire class. A second avenue is to create flexible small groups where students can learn together to understand certain techniques or methods. Finally, instructors can work to build a file of resources so that they can have materials ready for students who have a particular interest in an approach or aspect of the assignment.

The following is a progress monitoring document to assess overall creative thinking skills.

Creative Thinking Skills Progress Monitoring Document

Student Name: _____

Grade/Subject: _____

Teacher Name: _____

Date of Review: _____

Table 12.3 Creative Thinking Skills Progress Monitoring Document

Skill	Description	Baseline Observation	Goal	Evidence of Progress	Next Steps
Fluency	Ability to generate a large number of ideas or solutions.	Example: Student generates 3–5 ideas during brainstorming sessions but stops when prompted for more.	Example: Generate at least ten ideas in brainstorming within five minutes.	Example: Student generated 12 ideas during the latest brainstorming session, showing improved speed and volume.	– Introduce timed brainstorming challenges using prompts.
					– Use creative warm-ups like listing ten unrelated objects for unusual uses.
Flexibility	Ability to generate diverse ideas across categories or perspectives.	Example: Student tends to stick to one type of idea or solution during discussions.	Example: Create at least 3–5 ideas from different perspectives or categories.	Example: Student produced ideas from four distinct categories during a class activity.	– Present real-world case studies where diverse perspectives are essential.
					– Encourage "What if" scenarios to view problems from different angles.

(Continued)

Table 12.3 (Continued)

Skill	Description	Baseline Observation	Goal	Evidence of Progress	Next Steps
Originality	Ability to produce unique and innovative ideas or solutions.	Example: Student generates ideas that are common or already suggested by peers.	Example: Develop at least 2–3 unique ideas per activity that are different from peer suggestions.	Example: Student presented an original project concept for the class activity.	– Provide examples of unique solutions from innovators to inspire thinking.
					– Have students explore "wild" ideas before refining them.
Elaboration	Ability to add detail, depth, or refinement to ideas.	Example: Ideas are basic, lacking specific examples or detailed explanations.	Example: Add at least 2–3 layers of detail or supporting evidence to each idea.	Example: Student provided detailed explanations and supporting examples during their presentation.	– Use guided questions (e.g., "How would this work?", "What are the steps?") to deepen responses.
					– Incorporate storyboarding or diagramming to visually elaborate on ideas.
Evaluation	Ability to assess ideas for feasibility, effectiveness, or potential.	Example: Student has difficulty identifying the strongest idea or solution from a set.	Example: Use a checklist or rubric to evaluate at least 2–3 ideas for feasibility and effectiveness.	Example: Student successfully used a rubric to evaluate ideas and select the best solution.	– Teach students to use decision matrices to weigh pros and cons.

(Continued)

Table 12.3 (Continued)

Skill	Description	Baseline Observation	Goal	Evidence of Progress	Next Steps
					– Provide peer evaluation opportunities for feedback on strengths and areas for improvement.

Notes and Observations

- Strengths: _____
- Challenges: _____
- Progress Summary: _____

Signatures

Student Signature: _____

Teacher Signature: _____

Date: _____

Assessing Creative Collaboration

Assessing the creative collaborative process can take two forms: Formative assessment and summative assessment. For formative assessments, students can take the time to write a few sentences about what they completed and the performance of self and others. It is important to remember that students are responsible for their personal performance, and not the performance of other students. Students can also offer a verbal evaluation by ranking their commitment to task on a scale of 1–5 and by making goals for the next day. A positive approach in helping students work on these skills is to allow the opportunity for complimenting group members. Instructors can also keep notes while monitoring group work in order to provide specific feedback to each student about their strengths and areas that could be addressed.

For summative assessments, students should contribute in creating a rubric for the assignment or project. Rubrics can include specific avenues for effective collaboration within the overall project or separate rubrics can be developed for the project and for creative collaboration. Students should self-assess their personal performance. The opportunity to discuss any issues should be provided throughout the process and then again at the end of the experience.

The following table provides strategies that groups can use to assess collaborative efforts in order to improve collaboration.

Table 12.4 Collaboration Assessment Techniques

Self-Assessment Method	High School Assignment	Steps to Improve Collaboration Efforts
1. Reflective Journaling	Group project to design a sustainable community using 3D models or digital tools.	Reflect daily on your role and contributions. Write about what went well, any conflicts, and how communication can improve. Share key insights during team discussions.
2. Peer Feedback Forms	Collaborative lab report on environmental science experiments.	Distribute structured feedback forms to teammates. Focus questions on communication, fairness, and problem solving. Use the feedback to identify specific areas to improve, such as listening or sharing ideas more openly.
3. Contribution Tracking Chart	Team research paper on the causes and effects of a historical event.	Track individual contributions to ensure balanced workload. Analyze data to redistribute tasks or address gaps in accountability for the next project.
4. Goal Achievement Checklist	Plan and present a marketing pitch for a mock company in an economics class.	Use a checklist to track individual and team goals, such as meeting deadlines or brainstorming innovative ideas. Hold a group meeting to evaluate progress and adjust timelines.
5. Strengths and Weaknesses Grid	Group debate about ethical issues in technology.	Create a personal grid of strengths (e.g., research, speaking) and weaknesses (e.g., time management). Share grids with teammates to delegate tasks more effectively and build on each other's skills.
6. Team Dynamics Observation Form	Collaborative video project showcasing literary themes in a chosen novel.	Observe how team members interact during work sessions. Note participation levels, interruptions, or miscommunications. Schedule check-ins to address concerns like quieter members being overlooked.
7. Self-Evaluation Rubric	Group art installation based on a social issue.	Use a rubric with categories like communication, teamwork, and creativity. Score yourself honestly and review scores with teammates to create a shared improvement plan.

(*Continued*)

Table 12.4 (Continued)

Self-Assessment Method	High School Assignment	Steps to Improve Collaboration Efforts
8. Task Completion Log	Coding a group app or website for computer science class.	Maintain a shared log to track progress on assigned tasks. If delays occur, discuss as a group to improve planning or reassign responsibilities.
9. Feedback Loop Practice	Group presentation on the impact of a scientific discovery.	Practice giving real-time feedback using respectful and actionable language. Encourage teammates to ask clarifying questions to avoid misunderstandings.
10. "What I Learned" Reflection Prompts	Group essay analyzing literary devices in a Shakespearean play.	Use prompts like "What new ideas did I gain from my teammates?" and "What could I do differently next time?" to reflect on collaboration strengths and areas for growth.

EXAMPLE OF SELF-ASSESSMENT IN PRACTICE

Self-Evaluation Rubric for Group Art Installation

1. Students complete a rubric with specific categories like communication (e.g., "Did I actively listen to my team members?"), contribution (e.g., "Did I complete my assigned tasks on time?"), and collaboration (e.g., "Did I help resolve conflicts in a constructive way?").
2. After scoring themselves, students compare results with feedback from teammates to identify discrepancies (e.g., one person perceives themselves as helpful, but teammates feel otherwise).
3. Based on the results, the team discusses ways to improve group performance, like redistributing tasks or setting clearer expectations.

Team Dynamics Observation Form for a Video Project

1. During team meetings, one student serves as the observer, noting who participates and how ideas are shared.
2. Observations are shared with the group to highlight imbalances, such as one person dominating the discussion or others not contributing enough.
3. The group agrees on specific strategies, like time limits for each speaker or structured brainstorming sessions to ensure everyone's voice is heard.

By offering detailed self-assessment tools, students become more aware of their collaborative strengths and weaknesses and can make targeted improvements, ultimately leading to better teamwork and more successful projects.

SPOTLIGHT: INVENTORS UNDER 18

Fionn Ferreira, a young inventor from West Cork, Ireland, has made significant contributions to environmental science. Growing up near the ocean, Fionn developed a deep love for the sea and a passion for science. This combination led him to tackle the pressing issue of microplastic pollution in water. In 2017, he began developing a method to extract microplastics using a magnetic liquid called ferrofluid. His innovative approach won him the 2019 Google Science Fair.

Fionn's method involves adding ferrofluid to water, which binds to microplastics. Magnets are then used to remove the ferrofluid along with the microplastics, achieving an impressive removal rate of over 85%. Despite living far from any professional labs, Fionn built most of his testing equipment at home, demonstrating remarkable resourcefulness and determination. His work has not only garnered international recognition but also highlights the potential for young minds to contribute to solving global environmental challenges.

Currently, Fionn is a student at the University of Groningen in the Netherlands, where he continues his research on microplastics and other environmental issues. He aims to inspire greater interest in STEM fields and encourage more people to engage in scientific research. Fionn's journey is a testament to the power of curiosity and perseverance in driving innovation and making a positive impact on the world.

In addition to his scientific endeavors, Fionn is also an advocate for environmental education and awareness. He participates in various outreach programs and speaks at conferences to share his knowledge and inspire others. His dedication to both science and environmental conservation makes him a role model for aspiring young inventors and environmentalists alike.

CONCLUSION

Practical and learner-centered strategies emphasize the significance of empowering students in the evaluation process. By incorporating self-evaluations, students are encouraged to reflect on their creative growth, identify challenges, and take ownership of their learning journey, fostering both self-awareness and metacognition. The chapter also underscores the value of learner-generated goals, enabling students to set personalized, meaningful objectives that align with their unique creative pursuits, thus enhancing motivation and engagement.

Rubrics are presented as a versatile tool for assessing creativity, offering clear, structured criteria while allowing flexibility to accommodate diverse ideas and innovative approaches. Progress monitoring tools further enrich the evaluation process, providing a means to track development and celebrate achievements over time. Collectively, these strategies cultivate a classroom environment where creativity is nurtured, assessed, and continuously refined, ensuring that students are equipped with the skills and confidence to think critically and innovate effectively.

REFERENCES

Brookhart, S.M., & Nitko, A.J. (2019). *Educational assessment of students* (8th ed.). London: Pearson.

Long, H., Kerr, B.A., Emler, T.E., & Birdnow, M. (2022). A critical review of assessments of creativity in education. *Review of Research in Education, 46*(1), 288–323. https://doi.org/10.3102/0091732X221084326

Moon, T.R., Brighton, C.M., Callahan, C.M., & Robinson, A. (2005). Development of authentic assessments for the middle school classroom. *Journal of Secondary Gifted Education, 16*, 119–133.

VanTassel-Baska, J. (2013). Performance-based assessment: The road to authentic learning for the gifted. *Gifted Child Today, 37*(1), 41–47.

VanTassel-Baska, J., & Little, C.A. (2017). *Content-based curriculum for advanced learners* (3rd ed.). Austin: Prufrock Press.

For Product Safety Concerns and Information please contact our EU
representative GPSR@taylorandfrancis.com
Taylor & Francis Verlag GmbH, Kaufingerstraße 24, 80331 München, Germany

* 9 7 8 1 0 3 2 5 5 7 4 0 3 *